T0193667

ONE MINUTE
AFTER
SUNRISE

ONE MINUTE AFTER SUNRISE

THE STORY OF THE STANDARD OIL REFINERY FIRE OF 1955

JOHN HMUROVIC

ONE MINUTE AFTER SUNRISE
THE STORY OF THE STANDARD OIL REFINERY FIRE OF 1955

iUniverse books may be ordered through booksellers or by contacting:

iUniverse
1663 Liberty Drive
Bloomington, IN 47403
www.iuniverse.com
1-800-Authors (1-800-288-4677)

ISBN: 978-1-5320-1958-6 (sc)
ISBN: 978-1-5320-1959-3 (e)

Library of Congress Control Number: 2017903961

Print information available on the last page.

iUniverse rev. date: 04/20/2017

ACKNOWLEDGMENTS

Frank Vargo...Gayle Faulkner Kosalko...Chuck Kosalko.

These three people were essential in the creation of this book. Although I did the writing and much of the research, without them this book would not exist.

One morning in 2014, Frank and I were at the Whiting-Robertsdale Historical Society, where we volunteer our time. I suggested that we needed to capture the memories of those who lived through the 1955 Whiting Refinery disaster. The 60th anniversary of that event was approaching, and everyone who remembered it was easily eligible for Social Security. He agreed, and we talked it over with fellow-volunteers Gayle Faulkner Kosalko and Chuck Kosalko. The four of us hatched a plan.

The first step was to spread the word that we were looking for people who remembered the disaster. Eighty-two people stepped forward. We interviewed 34 of them on camera and gathered written memories from the others. Those interviews formed the foundation of our research.

With the editing help of Rob Schultz we produced a video which premiered before a standing-room-only crowd at the Whiting High School Auditorium. We have since sold hundreds of copies of the video. All proceeds went to the Whiting-Robertsdale Historical Society, just as will all proceeds from the sale of this book. Late in 2015, the Indiana Historical Society chose our project for their annual Indiana History Outstanding Organization Event or Project Award.

Frank, Gayle, and Chuck helped edit the book, as did my wife, Bev Hmurovic; my sister, Susan Hmurovic; and my friend, Kate Murphy. Carol Badenhoop did a thorough final edit.

Thank you also to those who helped by contributing photographs: Betty Delinck, Ann Devoy, Dennis Hittle, Pat Mazanek, Ronald Plewniak,

Cheryl Macko Rosen, Frances Vanek, and Gina Vitucci. Thank you also to Steve McShane of the Calumet Regional Archives at Indiana University Northwest. And thanks to John Lambert for his work on the maps.

I owe a great deal to my family. My father, John Hmurovic, loved his Slovak heritage. He loved history. He started me on the path that led to this book. My sister, Susan Hmurovic, another lover of history, also helped me along that route. I owe so much to them and my mother, Violet Lovrinich Hmurovic, for all the love and support they have given me. I was fortunate to have them as family.

But there is no one I value as much as my wife, Beverly Ramey Hmurovic. Thanks for your love and support. This project would not have been possible without it.

Thank you to all the wonderful people who helped with this book. I will always appreciate your friendship, love, and support

John Hmurovic
2017

WHERE WERE YOU?

Emily Timko was angry. And even though 13-year-old George Timko Jr. was still in bed on this Saturday morning, he could tell his mother was upset.

"What's the matter?" he called out, only half awake.

"That dog's been barking since two o'clock in the morning and hasn't stopped," she responded.

It was the beagle next door. The neighbors always kept it in the garage overnight. On a hot summer morning like this, they left the garage window open about six inches to give the dog some air. But the dog never barked. Emily wondered what was going on.

She walked down a short flight of steps to the back door. She planned to go to the neighbor's garage, open the door, and then let the dog out. When she got to her back door, much to her surprise, she saw the beagle standing just outside her door, barking and growling. Instead of looking at her it was looking toward the nearby Standard Oil Refinery.

She tapped on the door to get the dog's attention. The beagle turned his head but continued to face the refinery. Emily eventually got the dog to move. She watched him walk around the side of her house. She went back upstairs, into the kitchen, and got ready to put a pot of coffee on the stove.

It was then that she heard it.

BA-BOOM!

"Oh my God!" she screamed.

If George Jr. had been half asleep, he was now rapidly approaching 100 percent awake. It was the loudest sound he had ever heard. In a flash, he was on his feet. He must have put on a pair of jeans, but afterward he didn't remember doing that. He ran from his bedroom, out the back door and froze in place. He looked to the east, his head turned toward the sky. It was the kind of sight people saw on television, but not in real life. At least, not in his life. A huge cloud of black smoke billowed skyward. It was large, and getting larger by the second. And there were flames. Continuously, from beneath the black cloud, they shot out with the ferocity of an angry dragon.

Young George stood there in awe, but the words his father was uttering as he dashed to the back door also ran through his mind. Some of the words George Sr. used included language that George Jr. would not repeat before strangers, even decades later. What he would share was his father saying, "Don't tell me they messed up that new unit."

George Sr. worked at the refinery, located just east of where the Timko family lived. He knew right away that the explosion came from the plant where a large new unit, just a few months old, was ready to go back online after a maintenance shutdown.[1]

That was George Timko Jr.'s first memory of that day. Even 60 years later, he clearly remembered where he was at that moment.

We all have "Where were you?" memories. Where were you when he proposed? Where were you when a loved one passed away?

Nations have "Where were you?" memories. Almost every generation seems to experience at least one. Where were you when you heard the Japanese bombed Pearl Harbor? When JFK was assassinated? When terrorists attacked the Twin Towers on 9/11?

Likewise, many smaller communities share common memories. In Whiting, Indiana, the question is: Where were you at one minute after sunrise, 6:12 a.m., on August 27, 1955? For George Timko and everyone who lived in the Whiting area at that time, the answer to that question is as ingrained in their memories as Pearl Harbor, the Kennedy assassination, or 9/11. For them, it was a time of deep fear, of awe at the power of an explosion and the fury of the fire that followed.

On that day, at one minute after sunrise, the largest oil refinery in North America exploded. This is the story of that explosion – the most spectacular industrial accident in the history of Indiana and probably in all of Chicagoland. It is a story about people and their response to a disaster.

It is also a story about relationships. The Standard Oil Refinery and the people of Whiting had a decades-long relationship. Like most successful relationships, both sides benefited from it. In a town where almost every family depended on the refinery, the company paid its employees well and kept them on the payroll even in hard times. The workers responded with a fierce loyalty. A bond of trust developed.

That trust suffered a significant jolt on August 27, 1955. For the first time in the refinery's history, an explosion killed someone outside the company's property lines. For the first time, a refinery explosion obliterated a neighborhood. In the years that followed, for the first time, the company slashed jobs.

America was a different place in 1955. There were no cell phones and no internet. Only a few families had television sets, and even in a major media market like Chicago, viewers had only four channels available to watch. Most received their news from newspapers. Hardly any families in a working class community like Whiting had air conditioning in their homes. There were no video games to keep children occupied. Most children spent their playtime outdoors. Children walked to school and stayed out to play all day on weekends, and parents had little reason to worry about their safety.

Few families had more than one car, and quite a few had none at all. Interstates and expressways were coming, but not yet widespread. Just miles from Chicago, the main roads through Whiting were city streets doubling as U.S. highways. Traffic lights and stop signs choked the traffic.

It was a time when industry had fewer people questioning its actions and mistakes. There was no Environmental Protection Agency. Pollutants filled the air, saturated the ground, and drained into the waterways. There was no Occupational Safety and Health Administration. Employers were not required to answer to the government. Many did not even answer to their employees when workplace accidents occurred. There was also less pressure to cut costs and make larger and larger profits.

Some believe that life was never the same in Whiting after the explosion. But with TV, highways, and many other new developments on the way, life was gradually changing for all Americans in the 1950s. One minute after sunrise, then, was not just the time when an explosion occurred. It was not just the beginning of a new day. It was also the start of a new era in Whiting and many other communities across the United States.

THE CONDUCTOR

Everyone knew it was an important day. Thousands lined the streets of Chicago. A reporter for the *Chicago Democrat* said it looked like the entire city was there. William B. Ogden, Chicago's first mayor, was ready to give a speech; music played; a cannon was in position to fire a salute.[2]

What made this day important to the 38,000-plus residents of Chicago was the knowledge that their city was about to change. It was about to experience a population explosion. There was no guarantee, of course, but everyone felt it. It was coming as certainly as the train scheduled to arrive at 11 a.m. that day – February 20, 1852. It was coming because that train, operated by the Michigan Southern Railroad, would be the first to enter the city from the east. Once connected to the eastern United States, the population of Chicago would grow, and prosperity would follow. "Those who witnessed the first train would never forget it," wrote railroad historians Dave McLellan and Bill Warrick. "It marked the end of slow, water-borne transportation and the beginning of what was then an incredible speed for moving people and goods."[3]

Railroad operators and East Coast businessmen caught the excitement long before most Chicago residents. They knew they could make money by connecting the nation's midland to its eastern coast. They knew that Chicago could become the queen of the prairies, the gateway to the West. So, a race began. Both the Michigan Central and the Michigan Southern railroads wanted to reach Chicago first. It was a bitter battle. Both companies looked for an edge. They fought it out in courtrooms and state legislatures. They cut corners.

The home stretch of their race ran across northern Indiana. The Michigan Central hired workers to lay track between Detroit and Chicago to complete the company's route from the east. The rival crews from the Michigan Southern laid track between Toledo and Chicago.[4]

Laying track across Indiana was a challenge, especially near Lake Michigan in the state's northwest corner. About 145 million to 250 million years earlier, dinosaurs roamed what is now Northwest Indiana. Mastodons lived there in more recent times…just 10,000 to 12,000 years ago. But the most important event in prehistoric Northwest Indiana took place between two million and 12,000 years ago, when the series of glaciers that covered the area began to melt. As those glaciers melted and the ice sheet receded to the north, they left behind a sandy and marshy landscape. "The country falls off into pond[s] and marshes that can never admit of settlement nor never will be of much service to our State." That was the opinion of future U.S. Senator John Tipton in 1821, as he served as a commissioner to establish the boundary between Indiana and Illinois.[5]

Just east of the Illinois state line, Northwest Indiana was an outdoorsman's paradise in the 1800s. Lakes, sloughs, and swamps attracted flocks of ducks, deer, and wild turkeys. Strawberries and raspberries were abundant, and cranberries and huckleberries were plentiful. But as Tipton predicted, early 19th-century pioneers bypassed the state's northwest corner. Indiana became a state in 1816, but 36 years later its northwest corner had few inhabitants. Historian Powell Moore called it Indiana's "Last Frontier." Now, in the brutal winter of 1851–1852, railroad workers struggled to lay track over this no-man's land.

That winter, temperatures dipped to 15 degrees below zero. A winter storm hit the Chicago area. One newspaper described it as "the wildest and most inhospitable we have ever witnessed in this city." Through it all, the railroad crews kept working, laying track over the sand and swamps.[6]

At a few minutes before noon on February 20, 1852, the anxious crowd gathered in Chicago spotted smoke, which "gracefully curled up behind the trees in the distance." The sight of it created a stir "as animated as a beehive," according to a reporter for the *Chicago Daily Journal*. Young men climbed onto fences and rooftops to get a better view of the incoming train. Perhaps it was an omen for generations of passengers to come, but the train was an hour late.[7]

Soon the crowd began to cheer, and the cannons boomed. The train was in sight. The race was over. The Michigan Southern claimed victory. The Monroe, "a neat little engine," as a reporter for the *Western Citizen* described it, led the way. Attached were a few freight cars loaded with some of the men who built the track. Behind it was another engine, The Bronson, "large and beautifully decorated." It pulled two passenger cars filled with people who had gone out to meet the train, jumped on board, and ridden part of the way into the city. When the train came to a stop, the speeches began. Mayor Ogden talked about the prosperity that would follow, and he proposed three cheers for the Michigan Southern.[8]

As festive as the occasion was, the Michigan Southern did not really win the race. It changed the rules to make it appear that it won the race. The train that arrived in Chicago that day had not traveled from the East Coast, or even from Toledo. It started its journey in Michigan City, Indiana.

The swampy, sandy land of Northwest Indiana presented numerous problems for the men laying the track. They'd finished the section between Michigan City and Chicago, and the road from La Porte to the east was complete. But they had yet to finish an 11-mile stretch between Michigan City and La Porte. To beat the Michigan Central to Chicago, the Michigan Southern needed a different plan.

That plan involved a plank road that connected Michigan City and La Porte. The Michigan Southern put the Monroe, a small construction engine, on a sled. They then dragged it along that plank road to Michigan City. They most likely got the Bronson to Michigan City on a ship via Lake Michigan. They placed both engines on the track at Michigan City, and from there they rode into Chicago. Michigan City was not the East Coast, but that did not dampen the enthusiasm of the crowd. They knew the connection would soon be complete.[9]

The connection was completed three months later. On May 21, the first train carrying passengers from the east arrived. It was a Michigan Central with 500 first-class passengers and 300 others on board. Two days later, a labor force of 200 men and 60 teams of horses finished the Michigan Southern's link to Chicago.[10]

Passenger service to and from Chicago was ready to begin in earnest. Still, the rail link was not complete all the way to the East Coast. Passengers could go as far as Monroe, Michigan, and then board a boat that would take them across Lake Erie. It took almost another year – January 24, 1853 – before a passenger could travel solely by train from Chicago to Buffalo. Until then, the Michigan Southern bragged, a trip of 45 hours between New York and Chicago was the "quickest time yet." One of its trains clocked that time in mid-1852.

On board that train was a 31-year-old conductor by the name of Herbert Lloyd Whiting. Before his long career in the railroad industry ended, a city in Indiana would carry his name. But when he died, his obituary did not mention the city of Whiting. What made him most proud, it said, was being the conductor in charge of the Michigan Southern's first through train out of Chicago.[11]

Herbert Lloyd "Pop" Whiting never lived in the city in Indiana that bears his name. But he frequently passed through it as a conductor on passenger trains in and out of Chicago.

Most records, and even his tombstone, say Whiting was born in 1821. But an entry in the birth records of Brimfield, Massachusetts (a town between the Massachusetts cities of Springfield and Worcester) shows August 19, 1817, as his date of birth. He was the second child of Ezekiel Whiting and Azubah Moulton. Herbert's older brother was Homer. His younger siblings were Hudson, Herschel, Helen, Hersey, and Hermione. When Ezekiel and Azubah apparently ran out of names starting with an "H," they chose to call their youngest "Laura."[12]

In his early years, Whiting worked as a farmer and a laborer. After finishing his schooling, he looked for work in railroading, the growth industry of the time. Whiting worked as a conductor on the newly built New York and Boston Railway. As conductor, he became acquainted with many of the regular passengers, including the Barton family. Rosella Towne Barton was a cousin of Clara Barton, who later founded the American Red Cross. Herbert and Rosella married in 1850. In 1852, he took a position with the Michigan Southern as it began its service to Chicago.[13]

The worst day in Whiting's career came less than a year later. He was the conductor on board a Michigan Southern train that left Chicago on the night of April 25, 1853. Eight miles from the future city of Whiting, two railroad tracks crossed, almost at a right angle. The area later became known as Grand Crossing. Today, it is near 75th Street and South Chicago Avenue, on Chicago's south side. Then, it was a rural, unsettled area. One track belonged to the Michigan Southern. The other track belonged to its bitter rival, the Michigan Central.

The Michigan Southern left Chicago at nine p.m., eastbound. It was dark. The moon was not yet up, but the night was clear. The train made a stop not long after leaving the heart of the city, at an intersection where the Rock Island Railroad came into Chicago. Several passengers on the Rock Island needed to transfer onto the Michigan Southern, but the Rock Island was running late, and the Michigan Southern had to wait. The delay put the Michigan Southern a half-hour behind schedule.

Meanwhile, a westbound Michigan Central train was nearing the end of its long journey. It was coming toward the city of Chicago. It should have been there more than seven hours earlier.

When the Michigan Central stopped in Michigan City, Thomas Rackham, its engineer, noticed that his headlamp was out. Fastened in front of the train's smokestack, a headlamp helped engineers see better at night. Just as important, on a clear night with no obstructions, engineers on other trains could see these headlamps from 10 miles away. Rackham reported to a man named Jurat, the superintendent of the machine shop in Michigan City, that his light was defective. But, according to Rackham, Jurat said nothing and did nothing. Already far behind schedule, Rackham became impatient. He decided to move on into the night without a functioning headlamp on his train.

Around 10 p.m., at about 12 miles an hour, Rackham's Michigan Central train approached the spot where the two tracks crossed. A half-mile from the crossing, Rackham saw a light from the eastbound Michigan Southern train. He knew it was close. But Edward Davis, the engineer on the Southern, did not see the Michigan Central train. The area was open prairie with few obstructions. There was a slight fog around the swampy spot where the tracks met. Even so, Davis probably would have seen the Michigan Central if it had possessed a working headlamp.

Rackham figured he had the right of way. So, although he saw the oncoming train, he crossed the Michigan Southern track. Rackham assumed the eastbound train would stop. He slowed his train down to about four miles per hour. Engineer Davis, on board the Michigan Southern, stood on the footboard of his wood-burning engine, his head sticking out the window and his hand grasping the throttle. Less than a quarter-mile from the crossing, he saw sparks ahead. In this rural area, he knew the only thing it could be was sparks from another train. Davis blew the whistle – a signal for the brakeman to apply the brakes. At that moment, with his train only 10 to 15 seconds away from the crossing, the headlamp from his own train allowed Davis to see the Michigan Central for the first time. It was directly ahead of him.

The Michigan Southern, going 20 to 25 miles an hour, rammed into the side of the other train. The Michigan Central was 24 cars long, and most carried freight. But the engine of the Michigan Southern crashed straight into the passenger cars. Eighty people were on board those cars. They were called "emigrant" cars, one of the cheapest and most uncomfortable ways to travel long distances in the 1850s. The only thing inside most wood-framed emigrant cars was a wooden bench. Many of those on board this crowded Michigan Central train were Germans, heading to Chicago to start a new life in America.

The Michigan Southern split the emigrant car in half. Splintered wood and bodies flew through the air, some landing in the muddy water alongside the track. Herbert Whiting was standing near the back of a passenger car on the Southern when his train hit the Central's. The impact of the crash injured Whiting and damaged the car he was in, but he got off the train by going through the adjacent baggage car.

What Whiting saw when he emerged from the train was horrific. J.N. Flesh, a Norwegian passenger on Whiting's train, was hanging by his foot from the wreckage. The collision threw George Miner and Allen Richmond into the water near the track. They were both from Ohio and were both passengers on Whiting's train.

But the passengers on the Southern did not bear the brunt of the collision. For the occupants of the Central's emigrant car, the crash was deadly. People on board that car were "maimed and mangled, dead and dying," according to a report in the *Chicago Democratic Press*. In that remote area, "Shrieks...startled the midnight air," the reporter wrote. "Groans...were but a faint echo of the physical and mental anguish which the unfortunate sufferers endured."

Whiting did what he could to help the injured, but after about 20 minutes he realized he needed help. He took off on foot toward the junction with the Rock Island Line. He walked the same track his train had been on just before the crash. It was a two-and-a-half-mile walk in the dark of night.

When Whiting arrived at the junction, he told the people he found there about the accident. It was the first news anyone not on board the two trains had heard about the deadly collision. He and several others then returned to the accident scene on a locomotive.

A coroner's inquest convened the day after the crash. Michigan Central Engineer Thomas Rackham did not escape criticism for operating a train without a headlamp. He also admitted, in hindsight, to two errors. He should not have slowed down to four miles per hour. If he had maintained his speed, his train might have cleared the track before the Michigan Southern arrived. And knowing his headlamp was out, he should have stopped to give the Michigan Southern the right of way.

Engineer Edward Davis of the Michigan Southern also received criticism. Based on general practices, trains coming into Chicago had the right of way over trains leaving the city. Davis should have stopped. In his defense, Davis said he did not see the Central until it was too late. The coroner's jury charged Davis and Rackham with gross carelessness. Whiting and the conductor on the Central were charged with the same offense.

But the bulk of the criticism soon shifted to the two railroads. Why had they built their tracks in such a manner? The answer went back to the race between the Michigan Southern and the Michigan Central to be the first railroad to reach Chicago from the east.

The Michigan Southern was the first to lay its track in the Grand Crossing area, the scene of the collision. But the Michigan Central claimed it had priority rights over that ground. It based its argument on the fact that it was first to receive approval from the state of Illinois to operate in the state. The Michigan Central could have built a bridge over the Southern's track. But to do so would have cost more money and delayed the railroad in its effort to beat the Southern in their race to Chicago.

Officials from the Southern were not happy with the Central's decision. The Central sent armed guards to the site in fear that the Southern would send men in the dark of night to dismantle the Central's track. Less than a year later, the guards were gone, and neither railroad thought it was important to send a watchman to the intersection to prevent an accident. Twenty-one people died in the collision of the Michigan Southern and Michigan Central. Sixty were injured.[14]

Tracks going east-west and others going north-south crossed at an area that became known as Grand Crossing, now on Chicago's south side. This is what the area looked like in the early 1900s. About 50 years earlier, it was the spot of a horrible collision between two trains, one of them with Herbert Lloyd "Pop" Whiting on board as the conductor.

For the next 15 years, Herbert Whiting stayed out of the public record. He continued as a conductor on the Michigan Southern. He stayed on even as the railroad went through ownership and name changes, eventually becoming known as the Lake Shore and Michigan Southern. His job, however, didn't change much. As a conductor, he was the familiar face seen by travelers on the trains coming in and out of Chicago.

Sometime around 1868, the Michigan Southern built a siding along its track in Northwest Indiana. A siding is a pull-off, a place where trains can get off the main track. There are different reasons for sidings. They can serve as a place where trains load or unload freight or passengers, or a place where a slower train can get out of the way of a faster train coming up from behind. The siding built by the Michigan Southern in 1868 was about 15 miles from the heart of Chicago. They named it Whiting's Siding. Why did the railroad choose to name the siding after one of its conductors? In his job as a conductor, Whiting often passed through the area, but he never lived there and never owned property there.

In 1894, Whiting was 75 (based on his 1821 birthdate) and still working for the Lake Shore and Michigan Southern. A story appeared in the newspapers. Whiting got its name, an article in the *Whiting Democrat* said, after a "gray-haired conductor ran his train off the track…and thereafter the spot was known as 'Pap Whiting's Siding.'" The newspaper called him "an old grizzled conductor known to the boys as 'Pap' Whiting." It claimed, "he was known to every crew," on the Lake Shore and Michigan Southern, "and was quite a character."[15]

Although the 1894 article reported that Whiting ran his train off the track 25 years earlier, there is no known contemporary account of that happening in or around 1869. Yet, the story earns some credibility just by the fact that it has been so often repeated. The *Whiting Sun* repeated it in 1898. Whiting was the conductor of a train that wrecked here, the paper declared, and people referred to the site as "Whiting's" from that time on.[16]

In 1900, the legend of heroic train engineer Casey Jones first captured America's attention. In that same year, the *Chicago Tribune* told the story of "Pap" Whiting, with much embellishment. He was, the newspaper said, "one of the humblest men that ever pulled a throttle or ditched a train." Whiting was a conductor on passenger trains for most of his working life. In this version, he became an engineer on a freight train.

"Old Pap Whiting," the *Tribune* said, was "fearless...if not reckless." It was not infrequently that he "took large chances in order to make time." One day, the story went, he was hauling freight. He was "pounding along down the line with a heavy train, trying to make a certain siding to get out of the way" of a fast-moving passenger train that was coming up from behind. "His haste overcame his discretion and on a nasty bit of track he ditched his entire train, doing it all so neatly that he left the passenger as clear a track as if he had pulled in on the desired siding." From then on, the area where he ditched the train was known as "Pap Whiting's Siding."[17]

The story of "the humblest man who ever pulled a throttle" is the most colorful explanation of how the city of Whiting got its name. But other accounts also appeared. In 1907, early Whiting resident C.D. Davidson identified Whiting as a conductor on the Lake Shore Railroad, and this was "the place where the freight trains would sidetrack to let Whiting pass." Another story – also published in 1907 – said that after congestion had led to a wreck on the tracks, Herbert L. Whiting suggested to his employers that they put in a siding. The railroad liked his idea and called it "Whiting Siding" as a "compliment to the man who had made the suggestion."[18]

Another explanation seems to refer to the 1853 wreck at Grand Crossing, eight miles away, which reported that the area had taken the name of a conductor "who tried to conduct his train across the tracks of another railroad occupied by a train, the result being a disastrous wreck." And yet another seems to agree: "The wrecking of a train or freight, which crashed into another line's string of cars, was responsible for the building of a siding to avoid similar mishaps. The siding was called Whiting's Siding, Whiting's Turnout, or simply Whiting's."[19]

The *Whiting Democrat's* story estimated that Whiting "ditched his freight train" in 1869. But the name Whiting is known to have existed at least one year earlier. "Whiting's" was listed in the 1868 edition of the *Michigan Southern and Northern Indiana Rail Road Business Gazetteer*. Whiting's was described as a side track, used only for the meeting of trains. The publication also gave another version of how Whiting got its name, saying it "takes its name from one of the oldest conductors on the road." By at least 1868, the name was in common usage. That year, a newspaper reported a dead body "found on the lake shore near Whiting station," washed up from the lake.[20]

No one may ever know with complete certainty why "Pop" Whiting (as he became known to future generations) had a city named after him. Maybe he was a "fearless, if not reckless" railroad man. Maybe he was a conductor who had an idea for a siding that his employer liked. Maybe he was a longtime conductor who always received the right of way from other conductors. But one thing for certain is that naming a city after a man like him was unusual. The neighboring city of Gary, Indiana got its name from a powerful steel company executive. Nearby Hammond was named after the owner of the first industry to make that city its home. Whiting, by contrast, bears the name of a working man. He was not rich. He was not famous. He may not even have been "fearless." He was just a guy who showed up every day for over 40 years, did his job, and earned the respect of those who knew him. He was, in many ways, like the thousands of other men and women who later made their home in the city that bears his name.

Herbert Lloyd Whiting was born in Massachusetts and lived most of his adult life in Chicago. A foot stone marks his grave in Chicago's Oak Woods Cemetery. On the cemetery's east side is a railroad track. The track marks the same route through Chicago that Whiting traveled for 40 years as a passenger train conductor.

Herbert L. Whiting died on June 24, 1897, in the garden of his Chicago home at 2417 South Park Avenue, which later became Martin Luther King Drive. The dates on his tombstone indicate he was 76. Whiting had stopped working as a conductor 10 years earlier but continued to work in the Lake Shore Railroad's office until his death. He spent 45 years with the same company. "He was a very general favorite among his fellow employees and acquaintances," said an article in a magazine published by the Order of Railway Conductors after his death. Whiting's burial place is in Chicago's Oak Woods Cemetery. He rests in peace about a mile from the site of the 1853 wreck at Grand Crossing.[21]

THE MILLIONAIRE

The noise was deafening. "It was enough to wake the dead," was the line some members of the Eggers family used to describe it. It was so loud that the small children in their family could not sleep. Grandmother Eggers lost all patience. She grabbed a gun, stepped out of the house, and took a shot. The skies and the water were so filled with ducks and other waterfowl, "with that one random shot (she) brought down nine mallards." That was early Whiting. It teemed with noisy birds and waterfowl, and other than an occasional angry grandmother, there was little to disturb them.[22]

The area was nearly surrounded by water: Lake Michigan to the north, Wolf Lake to the west, George Lake to the south, and Berry Lake to the east. It was duck paradise. But for humans trying to settle in that area, Whiting was "one of the most uninviting portions of the region," in the words of historian Powell Moore. "The greater part of the area was a wilderness of sand and swamps covered with a luxuriant growth of marsh grass, wild rice, and scrub oak. Great sand ridges lay parallel to Lake Michigan and between these were deep sloughs and swamps."[23]

From the 1850s to well into the 1880s, Whiting was, at most, a dot on a railroad map. Its first settlers were rail workers. Carl Steiber was the section boss on the railroad that passed through the area. His job was to maintain the track and other railroad property. He needed workers to do that, and he was willing to pay a dollar a day. That was good enough for Henry Reese, a German immigrant who worked in Arlington Heights, Illinois at the time. Reese brought his wife and three-week-old baby to what is now Whiting and was hired by Steiber. That was the spring of 1854.[24]

When the Reese family arrived, they discovered there were no houses available in Whiting. To help the family out, the 15 men on the railroad section crew stopped work and built them one. It took them two hours to finish and get back to their jobs.[25]

Between the arrival of the railroad in 1852 and the census of 1880, the population did not grow significantly. In 1880 there were about 21 households at Whiting Station with about 100 people. Half of them were born outside the United States. By far, the largest group of foreign born were from Germany. Life was not easy at Whiting Station. Only about five percent of the population was over the age of 60. The most common occupations among the settlers were as laborers and railroad section hands. But there was a tailor – William Fisher. Henry Seehausen and Albert Poppen were shoemakers. Christian Vincents was an umbrella repairman. The telegraph operator was R.F. Scoffern. Henry Schrage ran the hotel and saloon, while Henry Eggers was an ice dealer with an ice house at Berry Lake.[26]

By all accounts, the area was beautiful. "There were all kinds of woods and birds, and the whole place was so pretty," said Emma Thamm. She came to Whiting in 1883. Beyond that, it was not appealing. "You bring me here to this sand hole!" her mother screamed to her father when they first arrived. The tramps scared Emma. They would jump off rail cars and look for anything they could get for free, no matter how they got it. Maybe even more frightening were the snakes. "There were always lots of snakes around here," Emma said. They were especially numerous around the many bushes where berries grew.[27]

James Perry Johnston was the operator in charge of Whiting's night telegraph office. He was also the first to mention Whiting in a work of fiction. He wrote about it in *Twenty Years of Hus'ling*, published in 1887. One 21st century reviewer of his book described Johnston as "a mountebank and charlatan who traveled the Midwest in the last quarter of the 1800s, selling furniture polish, cheap jewelry, patent rights to doubtful inventions, trading horses, and auctioneering." Johnston claimed his book outsold the works of Mark Twain, a contemporary. But the reviewer adds that Johnston "wasn't above lying." In the book, Johnston devotes several pages to the short time he worked in Whiting.[28]

"There was plenty of duck hunting and frog catching among the settlers" in Whiting, he wrote. Johnston, always looking for a way to make money, worked out a deal with the settlers. He would buy all the frogs they could get their hands on and he, in turn, would sell the frogs to a merchant in Chicago. One day, Johnston's boss, the division superintendent of the telegraph office, got off the train when it stopped in Whiting. He spotted Johnston loading boxes of frogs onto the train. "Does the railroad company pay you to buy frogs?" the superintendent asked. Johnston answered, "No, they pay my board to watch the station, and I buy and sell frogs to make my salary."[29]

More people in Whiting made their money cutting ice and gathering gravel than catching frogs. "In winter, there were about 100 men employed here cutting ice," said Henry Theobold, who came to Whiting in 1886. In the days before refrigeration, businesses used ice cut from lakes to keep food fresh and safe to eat. There were ice houses east of Whiting on Berry Lake and west of Whiting on Wolf Lake. Between them, on the northern shore of Wolf Lake and all the way to what would become Front Street in Whiting, there were woods and sand dunes. "There used to be a lot of wild grapes growing there," Theobold recalled. "We would go out and pick them and make grape juice and jelly. One winter we picked 75 gallons. Between the woods were swamps with plenty of water-lilies and frogs. We could almost dance to the concert the frogs and crickets broadcast from these swamps."[30]

Although the community's growth was stagnant, it was in the middle of a booming part of the United States. By 1869, railroad tracks stretched across North America from the Atlantic to the Pacific. With the railroad, Americans moved west in greater numbers. But while thousands passed through Whiting on the trains, few stopped. They were on their way to other places in the Midwest. In the 1880s, Chicago's population rose 119 percent. That growth was slow compared to Minneapolis at 251 percent, Omaha at 360 percent, and Duluth at 851 percent. Those numbers did not escape the attention of John D. Rockefeller.[31]

A generation earlier, Samuel Kier and his family owned a Pennsylvania salt mine. When oil started to leak into the mine, the family tried to sell the oil, but no one wanted it. The Kiers dumped it into a nearby canal, but the oil slick caught on fire. Kier then tried to figure out ways to make money from it. He tried to pass it off as medicine. "A few sips of Pennsylvania crude could help the blind see or the lame walk," was his advertising pitch. When consumers discovered that a daily sip of oil failed to produce miracle results, Kier searched for other ideas. That led him to a discovery. He found a way to produce kerosene from crude oil – inexpensively.

Until the mid-1800s, whale and coal oils fueled most lamps used to produce light. Kerosene was known as an alternative, but it was too expensive to produce until Kier came up with a way to do it. In 1853, one year after railroad tracks arrived in Northwest Indiana, Kier created the first oil refinery, in Pittsburgh.

But Kier soon had another problem: His product was popular, and he did not have enough oil to meet the demand. Kier relied on oil that seeped up from the ground, but the ground yielded only small amounts. No one had figured out a cost-effective way to get oil out of the ground by drilling. That changed in 1859 at Titusville, Pennsylvania, when Edwin Drake drilled the world's first oil well. The oil industry was born.[32]

Like gold in California a decade earlier, Drake's discovery triggered a mad rush to get rich from "black gold." Wells were drilled and oil deposits were discovered in Pennsylvania, Ohio, and Indiana. Refineries were built to process the oil. But of the many who tried to get rich, none succeeded as well as Rockefeller. Using oil from wells in Ohio, he built a refinery in Cleveland that produced lubricating oil, tar, paraffin for candles, and kerosene for lamps. He became a millionaire.[33]

Rockefeller noticed that America's booming population wanted kerosene. He saw that its prospering manufacturing plants wanted lubricants. Standard Oil, his company, also tried to convince owners of coal furnaces to convert to oil for heating. Oil was "the fuel of the future," their marketing department said. The idea caught on, especially in Chicago, with Milwaukee and Minneapolis close behind. The Midwest was thirsty for the products Standard Oil made.

Standard Oil's westernmost refinery was in Lima, in western Ohio, in the midst of Ohio's oil fields. But Rockefeller recognized that this was too far from the booming Midwest market. In 1888, Standard Oil began building a pipeline. "It is their intention," an 1888 *Chicago Tribune* article stated, "to place the fuel oil at the doors of the great Chicago manufactories at as cheap a figure as possible." The pipeline was the best way to do that.[34]

The pipeline was begun in Lima, and by July 1888 workmen were in Whiting laying a pipeline just north of the railroad track. Each section of pipe was 22 feet long and eight inches in diameter, and it took 1,050 railcar loads of pipe to finish the job.[35]

Just as it was with the arrival of the railroad 36 years earlier, Whiting was no more than a dot on the map along the pipeline's way. The end point was just a few miles west – a terminal on Lake Michigan on 50 acres at the foot of 100th Street in Chicago, in an area called Fleming Park. Years later it became Chicago's Calumet Park. Oil reached the Chicago terminal by pipeline and by rail. Before long, 15,000 barrels of oil arrived at the terminal each day, temporarily stored in large tanks. There was no problem selling it once it arrived. The demand for oil was still greater than the supply.[36]

Standard Oil soon recognized that it needed more than a terminal to serve Chicago and the Midwest. It needed a refinery. The company drew up plans to build one at Fleming Park, at its 100th Street terminal. Pipelines and storage tanks were already in place, and the site was well served by railroads and by shipping across Lake Michigan. But there was one big, smelly problem: Standard's oil came from Lima-area wells. Lima's oil was rich in sulfur. "If you got a drop on you," wrote Paul Giddens, a Standard Oil historian, "you smelled like a rotten egg." It also stank up the neighborhood, and residents of South Chicago complained.

"About this time," Lake County historian Thomas Cannon wrote, "one of the tanks split from top to bottom, pouring oil over the ground; this settled the question – the citizens there did not want oil as a next door neighbor." Standard Oil was not entirely disappointed to leave Chicago. Taxes were high, and there was not much room for future expansion of its planned refinery. The company began a thorough search for a new location. The site they found, as Giddens put it, was "in a desolate spot on the sand dunes along the southern shore of Lake Michigan about two miles east of the Illinois-Indiana line…at a place called Whiting, Indiana."[37]

The location was perfect. It was sparsely populated, so objections to the smell would be few. Surrounded by what was then considered useless sand dunes and marshes, the price of the land was low. With no other industry or cities in the immediate area, there was plenty of room to grow. There was an endless supply of water from Lake Michigan. Major rail lines and a pipeline were already in place.

The company quickly bought up land. Workers from Standard Oil's Cleveland plant and boilermakers from Buffalo provided the expertise needed to build the refinery. The company hired local residents to help with the construction. Henry Theobold cut trees along Berry Lake. He made $1.50 for a day's work. Crews also uprooted brush, drained swales, and leveled sand dunes. There were not enough workers living in Whiting to even come close to filling the many jobs. So, every day, the train brought throngs of men to Whiting. They showed up at the gate, hoping to get work and a day's pay. Many of them came from Chicago and other Illinois communities. Many of them were European immigrants.

Boardinghouses and dwellings soon went up. Front Street, near the plant and the track where the train to Whiting stopped, became dotted with saloons. The first retail stores opened on what became 119th Street – Whiting's main thoroughfare. Within two years, the refinery employed 2,000 men.[38]

For the new arrivals, life in Whiting was a challenge. "There were lots of fleas!" remembered Hannah Falkenthal, who came to town as a newlywed in 1889. "Whiting's pest, the sand flea, is almost unbearable this year," the *Lake County News* reported a few years later. "Nothing can be found with which to exterminate them." Besides the bugs, sand was a problem. "Those sand hills, I didn't like," Hannah added. "There were awful many sand hills on John Street, where we lived." Lena Vogel had the same complaint after arriving in 1891. "There were no sidewalks or streets. We waded in sand up to our knees."[39]

Despite the challenges, people flocked to Whiting. Between 1890 and 1900, the city's population jumped from 200 to 3,983, an increase of 1,892 percent. All signs indicated that the growth, fueled by Standard Oil, would continue. Oil was a booming industry. The Whiting Refinery produced kerosene, the best fuel for providing light. It produced heating oil, arguably the best fuel at the time for keeping a house or office warm. It produced lubricating oils at a time when industry was overtaking agriculture as America's primary employer. The refinery was prosperous even before the automobile took center stage in American life.

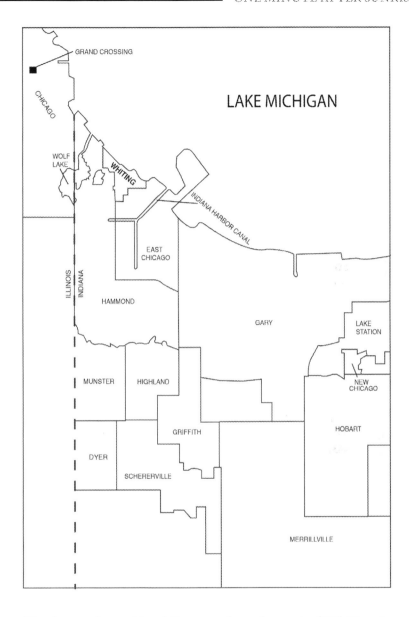

The far northern side of Hammond, to the west of Whiting, is the Robertsdale area. Whiting and Robertsdale share the same zip code and the same telephone exchange, and many of their residents attend the same churches and shop at the same stores. Even though they are not the same city, the two have, in many ways, been one community almost from their earliest history. (Map by John Lambert.)

"The real product is kerosene, kerosene for illumination," said a character in *Danger! Keep Out,* a 1943 novel by Edward J. Nichols. Although Nichols did not mention Whiting by name in his book, he did live in the city. Starting as early as 1914, he also worked several summers in the refinery. It was clear Nichols had Whiting and the early years of the refinery in mind when he wrote the book. "In addition to the all-important kerosene, we made oil for lanterns and railway headlamps. There were greases for locomotives, for the doctor's rig, and for the hay wagon on the farm. There was also a wax for candles and for the housewife's canning, and naphtha for varnishes and paints."[40]

Gasoline? Nichols' character said they produced gas in the early days of the refinery. But "we couldn't dispose of it, except as deodorized stove gasoline and for other minor uses." In 1910, the plant converted "as little as 10 percent of our crude" to gasoline.[41]

But that was changing. "There are approximately 2,400 machines in the state," said state Senator D.L. Crumpacker, of Westville, in 1905. He was not alone in trying to figure out what to call those "machines," as well as the "autoists" who drove them. When cars began to appear in Whiting, they were an irritation to most people. Many of those cars came from Chicago, manned by drivers going for a long spin in the country. "A scorching automobile was pursued by several irate citizens on Wednesday evening," the *Whiting Sun* reported in 1906. "They received nothing for their pains but a good supply of dust in their eyes. Autos are growing to be a menace to life and limb as they whiz thru town." In response, the city made it illegal "for any person to ride or drive any animal or vehicle within the limits of said city, at a rate faster than eight miles per hour."[42]

Manufacturers were making cars cheaper and more dependable. Between 1907 and 1912, they became affordable for farmers and laborers. The result was a tremendous increase in the sale of automobiles. Nationwide, there were four cars in the United States in 1895; 8,000 by 1900; 500,000 by 1910. While Whiting residents may have complained about drivers, John D. Rockefeller probably smiled at the sight of one. He knew that automobiles needed fuel, and he was confident that Standard Oil was in a position to be the primary supplier of that fuel.[43]

The refinery grew. As it did, other industries soon saw what Rockefeller recognized: Northwest Indiana had much to offer. Just to the east of Whiting, a steel mill went up in 1901, which became Inland Steel. Berry Lake vanished, filled in to provide more land for industry. Two years later the Indiana Harbor Ship Canal opened to the east of the refinery, improving access to Lake Michigan. In 1906, a little farther east, United States Steel opened the largest steel mill in the world in the new city of Gary. Heavy industry scooped up cheap land along Lake Michigan's southern tip and adjacent properties. In 1915, Sinclair established an oil refinery just to the south of Standard Oil's facility. Youngstown Sheet and Tube Company opened a mill in East Chicago in 1923. By 1938, more than 50 plants in East Chicago manufactured almost 400 different products. Hammond, just to the west and south of Whiting, had 74 manufacturing plants producing corn syrup, railway equipment, hospital supplies, tile roofing and many other products.[44]

The Calumet River runs through Northwest Indiana, south of Whiting. The Calumet Region, as the area came to be known, was on the verge of greatness in the early 1900s. At least, that's what some were saying. "The eyes of the world are on the Calumet Region," said one typical newspaper article of the period, as it was "triumphantly marching to its destiny...It will become the center of the iron and steel industry of the world, the greatest port in the world." Whiting's growth continued in the first decade of the 1900s, rising in population to 6,587 in 1910, an increase of 65 percent in 10 years. Neighboring East Chicago was up 460 percent to 19,098. Hammond was up 69 percent to 20,925. And nearby Gary, the newest of the four cities in the industrial heart of northwest Indiana, founded just four years earlier, was at 16,802 in 1910. The rate of growth was dizzying.[45]

From its earliest days, Whiting was a city of immigrants. Many in the generation that arrived before Standard Oil were German. A new wave of immigrants, from many different countries, came with the building of the refinery. Besides Germans, there were Irish, Turks, Russians, Croatians, Serbs, Hungarians, Greeks, Italians, and even a few Chinese. By 1920, Whiting's population had grown to 10,145. Almost 40 percent were foreign born. And if the number of native-born Americans with at least one parent who was born overseas is added to the mix, then a whopping 67 percent of Whiting was either foreign or first-generation American. In Indiana, only neighboring East Chicago had a higher percentage of non-native residents.

In 1920, Poles were the largest ethnic group in East Chicago, Gary, and Hammond, but not in Whiting. Ten percent of Whiting's residents were Slovak; 7.2 percent were Polish. There were more native Slovak residents in Whiting than there were in 24 of the 48 states in 1920. Other cities, like New York and Chicago, may have had more Slovaks, but there was no city in the United States that had a higher percentage of Slovaks. Whiting was the most Slovak city in America.[46]

A lot of the early Slovak residents were already living in America when they came to Whiting. Many of them had moved to the United States to work in the coal mines. Streator, 100 miles from Whiting in central Illinois, attracted hundreds of peasants from rural Slovakia who found employment in that area's mines. When construction began on the Whiting Refinery in 1889, Slovaks from Streator were among those looking for work. Slovaks from the coal mines of western Pennsylvania followed. Soon, word spread to their families still in Slovakia. Most of the newcomers were natives of Saris and Zemplin, two rural counties located in northeast Slovakia near the Polish border. They were peasants, accustomed to hard labor.[47]

Whiting did not have enough housing to handle this massive influx of new residents. Michael Kozacik, who later became a bank president, got a job with Standard Oil in 1892. He worked on the labor gang nine hours a day for $9 a week. He had to share a wooden shack with three other Slovak immigrants and slept on a bed of straw.[48]

The area was desperate for new housing, and many developers stepped in. Two of those were Chicago businessmen Gustav Stieglitz and George H. Heiberg. They filed their plans for the Stieglitz Subdivision with the Lake County Recorder's office on March 5, 1892. The plan divided their land into 233 parcels north of 131st Street and south of 129th. Indianapolis Boulevard, then known as Indiana Boulevard, was the eastern boundary. One block to the west of the Boulevard, the plan called for the creation of Berry Avenue; one block farther west, Louise Avenue. Most of the plots were 25 feet wide and between 110 to 130 feet deep.

The original plan also called for an additional 125 parcels to the east of Indiana Boulevard. Newly created George Street would intersect with 129th Street just one block east, and Forsyth Avenue would be two blocks east of the Boulevard.[49]

In 1895, Chicago real estate mogul Franklin H. Bierbach took over the marketing duties for the Stieglitz Subdivision. He was a man of many ideas, one of which was to change the name of the subdivision. He called it "Rockefeller Park." The name made sense to Bierbach. Nearby was Standard Oil's Whiting Refinery, owned by John D. Rockefeller, one of the most famous names in America. Never mind that some people said, "Scrub oaks and mosquitoes are the only living things which seem to enjoy the odor of oil which circulates there." Bierbach was a real estate developer. If he wanted to sell his property, he needed to create a different image in the minds of prospective buyers. Rockefeller was a name associated with the kind of rich, comfortable living that many Americans of the 1890s wanted. So, Rockefeller Park was the name he chose for his development.[50]

"If true happiness consists of independence and contentment," Bierbach said in his ads, "buy a home at Rockefeller Park and be the happiest of the happy." All you needed to buy into the happy life at Rockefeller Park was $5 for a deposit and payments of $1 a week on a lot. Lots cost $100 and up.[51]

To draw prospective buyers to Rockefeller Park, F.H. Bierbach and Company offered free train rides to the development every Sunday. Once there, they were regaled with the advantages of living on a street illuminated at night by electric lights. Every lady who visited on one of those Sundays received a special gift: a sheet of music called the "Rockefeller Park March." Professor Hjalmer Frithief Neilsson said the success and beauty of Rockefeller Park inspired him to write it. If the ladies and their husbands were lucky, they might be there on a day that Bierbach offered free concerts, with music by the Rockefeller Park Band.[52]

But Bierbach's sales pitch failed to win over at least one person. In June 1895, John D. Rockefeller sued. "People throughout the United States," his attorneys claimed, "are led to believe by the fraudulent use of his name and picture that he is connected with the so-called 'Rockefeller Park,' when in fact he has nothing to do with it." The courts agreed. Bierbach changed the name to Stieglitz Park, after Gustav Stieglitz, the owner of the development.[53]

Stieglitz had nowhere near the wealth that Rockefeller had, but he was a successful stone contractor in Chicago for many years. He built his business after coming to America from Germany in 1866. In 1893,

Stieglitz became secretary-treasurer of the American Metalware Company in Chicago. He remained there until his death in 1905. Like Bierbach and Rockefeller, Stieglitz never lived in the neighborhood that bore his name.[54]

In 1903, Whiting developer Charles D. Davidson began work on a section of land just north of Stieglitz Park. His plan called for 110 plots west of Indianapolis Boulevard and north of 129th Street. Ann Street was one block north of 129th, and 128th Street was just north of Ann. Grace Street was north of 128th. Even though it was Louise Street on the original Stieglitz Park map, Davidson called the street that formed the western boundary of both developments "Louisa." His plan also called for 16 plots of land to be sold on the eastern side of Indiana Boulevard, all of them north of 128th Street. Davidson's development originally was separate from the Stieglitz development, but both developments together became known as Stieglitz Park.[55]

Stieglitz Park, Goose Island, and Marktown were three neighborhoods on the southern end of the Standard Oil Refinery. Marktown was in East Chicago, Stieglitz Park in Whiting, and Goose Island partially in Whiting and partially in the Robertsdale section of Hammond. In this photo, a woman hangs her wash on a laundry line in her back yard in Stieglitz Park. (Photo courtesy Dennis Hittle.)

Most of the lots east of Indianapolis Boulevard never developed, but the other lots in Stieglitz Park sold. By 1955 there were about 180 houses in the neighborhood and over 700 residents. Stieglitz Park had its own grocery stores, gas stations, and tavern. Many who lived there worked at the refinery or at one of the other heavy industries located just a few miles away.[56]

Despite the foul smells and smoke-filled skies from the refinery, nearby steel mills, and other industries, there was security in the Calumet Region. It was a growth time for heavy industry. Jobs were available and most of the jobs paid well. For those who worked at Standard Oil, the security was even stronger. Standard Oil had a reputation for treating its workers well. In 1893, an economic panic hit the United States. Many lost their jobs. Wages in South Chicago, just a few miles east of Whiting, dropped to 10 cents an hour. Standard Oil, however, was hiring, and the minimum pay was 15 cents an hour. Whiting, according to Standard Oil historian Paul Giddens, had the distinction of being "almost the only town in the area in which wages did not fall during the panic." Standard adopted a policy of always paying about five percent more than other industries in the area.[57]

No one appreciated that more than the workers. John Locke arrived in Whiting in 1891 as a 22-year-old with $20 in his pocket. Based on his first impression, he was pretty sure he would need that money for the return trip home to Ohio. The temperature was 17 degrees below zero, and there were only two houses on 119th Street. But he stayed, and he never regretted it. "There is one thing I really liked about Standard," he said. "I've never been hurt by hard times."

Other companies shut down or laid off workers during the Great Depression of the 1930s. Standard, by contrast, spent $10 million on a plant rehabilitation program that kept its workers on the payroll. Locke remembered seeing up to 5,000 men at a time outside the company's main gate in those years, hoping Standard would hire them. As historian Powell Moore wrote: "Whiting, it was said in 1932, 'laughs at the Depression.' Ninety-eight percent of its taxes were paid, its banks were open, its teachers and city employees were being paid regularly."[58]

But what do you give up for security? "We didn't like it at first when we learned that Standard was coming," said Emma Thamm, who lived in Whiting before Standard Oil arrived. Like many others who came in the decades that followed, Emma learned to accept the bad to benefit from the good. "The odors weren't very pleasant, and fumes from the plant killed the oak trees. But they have been a good company."[59]

A 1906 *Chicago Tribune* article was highly critical of Standard Oil, Whiting, and its residents. "There is nothing at Whiting but the oil works," the report said. "Every soul in the place looks to the Standard Oil Company for bread and butter." The article conceded that at $1.35 to $1.80 a day, laborers were making good money and that working conditions were better than in most industrial plants of the time. But it argued that Standard's generosity had nothing to do with a desire to be fair to its workers. It was only a "good employer" because it wanted to avoid negative publicity and keep its employees quiet.

"There is plenty of discontent and anger in the stockyards of Chicago," the writer said, "but there is none of this in Whiting. The mouse does not struggle in the grasp of the cat. It knows that the cat is the master... This is the situation in Whiting. The Standard takes no chances. When it seeks control of a field of oil wells, of a pipeline, of a railroad, of a community, it takes precaution to make that control so absolute as to leave no possible chance for strife or dissension. There must be no room for doubt as to who is master."

Reflecting the bigoted attitudes of the era, the article claimed that was the reason Standard hired a Slavic workforce. They are "workers who are too ignorant of the customs and privileges of the country to 'make trouble.'" These Slavs, it said, are "the typical immigrant kind... unable to speak more than a few of the simplest words of English. Such men are used in all capacities where their lack of intelligence does not render them unavailable." Paying them well does not necessarily provide loyalty, the article said, "but it provides a peg upon which to hang a threat which does."[60]

The *Whiting Sun* defended its city: The "dirty slander...was uncalled for." And it supported Standard Oil, which "continues to be one of the best and highest paying corporations in the country."[61]

THE NEWSPAPER BOY

The summer of 1955 was a busy one for Dennis Hittle. It was a season of change in his life. In June, he graduated from grade school. In July, he turned 14. In September, he would begin high school at Bishop Noll in Hammond. But one thing he hoped would not change was his job as a newspaper delivery boy. He liked it.

Dennis was hired when he was 12 – taking over the route from Jerry Ward, who had taken over from his older brother. That's how it worked. Who you knew could make a difference in getting a good job, and once you got it, you did everything you could to hold onto it. Now that Dennis had a good job, he wanted to keep it until he was old enough to find something better. But he was still a boy, and it was summertime in the Stieglitz Park neighborhood of Whiting.

Dennis Hittle

There were probably better places for a kid to grow up. Still, few who lived in Whiting in 1955 would disagree with Tom Marciniak, who was 15 years old at the time. "Growing up in Whiting back then," he said, "was pretty damn good for a kid."[62]

Ten-year-old Dennis Zelenke would agree. But to ask him that question you would have to go to the beach. If the sun was out and the temperature was right, that's where he always was. Whiting Park, situated on the shores of Lake Michigan, was less than a mile away from Dennis' home on 119th Street. The lake was one of the best swimming holes in the world. On a clear day, Dennis could see the Chicago skyline across the water just 11 miles away. The brand new Prudential Building stood out. Topped off by the WGN television tower, it rose 912 feet from the ground. It was the tallest building in Chicago and one of the tallest in the world.[63]

Seven-year-old Lynn Larsen would also agree. She lived in Stieglitz Park, and at that age, a typical summer day would have found her riding her bicycle with her friends. "As long as we were back before it got dark, it was fine."[64]

Whiting was in an urban area, but it felt like a small town. "We were pretty much free to go anywhere," Tom remembered. "There were no safety issues. Everybody pretty much knew who you were in town. You really couldn't get into too much trouble. But if you did, everybody would know about it."

"Close" was the word Justine Moskalick Bircher used to describe Whiting. She was eight years old in 1955. Her recollection was, "We knew everybody." That closeness had its advantages and disadvantages for children. If everybody knew you, your parents would soon know if you did something wrong, and many parents of that era knew how to teach their children a lesson. Lynn Larsen learned that when she broke the family rule for riding her bicycle. "I didn't get home early enough, and my mom locked the doors on the house to teach me a lesson."[65]

By 1930, Whiting had reached its peak population of 10,880. Immigration slowed down as war devastated Europe, and new American immigration laws slowed the flow of newcomers. The foreign-born portion of Whiting's population, which had been 40 percent in 1920, dropped to 16 percent by 1950. Of those who were foreign-born, 39 percent were Slovak and 11 percent were Polish. And of its 9,669 people in 1950, only five were African-Americans.[66]

The immigrants who formed the working backbone of the refinery in the early decades of the 20th century were aging by 1955. But many of their first-generation American children also worked in the plant and strongly identified with the homelands of their parents. In 1961, a door-to-door census by the Roman Catholic parishes in the area indicated the foreign-born population was down to 13 percent. Most of those were elderly. About 60 percent of residents belonged to one of the five Catholic parishes in the community. About 33 percent identified as Protestants. Of the Catholic households, 82 percent said they identified with a particular ethnic group. Of those, 44 percent identified as Slovak, 19 percent as Polish, and seven percent as Croatian.[67]

Life seemed good in 1955 Whiting, although many outsiders could not understand why. James Hazzard was 19 years old in 1955. He grew up in Whiting and became a writer. He composed a poem titled, "A Girl from Connecticut Visited Whiting, Indiana."

> Later, safe in Evanston, she said, "People are so ugly there." She meant how they look, so many arms and legs given away for factory wages, and lumpy Slovak faces that don't hide a thing shift-work has pulled on them.[68]

Certainly, life was not easy. Living close to an oil refinery was not anyone's idea of paradise. Whiting's pioneers adjusted to life with sand, swamps, snakes and fleas. Over six decades later, people adjusted to smoke, smells and other forms of pollution. Yet, there was no doubt that life was better for them than it was for earlier Whiting residents.

"Charles Dunlap has gone to work in the office of the Standard," the *Whiting Sun* reported in 1904. "He was doing good work in the seventh grade, and it is very unfortunate that he should be compelled to leave school." By 1950, like Charles, 25 percent of Whiting's adults had never made it past the seventh grade. But 33 percent had made it through high school. That was progress.[69]

In 1906, the *Lake County News* identified the "large foreign family" as a problem in Whiting. "As high as 17 people eat, sleep and live in two small rooms; where the best of liquor is drunk by every member of the family as freely as water." The newspaper described the children of those families as "miserable little urchins…shivering in the cold without shoes, underclothing or wraps." By mid-century, those foreign families were doing better. While the median household income in 1950 Indiana was $2,827, in Whiting it was $4,096. In fact, only four cities in Indiana had a higher median household income than 1950 Whiting, and three of those (Munster, Griffith and Highland) were neighbors just a little south in Lake County.[70]

Industrial wages were responsible for lifting many of Whiting's families out of poverty. The typical Whiting family in 1950 was not wealthy, but they were in a better financial situation than their immigrant grandparents less than a half-century earlier. Many were willing to give credit for that to Standard Oil.

"It was good. They were good to their employees," said Robert Herakovich. Leo Kus also worked at the refinery. He called it "one of the jewels of the working force." Standard Oil's pay and benefits were among the best. "Most of the people that were working in the steel mills, every time they got a chance…they would run to Standard Oil." Just about everyone Evelyn Kortokrax knew in Whiting worked at Standard Oil, or so it seemed. If "What does your Dad do?" was the question, then "Whiting, Standard Oil," was how she described the usual response.[71]

Standard Oil "was one of the best things that ever happened to Whiting," said Michael and Julia Pukac. They "gave jobs to our parents' generation from Czechoslovakia…as they retired, their sons came in and their grandsons." John Locke came to Whiting in 1891 and retired after 47 years. He was still living in 1956, when his 65-year old son, George Locke, also retired from Standard Oil after 47 years.[72]

In his novel, Edward Nichols said there was loyalty in the relationship between the people of Whiting and the refinery. And it went both ways. "The town lives by this refinery and practically everybody works in it. They all feel as responsible as any boss in the plant." Joseph Hmurovich came to Whiting as a 26-year-old from Slovakia in 1926, got a job as a bricklayer at Standard Oil, became a foreman and retired at age 65. He learned to drive a car at age 57. For the rest of his life, even if his gas tank was near empty, he would drive past every gas station in town so that he could get to one selling Standard Oil gasoline.[73]

Despite the loyalty, there was widespread recognition that Standard Oil had its shortcomings. Few knew those better than the people of Stieglitz Park. The refinery started on 235 acres along the shores of Lake Michigan. By 1955, it covered 1,680 acres. Stieglitz Park was on the southwestern edge of that property. The neighborhood was across the street from the refinery. The only thing between them was Indianapolis Boulevard, a major north-south, four-lane street. On the east side of "the Boulevard," as the locals called it, was the refinery. On the west side was a line of houses and small shops, and more Stieglitz Park homes were behind them.[74]

Indianapolis Boulevard was the main north-south street in the neighborhood. 129th Street was the major east-west road. A mile east on 129th was Marktown, another small community in neighboring East Chicago. Even closer, to the west on 129th Street, was the community of Goose Island. Only a railroad track separated Goose Island from the western side of Stieglitz Park. Part of Goose Island was in Whiting, but the other part was in the Robertsdale section of neighboring Hammond.

Robertsdale was in the far northern part of Hammond, with Chicago on its western border and Whiting on its east side. Socially, economically and culturally, Robertsdale was more closely connected to Whiting than to Hammond. The Post Office reinforced those ties. All mail to Robertsdale residents went to the Whiting Post Office. When they gave their addresses, Robertsdale residents said "Whiting" as the name of their city, even though they lived in Hammond. They also shared the same "659" telephone exchange.

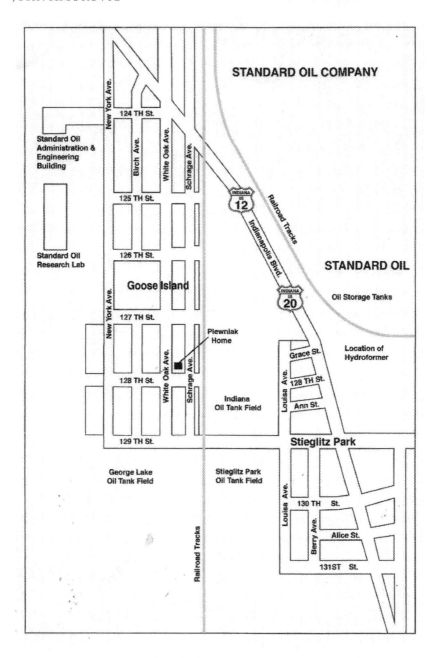

Stieglitz Park was surrounded by oil refineries. Standard Oil was across the street to the east, and the company had oil storage tanks to the north and west of the neighborhood. To the south of Stieglitz Park was the Sinclair Oil Refinery. (Map by John Lambert.)

But other than Goose Island and Marktown, there were no residential neighborhoods close to Stieglitz Park. Its neighbor to the south was the Sinclair Oil Refinery. Youngstown Sheet & Tube and Inland Steel were to the east. The sprawling Standard Oil refinery was Stieglitz Park's neighbor to the north. On the western edge of neighboring Goose Island was Standard Oil's new research lab. From the sky, Stieglitz Park, Goose Island, and Marktown looked like small islands of houses in a sea of industry.

The people who lived in those houses lived and breathed the noise, smells, dirt and grime produced by their industrial neighbors. "To them," wrote Andrew Jefchak, a native of Stieglitz Park, in a novel in which his old neighborhood was the setting, "the sounds and smells of the plant were the price they paid for an otherwise convenient life of good wages and low taxes."[75]

The houses in Stieglitz Park were, for the most part, nothing out of the ordinary. Marktown, a mile to the east, was an architectural landmark designed by Howard Van Doren Shaw, one of Chicago's leading architects of the early 20th century. Chicago industrialist Clayton Mark commissioned Shaw to build a neighborhood to house the workers in his steel plant. Mark had a dream of building a large community that was an easy walk to work. Shaw created an English village feel to the neighborhood they called Marktown. But Stieglitz Park was nothing like that.

"That whole end of town," Larry Jennings remembers, "used to be little, framed homes." Jefchak wrote, "Aside from a few small businesses, the houses looked like each other, facing off like fat arrows pointing upward." When newspaper boy Dennis Hittle made his morning deliveries, he had to deal with the fact that "All of the houses had fences around them. Most of them were the typical white picket fences." And, he said, the houses were close together, "with walks from the front yard to the back of the house."[76]

Jefchak called Stieglitz Park a "square mile of simplicity, stuffed inside the gut of heavy industry." He went on to describe it as a "flat place without ridges or slopes…Streets and alleys were both narrow, often looking like each other. The same sort of gravel covered both, and the same dark specks of oil and tar covered all the grass that managed to grow." The streets were never plowed in the winter, and snow and ice often built up on them. Dennis Hittle said the gravel-covered pitch that covered the streets was "very difficult to ice skate and sled on." In the summer, "learning to ride a bike on this kind of surface was tough, especially if you didn't catch on to the balance the first time." About 60 years later, he still had gravel in one elbow from a fall he took while catching his balance.

Some of the backyards in Stieglitz Park were little farms, places to raise animals or grow food for the table. "It seemed that everyone had some sort of animal, or animals in their yard," Hittle said. Ray Gajewski said his family referred to his grandparent's Stieglitz Park property as "the farm." In the first part of the 20th century, his grandmother had four or five cows and raised pigs there, as well. Even in 1955, Hittle remembers chicken coops in some yards, while Mary Ann Stofcik Dominiak remembers chickens running freely. "It was a little country in that area," she said.[77]

But even with oil storage tanks almost surrounding the neighborhood, the children who grew up there found ways to enjoy the outdoors. A fenced-in playground on May Street had swings, slides, teeter-totters, a jungle gym, and a little merry-go-round. Kids rode their bikes or walked to Todd Park in East Chicago, just a mile south, where there was a swimming pool and other activities for children.

Although they enjoyed the playgrounds and parks, some Stieglitz Park children found new places to have fun. One of those was "Pollywog Pond." The pond was south of 131st Street – the southernmost street in Stieglitz Park – and north of the storage tanks of the Sinclair Oil Refinery. Ann Karin Gregorovich, who grew up in nearby Goose Island, remembers going with a Stieglitz Park friend to that swampy area "to catch pollywogs in Mason jars" and bring them home. Besides pollywogs, also known as tadpoles, Dennis Hittle said he and his friends found fully grown frogs, crawdads, and turtles there. In the autumn, they collected wood and carried it to Pollywog Pond to make a bonfire, roast potatoes and sit around the campfire. In the winter the water froze, giving them a chance to ice skate. In the summer, the cold waters of the pond, about 40 by 50 feet in size, served as an excellent swimming hole.[78]

There was no neighborhood movie theater for the children of Stieglitz Park or Goose Island. The 41 Outdoor Theater was just a short drive down rutted and potholed 129th Street, but you needed a car to get there.

They could see a movie in downtown Whiting, but that was a mile-and-a-half to two miles away, and it cost 11 to 13 cents to get in. To make up for the lack of movie entertainment, the Kubacki Grocery Store offered free movies and popcorn on some Friday evenings. Leilani Suchanuk said the grocer would put up a screen behind his store and show a film for anyone who wanted to come. The movies drew a good crowd of young moviegoers who sat on wooden grocery boxes, their own chairs, or the ground. The movies, Gajewski said, "kind of kept the kids out of trouble." They usually had crowds of 40 to 50 children.[79]

Stieglitz Park had a handful of other businesses. Pete Strezo operated a Sinclair gas station on Indianapolis Boulevard south of 129th. John Perunko's Clipper tavern was on the southwest corner of 129th and Indianapolis Boulevard. Besides Kubacki's on 130th Street, there was the Stipulin grocery store on 129th. Lynn Larsen said her family frequented Kubacki's. It was where they got their fresh meat and canned goods. "Since my mom didn't drive, we could just walk there and get our groceries. We didn't go downtown to the A&P."[80]

According to neighborhood resident Ray Gajewski, the free movies at the Kubacki grocery store on 130th Street in Stieglitz Park were a treat for the neighborhood children. A large screen was set up outside, in the back lot of the little grocery store, usually on a Friday night. (Photo by Vrabel Studio. Courtesy of Calumet Regional Archives, Indiana University Northwest.)

As was the case in every other neighborhood in Whiting and Robertsdale, many entrepreneurs drove up and down the streets of Stieglitz Park selling their products. "I remember Farmer Bill coming around on his truck with the vegetables all the time," said Justine Moskalick Bircher, who lived nearby in Goose Island. She remembers him beeping his horn to let people know he was in the neighborhood. There was also the milkman, delivering his product to the neighborhood's doors, and coal and heating oil deliveries to many houses to keep the home furnaces burning. The ice man still visited homes in 1955, before refrigerators replaced iceboxes and made his job obsolete. There was also a junk man, yelling "Rags and old iron," as he went down the streets buying and selling.[81]

And there were more sinister visitors to the neighborhood. Whiting was a regular stop for hobos who hitched a ride on boxcars passing through. They came to the doors of houses looking for a meal or a handout. Many residents, with memories of the Great Depression of the 1930s still fresh in their minds, were willing to help. Some hobos camped along the tracks that ran alongside Stieglitz Park, but they were often chased off by railroad detectives.[82]

Gypsies also roamed door to door. Some camped out on the vacant lot on the northeast corner of Indianapolis Boulevard and 129th Street, just feet away from the refinery boundary. Their camp consisted of makeshift houses built from old boxcars, canvas tarps and anything else they could find, including a run-down trailer that sat on their campsite. Stereotypes of the time said that gypsies survived by stealing.[83]

Tom Marciniak remembers a gypsy fortune teller with a storefront shop on Indianapolis Boulevard just across the street from the refinery. James Hazzard wrote a poem about it that he called, "Gypsies in Whiting, Indiana."

> Every year we were surprised. Why would a gypsy live
> here, of all places, and in a storefront?
> "They must know something we don't," we agreed.
> That made us hate them, and be afraid of them.[84]

Dennis Hittle was afraid of them. They were different and mysterious – scarier to him than the oil tank fields that surrounded Stieglitz Park. Occasionally, one of the boys in Stieglitz Park lost a kite when it flew into the tank field. "Of course, we could not lose our kites," Dennis said. So they climbed the fence and went into the tank field to retrieve them. Other boys, older and bolder, climbed onto the tanks for the fun of it, trying to stay out of sight of Standard Oil's security guards.[85]

The proximity of the refinery also provided an opportunity for those who wanted to make a few extra dollars. Justine Moskalick Bircher grew up in the Goose Island neighborhood, where she delivered newspapers for a time. During the lunch hour, several refinery workers usually sat along the curb on Indianapolis Boulevard to eat. In the days before aluminum and plastic beverage containers, glass bottles were common. Each bottle came with a two-cent deposit in 1955. But return the bottle to a grocery store, and you could get your two cents back. Justine would sling her newspaper delivery bag on her shoulder and take off for Indianapolis Boulevard with her younger siblings during the refinery's lunch hour. They walked the Indianapolis Boulevard boundary of the plant, picking up empty pop bottles along the way. "Two cents apiece," she said, "that was a lot of money in those days."[86]

Jim Sandrick recalled that just 10 blocks north, policeman Emil Walsko stood at the corner of 119th and Indianapolis Boulevard to manually control the traffic light. It was, Jim said, "the busiest intersection in America. It was the crossroads of America." Traffic on the Boulevard usually had the green light until Officer Walsko decided that traffic on 119th Street was building up.[87]

The Federal Aid Highway Act, which created the Interstate system, did not become law until 1956. When drivers went on trips to places like Chicago in 1955, they usually traveled on the U.S. Highway system. Unlike the Interstates, the old U.S. Highway system used existing streets and roads. In cities like Whiting, the intersections of those streets had traffic lights. Houses and businesses lined the streets, and parking places took up space along the sides. In Whiting-Robertsdale, two of the primary streets were U.S. Highways: Indianapolis Boulevard and Calumet Avenue. Both were major routes from the east into Chicago.

U.S. 12 ran between Detroit and the Pacific Ocean, ending at Aberdeen, Washington. U.S. 20 was a coast-to-coast highway, the longest in America at the time, running between Boston on the east to Newport, Oregon in the west. Indianapolis Boulevard was part of both routes. Just a mile west was U.S. 41, or Calumet Avenue, a north-south road that ran between Miami to the south and the Upper Peninsula of Michigan to the north. U.S. 41 intersected with the combined U.S. 12 and U.S. 20 just a few miles north of the refinery, and all three went across the state line into Chicago.

Since U.S. 12 and 20 ran next to Stieglitz Park, residents had to deal with huge volumes of traffic. "The refinery was there, too," Betty Small Delinck recalled, "and people were going to work…so, Indianapolis Boulevard was very busy." Leilani Suchanuk remembers heavy traffic during the summer on Sundays, the day her family visited friends in Stieglitz Park. They sat on the front porch of the house, watching "the traffic coming from Michigan, going back to Chicago, bumper to bumper, starting around four or five in the afternoon. Traffic was backed up like you wouldn't believe…and that went on for a couple of hours."[88]

The noise was another annoyance. Dennis Hittle remembered "the occasional 'bang' of tank cars coupling together." For Jim Hoelzel, living in nearby Marktown, one of the most memorable sounds came from one of the refinery's most recognizable structures, the Flare Stacks – the towers topped by flames that burned off excess gasses. "You hear them hissing, and really blowing." He also remembered hearing fire sirens sounded from throughout the plant. "There's nothing more eerie than that wailing sound at night, especially in the summer when all the windows are open." No one had air conditioning in those years, so as Andrew Jefchak wrote, "People sat on their front porch, staring out through industrial mist, listening to factory rhythms."[89]

Residents also were inundated with noxious odors. "There was always a pungent smell that I really can't describe," Dennis Hittle said. "'Acid Rain' had a real meaning in Stieglitz Park." Fear was also in the backs of many minds. But if you lived there, you dealt with it. "Living in that area," Bill Haddad said, "we had a lot of minor explosions and fires…It was something we were used to." Frank Vargo Jr., who lived in nearby Goose Island, followed the advice of his mother. "My mom would always say, when you hear the fire sirens, you come home. I don't care what you do the rest of the day, if you hear the sirens you come home because you never know."[90]

There was no reason for Dennis Hittle, or his parents, to worry on the morning of August 27, 1955. It was an ordinary morning. A newspaper delivery boy's job required early hours. Dennis Hittle was awake well before 6 a.m. – his deadline for getting out the door and onto his bicycle. But his workday began earlier than that. John "Dutch" Serafin, the route coordinator who worked for the Whiting News Agency on 119th Street, delivered the usual load of 74 newspapers to Dennis's home well before six o'clock. Once he had the papers, Dennis could begin to roll each one. He made the rolls tight. That way, he could fling the papers onto the porches of the neighborhood homes without having to climb any steps or pass through any gates. He was out the door by six.

Thanks to the money he made delivering newspapers, Dennis had a new Schwinn Varsity three-speed bicycle. He liked the new bike, but he was still getting accustomed to the differences. On his old bike, the brakes worked by pushing backward on the pedals, but his new bike had brake handles on the handlebars. He had been able to hang his sack of newspapers from the handlebars of his old bike. With the handle brakes on his new bike, it was a challenge to hang the sack in the same place. Despite the problem, by 6:11 a.m., he had finished the south end of his route. The sun was rising in the east. Dennis was getting ready to cross 129th Street at Indianapolis Boulevard.[91]

THE REFINERY WORKERS

Al Plant and Thad Bogusz were at work as sunrise approached Standard Oil's Whiting Refinery on August 27, 1955. They were sweating through another hot day on the job. Sixty years later, meteorologists said that temperatures in the Chicago area usually reach 90 and above an average of 16 times a year. According to the forecast, it was going to pass 90 on August 27, 28, and 29, which would bring the number of days at 90 or above to 40 in 1955. That would put 1955 in the record books as the second hottest year in the area since the Weather Service began keeping records in 1871. It was second only to the 42 days of 90-plus in 1952. It was already 71 degrees at 6 a.m.[92]

But for Al and Thad, working in the worst of the heat would not be their problems. Their eight-hour shift was winding down, and soon they would be able to go home. All they had to do was finish one more job. Together with 11 other men, they made up a crew assigned to bring the refinery's new hydroformer back online that morning. It had been down for maintenance.

The hydroformer was a sight to see. The unit was just a few yards from Indianapolis Boulevard, at a point where the road made a 13-degree turn. Because of that angle, you could see the hydroformer for four or five miles as you traveled up the Boulevard. You could also see it because it was not only the tallest structure in the refinery but the tallest in the Whiting-Robertsdale community. The Central State Bank Building, located at the corner of 119th Street and Indianapolis Boulevard was six stories tall and 72 feet high. When they built it in 1928, it was the largest structure in Whiting. Standard Oil's new research building, built in 1949 on the western end of Goose Island, was just a few inches taller than the Central State Bank Building. But the tallest structure in Whiting-Robertsdale was the steeple of St. John the Baptist Catholic Church, built in 1930, which stood at 190 feet. The hydroformer soared past them all. It was 26-stories in height, 262 feet tall.[93]

Standard Oil developed the hydroformer to transform low octane naphtha gas into a high octane fuel. It was part of the company's effort to keep up with American automakers. By the mid-1950s auto sales were skyrocketing. Even in Whiting, a city of just 9,600 people, there were six car dealers. To meet the public demand, automakers manufactured bigger and more powerful cars. To fuel those high-compression engine automobiles, oil companies needed to produce a higher octane fuel. The hydroformer was Standard Oil's solution to that challenge.[94]

The word "hydroformer" combines the words "hydrogen" and "reforming." In the hydroforming process, gasoline was chemically "re-formed" by exposing it to a special catalyst in the presence of hydrogen. In the unit where Al Plant and Thad Bogusz worked, this process took place in a catalytic reactor and a regenerator built one on top of the other, so that the catalyst could travel in a straight line. There were other hydroformers, including an older one already inside the Whiting Refinery, but this design was the first of its kind.

On top was the regenerator, shaped like a cylinder, 130-feet tall and 24-feet in diameter, with walls made of steel two-and-a-half inches thick. A three-inch thick steel head connected the regenerator to the reactor below it. The reactor weighed 600 tons, making it one of the largest vessels ever made for use in the oil refining process. Thirteen feet in diameter, its walls were solid steel, one-and-a-half inches thick. The reason the walls were so thick was that the pressure inside the vessel was extremely high. The thick steel walls were needed to withstand that pressure and prevent an explosion. Standard Oil was a leader in the hydroforming process, and the Whiting Refinery's Fluid Hydroforming Unit No. 700, as it was officially called, was the company's gem.[95]

The hydroformer was another step in Standard Oil's proud history in oil refining research. Less than a half-century earlier, researchers at Standard Oil's Whiting Refinery essentially saved the gas-powered automobile. In the late 1900s and early 1910s, the supply of gas was not keeping up with the demand for cars. When supply does not equal demand, prices soar. From the end of 1911 to the start of 1913, the price of gas per gallon almost doubled, from 9½ cents to 17 cents. In parts of Europe, the price was over a dollar a gallon. At those prices, people could not afford to operate cars.

William Burton, the general manager of manufacturing at Standard Oil, knew what the answer was. He just did not know how to get there. In 1909, Burton pushed for research on how to increase the amount of gasoline that a refinery could get from each barrel of oil. Robert Humphreys, the chief chemist at the research lab in Whiting, joined Burton's effort. What came of the research lab's work was the cat cracking process. They discovered that if you use high pressure and high temperatures you can double the amount of gasoline per barrel of oil. Because of their discovery, and the development of cat crackers to do the job, the supply of gas was able to meet the demand. That made the price of gas cheaper, which in turn saved the early automobile industry and allowed it to prosper.

"By virtue of its discovery, the company acquired a place in the sun. It became the center of attention," wrote company historian Paul Giddens. "The small pioneer laboratory at Whiting emerged as the outstanding research laboratory in the petroleum industry." The Smithsonian Institute in Washington, the keeper of America's history, recognized the revolutionary nature of the discovery. It purchased the first cat cracking still that the Whiting researchers developed and put it on display along with the Wright Brothers first plane and other major American inventions.[96]

Standard Oil believed its hydroformer was another significant advancement in the oil refining industry. The hydroformer went up just a short distance from two large cat crackers. "While the cat crackers stood bulky and wide like a pair of refrigerators, the hydroformer was a sleek bottle," Andrew Jefchak wrote in his novel. An article in a Standard Oil Company magazine said that "The Fluid Hydroforming Unit No. 700…and two cat crackers formed an impressive sight for motorists on Indianapolis Boulevard. A sight that they, their children, and their children's children may be seeing for decades to come."[97]

M.W. Kellogg Company of New York was the primary contractor to build the unit. Workers started clearing the site for the hydroformer on June 1, 1953. By April of 1954, it was ready for excavation. The first structural steel went up in May. A 290-foot-high construction derrick, one of the biggest ever seen up to that time at the Whiting Refinery, helped lift loads up to 200 tons. It took 10 steel guy cables to anchor the derrick. Some of the cables stretched over and across Indianapolis Boulevard. During the height of construction, M.W. Kellogg had 660 men building the hydroformer. On March 16, 1955, it was ready to go online. It was ready to produce as much as one million gallons of high octane gasoline per day. The estimated cost of the project was $23-million.[98]

Standard Oil felt the hydroformer was perfect. It would put the company where it needed to be in the competitive oil industry of 1955. "Our company," said Dwight Benton, vice-president of sales, "is now refining the highest octane gasoline in its 66-year history." Whiting was the perfect place for the hydroformer because it was the heart of the company's operations. Standard had five other refineries. But the 7,000 workers in Whiting were more than the company had employed in the other five plants combined.[99]

The Whiting Refinery was "a panorama of towering stacks, stills, buildings, and innumerable storage tanks, many of the one-million-gallon capacity," the *Chicago Tribune* said in 1955. It was, "one of the industrial giants of the world and a landmark of the Calumet industrial district." The facts proved it. The refinery produced 1.3-billion gallons of gasoline each year. It produced 500-million gallons of domestic fuel oil and 300-million pounds of greases. It also produced 50-million pounds of asphalt. On top of that, it produced jet aviation fuel, diesel fuels, and kerosene. Insecticides, solvents, and oils for printer's ink were also produced. So were 2,000 other types of oil, petroleum coke, many chemical products, and more than 150 varieties of candles. "The plant is one of the world's largest complete refineries," the *Tribune* said, and "represents an investment running into untold millions of dollars."[100]

As Thad Bogusz took an elevator to the top of the hydroformer on August 27, 1955, almost everyone shared the belief that the refinery would continue to prosper. "Standard is reaping the harvest of the large investments made at its refineries in ultra-modern processes that upgrade straight-run gasoline," sales vice-president Benton stated. The hydroformer was the newest, sleekest, most modern example of that investment.[101]

On top of that engineering masterpiece, Bogusz checked the instruments to make sure everything looked good. It did. They were ready to bring the hydroformer back online. By 6:11 a.m. he was down from the top of the hydroformer with Al Plant and the rest of the crew. All across the refinery, the men on the graveyard shift were wrapping up their work and getting ready to go home, as workers on the day shift trickled in.[102]

THE GENERAL MANAGER OF MANUFACTURING

Like many others in Whiting and Robertsdale, Jesse Ducommun was asleep in his home at 6:11 a.m. on August 27, 1955. The windows in the bedroom of his Amy Court home faced south, toward the refinery, where he worked as Standard's general manager of manufacturing.

The clock changed to 6:12 a.m.

"It was a boom, boom that went up," said Mary Ann Stofcik Dominiak. "You had to be put under with heavy sleeping pills or something not to feel that. Because we felt it, heard it."[103]

Others chose the same word to describe it. "And all of a sudden...BA-BOOM," was George Timko's description. "You just felt this incredible BA-BOOM!" said Dennis Zelenke.[104]

It was the sharpest sound Jesse Ducommun had ever heard. Months later, to describe it, he clapped his hands together as hard and as loud as he could manage. "It was a sharp clap," he explained, "multiplied a thousand-fold." Almost immediately, he knew what it was.[105]

He jumped out of bed and started getting dressed. Maybe it was intuition. Maybe it was the experience of working in a refinery most of his life. But as he put on his socks and shoes, he was thinking about the hydroformer. He knew it was going back online that morning. He also knew "that the most dangerous time in the life of a unit is when it is coming on-stream." He knew he had to get to the refinery immediately.[106]

Although some knew the blast must be Standard Oil, not everyone did. Yes, there had been explosions at the refinery in the past, plenty of them, but none had ever been this loud. Many residents of Whiting,

Robertsdale, and East Chicago found themselves on the floor next to the bed they had just been sleeping in. This was a new experience.

"What happened? Why am I on the floor?" wondered 15-year-old Bonnie Wilson Faulkner. She shared a bed with Brenda, her younger sister, in their 121st Street home, just 0.9 miles from the blast. Brenda had the side against the wall. Bonnie woke up on the floor. Next to her were the flowerpots her mother kept on the windowsills, broken into pieces. Eleven-year-old Shirley Pullo Christ was in her Robertsdale home in the 1700 block of Lake Avenue, 1.7 miles from the center of the blast. She was also thrown out of bed. Joe Mazanek was still in bed, 1.1 miles from the blast, on one of the most important days of his life. An instant after the explosion he found himself on the floor...just hours before his wedding.[107]

Robert Herakovich, Sr. was sleeping on the front porch of his Robertsdale home on 119th Street. It wasn't where he usually slept. But this was a hot morning, and with no air conditioning it was more comfortable than his bedroom. His son, five-year-old Robert, Jr., was awake but still dressed in footed pajamas – seated on the cedar chest his mother got as a wedding gift. He was playing with a set of toy dinosaurs. The blast knocked father, son, and dinosaurs onto the floor.[108]

Thirteen-year-old Sharon Fernando Reinke lived in the Marktown neighborhood of East Chicago. It was a little farther from the hydroformer site than Stieglitz Park and Goose Island, but it was still only 0.8 miles away. The power of the explosion threw Sharon out of bed.[109]

Joe Gray was at work at the nearby Youngstown Sheet & Tube Tin Mill. His wife, Helen White Gray, was at their home in the 1900 block of New York Avenue, 1.1 miles from the blast. With her was their seven-day-old son, Jody Gray, and Helen's mother-in-law, Clorine Gray. Clorine stayed the night to help Helen with the new baby. When the hydroformer exploded, Clorine thought the house's water heater had blown up. Helen ran down the hall of their second-floor apartment to check. But when she reached the end and opened the door, she saw a sight she never forgot. Huge flames were shooting up to the sky and black smoke was billowing upward. She then ran back to her apartment and checked on Jody. A large picture of Jesus had hung on the wall above his bed.

"Thank God!" she said when she saw it. The blast knocked the picture of Jesus off the wall. She was grateful Jesus fell behind the baby's bed, and not on it.[110]

Four-year-old Pam Cummings was just 0.8 miles from the blast in the 2200 block of White Oak Avenue. She was sharing a second-floor bedroom with her sister. Their window faced the refinery and was open on that very warm morning. But they had the venetian blinds pulled down to keep the rising sun from waking them up. The blast shattered the windows, but the blinds kept the glass from hitting the sleeping girls.[111]

"The smoke started getting bigger and wider," remembered Betty Small Delinck. "And as it got dark you could see flames way up in the air, in the smoke...It was enormous. Just enormous." (Photo courtesy Betty Small Delinck.)

Glass windows throughout the area broke. The Hoelzel family lived in nearby Marktown, just across the city limits in East Chicago. That night, five-year-old Jim Hoelzel had slept next to the window at the foot of his bed. His father ran into his son's bedroom after the blast. Amazingly, young Jim was still asleep. His legs dangled off the side of the bed, and glass from the shattered window laid next to him on the mattress. Paul Stofcik had spent the night at the home of Joseph and Mary Perz, his grandparents, in the 1800 block of 129th Street. Glass from a broken window covered the sheets on his bed.[112]

The windows did not break in the home of Grace Kovach in the 1500 block of John Street, just slightly over a mile from the blast. She had long drapes on her bedroom window. But when she looked up just seconds after the blast, she saw that the bottom of the curtains, the part that covered the open portion of her window, had been blown inward at a nearly 90-degree angle. "They looked like the letter 'L'," she said. "How could they be standing straight out?"[113]

Donald DeLong was 24 years old in August 1955 and living in East Chicago. He worked at a steel mill, but also drove a taxicab. He was in his cab on Main Street in the Indiana Harbor section of East Chicago when the blast caused his car to "jump." He drove just a few feet before it jumped again. He stopped in front of the Levin Furniture store and saw plates and dishes rolling across Main Street. They came from the broken display window of the shop, and to DeLong "they looked like ducks or geese, all moving in the same direction."[114]

When they heard the initial blast, many people had no idea what it was. Larry Jennings, 12 years old at the time, was sleeping at his sister's apartment on the corner of Fischrupp and White Oak, about 1.1 miles from the blast. It was the 1950s, the Cold War era. "Holy moly," he thought, when he looked out the window and saw a mushroom cloud, "they dropped the atom bomb!" The same thing occurred to 18-year-old Larry McClelland. "The Russians bombed Standard Oil, sure as hell."[115]

It was a natural conclusion for anyone in their age group. In the 1950s, at the height of the Cold War, many Whiting residents believed that if the Soviet Union attacked, the Standard Oil Refinery would be a prime target. "We were always told that if there is a war and they do attack America," Jennings said, "Standard Oil is going to be the place that they're going to drop the bomb because of all the fuel for the services and everything. So when I saw that, when I saw the mushroom, I said, here it is."[116]

Dennis Zelenke had the same impression. "I just remember going outside and looking around, and people gathering on 119th Street and looking up in [that] direction," he said, "and then thinking...yeah...we have been attacked. Standard Oil, Whiting Refinery, probably was the world's number one oil refinery. If not number one, certainly in the top two or three." Zelenke recalled, "And this area, northwest Indiana, was highly industrialized. And the steel mills were probably number one or two in the world. So we were considered a number one bomb site, and we're talking nuclear, in the United States."[117]

The possibility of an atomic bomb attack on the city was not just burned into the minds of Whiting's young people; it was also burned into their bodies. In the years before the refinery explosion, the Whiting schools – as well as some other schools in the area – lined up every child and tattooed their blood types on the sides of their bodies, just in case a nuclear attack left the child alone and in need of medical care. Dennis Zelenke got his tattoo in kindergarten. Tables were set up in the Whiting school gymnasium. Children and teenagers filed in to receive their tattoos. The device used to apply the tattoo looked like a gun to Dennis. More than 60 years later, he remembered how much it hurt.[118]

The movie showing at the Hoosier Theater in downtown Whiting that day was *It Came from Beneath the Sea*. The film told the story of a giant sea creature driven from its home in the deep ocean by the underwater testing of hydrogen bombs, and then terrorizing people along the Pacific coast. "Monster Strikes...It Is Out to Destroy the World!" read the Hoosier Theater's ad in the *Hammond Times* that day. The thought of the world coming to an end was not far-fetched in the minds of 1955 Whiting residents.

"I thought the sun had exploded and that this was the end of the world," said Margaret Salle, who lived 0.8 miles from the blast in the 2300 block of New York Avenue. "There was a terrible noise and a big red flash."[119]

At a time when most people in Whiting attended church on Sundays, the explosion was loud enough to make some think a biblical prophecy was at hand. "Daddy thought it was the end of the world," said Brenda Wilson Felton. "We're Christians. We believe in Jesus Christ as our savior, and the Bible speaks of the end of the world, so, of course, that's what daddy thought right away. It's the end of the world." Brenda and her sister Bonnie peered out their window onto 121st Street. To Bonnie, it looked like the chaos that must accompany the end of the world. People were in their nightgowns, running up and down the sidewalks. "It was a very scary, very scary time," Brenda said.[120]

The situation was no different in the 2600 block of Birch Avenue. Bill Haddad looked out the window and saw the streets "full of neighbors standing around in their nightclothes, looking at the growing wall of flames and black smoke as sirens blared incessantly."[121]

"I got all my kids out of bed, and I started passing out rosaries and started praying," Helen Dudzik said. "Standard Oil is going up in flames. We were very scared. We sat here; we waited to see what would happen."[122]

While most knew that something horrible was happening, many just did not know what. George Plutko, age 43, was listening to the radio in his home in the 2100 block of Lincoln Avenue when his chair started to shake and he heard the blast. He rushed to his basement, thinking the gas heater had blown up. When that proved incorrect, he ran outside and saw the huge flames. His next thought was that Whiting was under nuclear attack. Shattered glass was all over the sidewalks, the sky was bright red, and people were running out of their houses in their pajamas. Some neighbors tried making phone calls to see what had happened, but the phone lines were jammed.[123]

The blast was so powerful that it woke people up miles away. Sharon Ross, 16 years old and living in Leroy, Indiana, was asleep at her home 24 miles from the blast. The noise jolted her out of a sound sleep. She thought it was thunder, so she got out of bed to close the window and keep out the rain. She was surprised to see mostly clear skies as the sun rose in the east.[124]

When he came home later that afternoon, Don Smith's father told his seven-year-old son about his day at work. Mr. Smith was an electrician who worked for the Bell Telephone Company. At 6:12 a.m., he was on a telephone pole in Highland, Indiana, about eight miles from the blast. A loud clap caused the pole he was on to shake, and he instantly feared he might fall. He also thought it was thunder, but from his vantage point he was soon able to see the smoke rising in the sky to the north.[125]

Rosemarie Gomez, age 20, lived on Drummond Street in East Chicago. She was about to sit down on a chair with her newborn baby in her arms when the explosion occurred. It caused her to miss the chair and hit the floor, but she kept the baby safe in her arms.[126]

They felt the blast 15 miles away at Adler Planetarium on Chicago's lakefront. Windows broke in Crown Point, Indiana, 18 miles away. In Mokena, Illinois, 24 miles southwest, George Dath felt his ranch-style house shake. He thought it was an earthquake. And in Lowell, Indiana, 26 miles away, Richard Davis thought a car had hit the side of his house as it shook from the blast.[127]

The explosion caused reverberations all along the lower shoreline of Lake Michigan. Virginia Galvin was having a baby at St. Anthony's Hospital in Michigan City, 30 miles to the east. She felt the hospital shake, but had a more pressing matter to deal with. It wasn't until she came home with her baby boy and glanced at a newspaper that she realized what she'd felt in the hospital was not an earthquake.[128]

Ottawa Beach, Michigan, is 101 miles from the hydroformer site in a straight line across Lake Michigan. Forty-two-year-old Gerald Ford was vacationing in a cabin there that morning with his wife, Betty, and their two boys, five-year-old Jack and three-year-old John. The Michigan congressman and future U.S. President joined his neighbors in thinking they also had experienced an earthquake. One neighbor, Wenzel Milanowski, an Ottawa Beach resident for 16 years, described it as a "strong tremor," much stronger than other tremors he had experienced there. Dishes rattled, the house shook, and many Ottawa Beach residents ran outside, fearing that their homes might get damaged.[129]

Everyone had their immediate theory about the noise they'd heard or the shaking they'd just felt. Joe Gray wrapped up his midnight shift by washing up inside the Youngstown Sheet & Tube Tin Mill in East Chicago. To him, it sounded like a bomb had dropped nearby. But as the steel mill shook and dust began to fall on him, he came to a different conclusion. He thought the operator of the factory's overhead crane must have accidentally crashed the crane through the walls of the building.[130]

Ten-year-old Michael Goodson lived about five miles away in the Hessville neighborhood of Hammond. He was on his way to the bathroom at 6:12 a.m. when he walked past the basement door and heard it shake from the explosion. As Michael looked, it appeared that the doorknob was turning. He ran back to bed and pulled the covers over his head. The previous day he'd been with a friend who tried to bust a lock on what appeared to be an abandoned house. Two men caught them and threatened to call the police, contact their parents, and give them a beating. Michael went to bed with terrible guilt and fear. So, it made sense to his 10-year-old mind that they had discovered where he lived. The rattling doorknob was the two men, trying to get inside to teach him a lesson.[131]

But for many, the first thought was not of the world ending, an earthquake, a bomb dropped on the city, or two men trying to get in the basement door. With millions of barrels of oil passing through their city every year, the people of Whiting knew an explosion at Standard Oil was always a possibility.

Betty Small Delinck, 14 years old, was 1.7 miles away in the 600 block of Burton Court, sharing an upstairs bedroom with her sister. The blast woke them up, and before long they "heard the sirens, just going and going, and going and going." Their mother answered their question immediately. "I think something happened at Standard Oil," she told them.[132]

One group of people who are often up and about before sunrise had no question what had happened. Fishermen along Lake Michigan watched in awe as flames shot into the sky. John Migas of Chicago was one of five men on the 95th Street breakwater. Just 4.6 miles from the blast, the cement breakwater on which they stood trembled, and they could feel the heat of the flames. "The clouds which rose after the explosion," Migas said, "looked to us like the mushroom formation of an atomic blast."[133]

Joseph Brown, a carpenter from Calumet City, was fishing for bass at George Lake, standing on a small wooden pier a little over a mile from the blast site. The explosion knocked him into four feet of water. "I got up, leaving my car and my fishing pole behind, and ran to Calumet Avenue. I thought they had dropped an atomic bomb." He joined 10 or 12 other fishermen who also ran for safety.[134]

On Lake Calumet, a little over five miles from the explosion, Ben Darnell of Hammond was laying out his fishing lines when the sky suddenly turned red. "The noise was terrifying. For two or three minutes I couldn't hear anything. It looked like newsreels of the Bikini bomb tests." He quickly pulled in his lines, got in his car "and drove away fast."[135]

The phone lines were busy, so Jesse Ducommun could not get a call through to anyone at the refinery. As he rushed out the door of his home and got into his car, he still believed the hydroformer had blown up. His thoughts were confirmed as soon as he reached Indianapolis Boulevard. Every morning for the past several months, since the construction of the 26-story hydroformer, he had seen it as he drove to work. But as he turned onto the Boulevard and looked ahead, it wasn't there. Standard Oil's most modern piece of refining equipment was gone.[136]

He drove down Indianapolis Boulevard, past the 1700 block. Marge Milligan operated a small grocery store there and lived in an apartment behind the shop, 1.7 miles from the explosion. The loud boom, followed by the sound of cans and other grocery items falling off the shelves, had woken her up. She was inside the store examining the damage as Jesse drove past. He began to notice other cars screeching onto the Boulevard. He realized that traffic would soon block the main roads, so he took off on side streets to reach the plant.[137]

When he arrived, he drove toward the site where the transformer had stood. He saw dense, black smoke and hot, soaring flames, and he hesitated. "Be careful." That's what his neighbors on Amy Court had told him as he got in his car to drive to the plant, and now their words were replaying in his mind. But he knew he needed to do this. He knew he needed to get close to the flames because he knew each of the men who were starting up the hydroformer that morning. Some he'd known for years. He kept driving through the refinery grounds and parked his car just north and east of the hydroformer site.[138]

Among the first men he saw were some of those who had been at work in other parts of the refinery at the time of the blast. "Have you released as many men as possible to help fight the fire?" he asked them. Fighting the fire would soon become his primary mission. Right now, however, he kept moving, on foot, toward the hydroformer site. His priority was to find the crew assigned to bring the hydroformer online that morning.[139]

He spotted one of them near the cat cracker, adjacent to the hydroformer site. It was Lester Ready, the shift supervisor of the hydroformer crew. Ducommun noticed Ready had a gash on his forehead and blood partially covering his face, but the wound was superficial. Ready was also darkened by soot and dirt, "looking as if he had just come out of a coal mine," Ducommun thought. That's also how Al Plant, the stillman on duty at the hydroformer, looked. Both men seemed dazed and shocked, but they tried to remain calm as they went with Ducommun to search for the others.[140]

There are no known records of injuries to the five others on duty at the hydroformer: helpers Alton Ashworth, John Morrison, Bill Karpinski and Robert Redlarczyk, and Instrument Department foreman Frank Miller. Miller was in the hydroformer control room at the time of the blast.[141]

Ducommun and the others narrowed the number of missing to two or three. When they reached the hydroformer site there was not much fire, but the area was in shambles, and the destruction was indescribable. The giant hydroformer had been reduced to a pile of rubble no more than one story high. When reporters were later allowed into the area, one from the *Chicago Tribune* said some light bulbs and meters on the lower part of the hydroformer were still intact with no sign of damage. But pipes from the hydroformer hung on the sides of other nearby structures "bent and crumpled and looking like spaghetti." He said the upper part of the hydroformer was completely gone, blown away. "One strange sight," he wrote, "was a piece of steel from the hydroformer about three feet by four feet, which stuck into concrete a block away. It looked somewhat like a garden spade jabbed into the ground."[142]

Ducommun tried a nearby telephone to see if anyone else had caught sight of the missing men, but none of the phones worked. He waded through the rubble, which was knee-deep, fearing that he would find a body. To his relief, there were none.[143]

Thad Bogusz was 100 feet away when the unit exploded. The blast threw him against a hand railing. He saw nothing but smoke and flames in the seconds that followed, and he could feel the intense heat. "The smoke was so dense that it was really hard to see exactly what had blown up. We had no warning of the explosion. Everything was normal as usual." He said he and others on the crew took off running, going "several blocks" mostly to escape the heat. He then realized he'd suffered a knee injury, sustained when the blast threw him against the railing. Other workers took him to St. Catherine Hospital in East Chicago for treatment, but he was back at the refinery within an hour.[144]

Instrument man Mick Macko, of Gary, was also taken to St. Catherine's with an injury. Rocky Kottka of Hammond, a 52-year-old helper, was judged to be in fair condition by hospital physicians. The most seriously injured member of the hydroformer crew was 23-year-old fireman Jack Kosarko, of Chicago. He suffered a skull fracture.[145]

Hours after the explosion, 39-year-old Al Plant sat in the quiet and security of his living room with just a few scratches on his face. "I never saw anything so horrible in my life," he said, when asked about the hydroformer that had exploded just 20 feet from him. "I was right outside the unit control room getting ready to make an inspection when everything let loose." The blast knocked him to the ground; metal flew through the air all around him, and intense flames shot through the area. "I got up and ran for the nearest building." He didn't even look back to see what had happened to the hydroformer's control room. He stayed at the refinery for three hours to fight the fire before he went home, still in shock. His landlady, Mrs. Leland Buckmaster, saw him come up the front walk. "I thought I was seeing a ghost," she said.[146]

Ducommun went inside the control room of the hydroformer. With all the men of the hydroformer crew accounted for, he needed to shift his attention to fighting the fire that was raging all around him. Before he left the control room, he offhandedly looked at the control room clock. It was frozen at 6:12 a.m.[147]

THE TWO LITTLE BOYS

Eight-year-old Ron Plewniak was asleep in his upstairs bedroom at 2638 Schrage Avenue. Schrage was in Goose Island, the first street west of Stieglitz Park. Ron shared the room with his little brother, three-year-old Ricky Plewniak. On the wall of their bedroom hung a framed picture bearing the words, "God Bless Our Home."

In many ways, the Plewniak family was blessed. Frank Plewniak, Ron and Ricky's father, was a skilled carpenter. He had a talent for cabinet work and for fixing problems on construction projects. Born in Calumet City, Illinois, he served in World War II. At Normandy, an artillery shell killed many others in his platoon. Frank survived and earned a Purple Heart. Back home after the war, he married Sophia Joan Marek in January 1946.[148]

Joan, as she was known, was a lifelong resident of Whiting, attending Whiting High School as a girl. She did her part in the war effort at a plant in East Chicago. Her job was to camouflage tanks for combat duty. She also worked at the Marek and Hajduk family grocery stores on Schrage Avenue. Joan grew up on Schrage Avenue. Her parents, Martin and Anna Dybel Marek, were Polish immigrants who operated a little grocery store on Schrage. Her two sisters, their husbands, and their children all lived in the same block. When Joan married Frank Plewniak, they moved into a home on Schrage Avenue just doors down from the rest of the family.[149]

For little boys like Ron and Ricky, having the aunts and grandmother close by was like growing up with four mothers. That could be a plus, could be a minus. It was mostly a plus, especially with their grandmother's cooking and all the cousins to play with. For Joan, it was exactly where she wanted to live her life, close to the people she loved.[150]

Ron was born in 1947; Ricky in 1952. They both can be seen in this family photo from December 1954. Their parents are behind them. All are wearing their winter coats, smiling, standing in front of a large Christmas tree. Joan is behind Ron, her hands on his shoulders Ricky is standing in front of Frank, holding a teddy bear by one of its legs. The stuffed animal dangles upside down. The teddy bear was in bed next to Ricky on the morning of August 27, 1955.

From left to right: Joan, Ron, Ricky and Frank Plewniak, Christmas 1954. (Photo courtesy of Ronald Plewniak)

Just before Ricky and Ron went to sleep on Friday night, their parents told them they might be going on a picnic on Saturday. Ricky slept in a crib, Ron in a bed next to him. On this hot, humid summer night, the window was open. Typically, they both slept with their feet, rather than their heads, closer to the window. Ricky stayed that way, but Ron wanted to take advantage of any relief the open window might provide. He switched ends of the bed, moving his pillow and his head close to the window. That's how they were positioned at 6:12 a.m. Four-tenths of a mile away was the hydroformer.[151]

At that same moment, Dennis Hittle was on his bike just across the street from the hydroformer. He was about halfway through his Stieglitz Park newspaper route. At 6:12 a.m., Dennis felt something odd. Everything "seemed to stop." He later described it as "a terrible pressure that seemed to compress everything" around him. It all happened in a second. An ear-shattering explosion deafened him. He looked slightly northeast from where he was, toward the hydroformer. It was built to be strong; made of solid steel, two to two-and-a-half inches thick. But the power of the explosion ripped the 26-story structure into little pieces. The strength of the blast sent those pieces flying in all directions. Debris, bent and twisting in flight, rained down. On the corner of 129th and Indianapolis Boulevard, Dennis was about a thousand feet from the hydroformer site. Everything appeared in slow motion to him. Smoke and fire quickly filled the sky.

Confused and scared, Dennis turned his bike around and headed south down Indianapolis Boulevard to May Street. He sped past frightened neighbors who had come out of their homes to see what had happened. Dennis tried to avoid the broken glass and pieces of metal on the streets. His parents were already looking for him, almost hysterical until they saw that he was safe. Dennis escaped without even a scratch from the steel that fell all around him.[152]

Others in Stieglitz Park escaped injury, or death, by a matter of minutes. Douglas Stipulan was on his way to his grocery store at 1829 129th Street. It was scheduled to open at 6:30 a.m. At 6:12 a.m., a 50-ton chunk of steel flew two city blocks and flattened the store when it landed. He arrived at the scene a few minutes later. Only a small part of his store was still standing. On top of the rubble was a slab of steel. It looked "like a weird machine from outer space," according to a reporter for the *Hammond Times*. A car was under the slab. The steel slab crushed the car and reduced it to a one-foot-thick piece of scrap. Just its chrome-plated bumper was visible beneath the load of steel. The front fender was in a street gutter, half a block away.[153]

The power of the explosion launched a wooden two-by-four through the sky and drove it into the side of a brick wall, where it became embedded. Another two-by-four cut through a mattress.[154]

Some of the steel fragments that struck Stieglitz Park and Goose Island were as long as 75 feet. One chunk of steel dug a 10-foot wide by six-foot deep crater in the backyard of the house where Joe Dulik lived at 1822 Ann Street, about a block from the hydroformer. The chunk of steel also demolished his small home, leaving only the bed and the television set intact. Joe wasn't there. He had left for work at the American Maize plant less than a half-hour before the explosion. A three-week old car was in the garage behind the house. Somehow, the blast lifted the car off the ground. It then flipped the car upside down. The car landed on top of the garage in which it had been parked.[155]

This house in the 2800 block of Indianapolis Boulevard was knocked off its foundation by the refinery explosion. The side of the house was hit by a huge chunk of steel that broke off from the hydroformer. That piece of steel can be seen in the foreground of this photo. To the right is a damaged automobile. Smoke from the refinery fire burns in the background. (Photo by Joseph Dudzik. Courtesy of Gina Vitucci.)

Twenty-nine-year-old Thomas Jurbala worked at the Union Tank Car Company in East Chicago. At 6 a.m., he kissed his wife good-bye to get to his job. He left his house in the 1500 block of Atchison Avenue and took his usual route down Indianapolis Boulevard. Just a minute or two after passing the Standard Oil Refinery, he heard the massive explosion. He looked in his rear-view mirror to see a towering inferno close behind. He floored the gas pedal to get as far away as fast as he could.[156]

Clifton Smith lived on Kenwood Avenue in Hammond, about 4.5 miles from the blast. He was on the next shift at the refinery and was ready to leave home, except for one problem: His car wouldn't start. A neighbor came by to help. Clifton's sons, seven-year-old Darryle and four-year-old Gregory, were standing by the open window in their bedroom watching the two men work on the car. A sudden blast blew the boys backward and knocked the two men to the ground. Clifton later thanked God his car hadn't started. He would have been driving down Indianapolis Boulevard right past the blast on his way to work in the area near the hydroformer. The family always felt that their old car saved his life.[157]

While some missed serious injury or death by minutes or seconds, others missed it by feet or inches. Elmo Sparks lived at 2838 Indianapolis Boulevard with his wife and four children. An immense piece of the hydroformer slammed up against their house – knocking the house off its foundation and moving the house six feet. Water pipes burst, flooding the basement as the family scrambled to get out. They went to one door; it was jammed shut. They went to the other door in the house; it was jammed. They escaped by crawling out the window, leaving everything behind.[158]

Just a few doors down, at 2812 Indianapolis Boulevard, John Springer and his family ran to the garage. They got in their car to escape the destruction and flying debris, but a giant piece of steel was blocking the alley at the back of their garage. They were not able to get the car out. Relatives who lived in Stieglitz Park had to drive them away.[159]

Also in Stieglitz Park, an eight-foot long pipe struck the roof of the Nicholas Smith home at 2921 Berry Avenue. Incredibly, it did not break through the roof – instead, it bounced off and flew down the street, crashing into the concrete block foundation of Frank Macsimik's home at 2927 Berry Avenue. Frank's brother, Anthony Macsimik, usually parked his car where the pipe landed. But Anthony had left for work at the Continental Foundry in East Chicago just a short time earlier.[160]

There were many close calls in Stieglitz Park. Arana Eidson was expecting her husband, Elmer Eidson, home soon from his job at the nearby Sinclair Oil Refinery. Just a short time before the blast, she got out of bed to unlock the rear door of their house at 2923 Indianapolis Boulevard. Seconds later, the hydroformer exploded. When she returned to her bedroom, she saw shattered glass from the bedroom window. It covered the pillow where her head had been resting just moments earlier.[161]

The Haluska family lived just 500 feet from the explosion. Twenty-six-year-old Ann Haluska was home with her five children. Her husband, Andrew, was already at work at his filling station job. The explosion knocked Ann and her children out of their beds and onto the floor. Falling plaster and broken glass rained down on them. The children screamed. Ann was afraid the house was going to collapse, so she hurried them outside. "We thought it was the end of the world," she said. "The house shook violently. Plaster fell, and I could hear the sound of breaking glass as the house rocked." The wood frame of their one-story house blew in and the house was pushed off its foundation.[162]

It was miraculous that no one inside the refinery was severely injured by the blast. It was every bit as miraculous that no one in Stieglitz Park was severely injured. But one family in Goose Island suffered a tremendous loss. One of the many fragments of steel propelled through the sky was a 10-foot pipe. It soared over the entire Stieglitz Park neighborhood before it hit the home of Thomas and Fran Demkovich at 2640 Schrage Avenue. While it caused considerable damage, the pipe did not rupture their exterior wall. It bounced off and hit the Plewniak home next door at 2638 Schrage Avenue – slamming through the bedroom where the two little boys slept.

The pipe hit three-year-old Ricky, killing him instantly. The same pipe landed across eight-year-old Ron's leg. Ron had switched ends of the bed to take advantage of the cooler air on a hot summer night. If he had slept where he usually did, the pipe would have hit the upper part of his body and probably killed him as well.[163]

"My wife and I were sleeping when there was a terrible roar that shook our house and knocked the plaster off the walls," Frank Plewniak told a reporter, just hours after it happened. "The plaster fell on us as we awoke. I rushed into the other bedroom where the two boys were sleeping." The boys' room was just across the hall. Frank and Joan also heard the screams of their oldest son, Ron, who woke up to a room full of dust. He was unable to see much more than the fog of plaster particles that filled the room. Ron got out of bed and crawled on his hands and knees, unaware that the pipe had sliced off one of his legs just below the knee. He knew where the doorway was, so he crawled toward it.[164]

When Frank Plewniak reached the room, he saw both of his sons covered in blood. The pipe was still hot, but he frantically tried to lift it off of his youngest son's body, seriously burning his hand in the process. Meanwhile, according to Larry McClelland, who lived just five doors down the street at 2610 Schrage Avenue, Joan Plewniak ran down the street screaming for help. Larry was one of about a dozen neighborhood men who rushed to the house to help Frank lift the heavy metal pipe off of Ricky. The pipe was too heavy for the rescuers to lift, so they stuffed debris into the end of it in order to use a jack to lift the pipe and remove Ricky's body. Newspaper reports the next day said that when they were able to free Ricky, Frank Plewniak lifted and then carried the body of his son outside.[165]

The powerful refinery blast sent a 10-foot long metal pipe flying through the air for 0.4 miles before it crashed into the bedroom where Ron and Ricky Plewniak slept. The pipe killed three-year old Ricky and sliced off the leg of eight-year-old Ron. In this photo of their bedroom, the end of the metal pipe is seen in the center-right portion. The mattress from Ron's bed is in the center left of the photo, just below the "God Bless Our Home" sign that hung on the bedroom wall.

At some point, it became apparent to Ron that the metal pipe had severed the lower portion of his leg. His Aunt Julia Dickey, who lived just a few doors down, rushed to the home of her sister's family when she realized their home had been hit. She heard Ron's anguished cries for his mother before an ambulance rushed him to St. Catherine's Hospital in East Chicago.[166]

Frank Plewniak had a leg injury, as well as cuts and bruises. Both he and Joan were treated for shock. Family, friends, and neighbors gathered in the Plewniak home to see if they could help Frank and Joan. The house was in ruins. The "God Bless Our Home" picture still hung, crookedly, on the wall near Ricky's crib.[167]

THE FIREFIGHTERS

Eight-year-old Cheryl Macko Rosen thought she heard a tremendous clap of thunder at 6:12 a.m. She opened her eyes and looked toward her bedroom window. Cheryl saw drops of moisture on the glass, which seemed to confirm her thought. She later realized that those were not raindrops on her windowpane, but drops of oil.[168]

But someone else in her household immediately knew the sound was not thunder. Cheryl's 37-year-old father was the Whiting fire chief. "The minute I heard the explosion, I knew it was the refinery," said George Macko. He was able to reach that conclusion so quickly because of one big advantage: The Macko family lived less than 0.5 miles from the blast, at 3049 Berry Avenue in Stieglitz Park. "I looked out of my bedroom window and saw it was an inferno."[169]

Whiting Fire Chief George Macko. (Photo courtesy of Cheryl Macko Rosen.)

Frank Horlbeck's view was not as close. He lived in the 1800 block of Calumet Avenue, 1.7 miles from the explosion. But he did have a lifetime of experience as a firefighter inside the Standard Oil refinery. The 57-year-old Horlbeck started working in the refinery's firefighting unit in 1932. By 1942, he was the refinery's fire marshal. His genial personality and his deep knowledge of refinery fires earned him the respect of those familiar with his work. His colleagues said he lived, ate and slept with fire. With a pipe almost always dangling from his mouth, they joked that he breathed fire as well. He could take a joke. Horlbeck was in bed when the blast woke him up. He quickly got dressed and rushed to the refinery. He knew at once that this was the biggest blaze the Whiting Refinery had ever seen.[170]

George Macko's first decision of the day came instantaneously. He told his wife, Louise, that she needed to take their three children and get out of Stieglitz Park. Cheryl, fully awake by now, walked down the hallway and looked into her parents' bedroom. Her father was putting on his uniform, Louise at his side. Once dressed, he walked outside with his wife and stopped on the sidewalk to kiss her good-bye. She clung to him as long as she could, telling him to be safe. He stressed again that she needed to pack, take the children, and get to her mother's house in the southern part of Hammond.[171]

As he drove past the refinery on his way to the Whiting Fire Station, Chief Macko got a closer look at the enormity of the fire. It wasn't just his own family's safety that worried him. He knew this was a fire that threatened the safety of everyone in his city.

Both Macko and Horlbeck headed first to their bases in order to organize their efforts. Both knew their boundaries. Horlbeck was responsible for dealing with fires inside the refinery, and Macko was responsible for fires within the city of Whiting. But they also knew this was not a typical fire. They were about to put to the test every lesson they learned from years of experience and training. And they knew this effort would suck up every ounce of energy that they could muster from within.

When the hydroformer exploded into pieces, many of the fragments shot into Stieglitz Park. Some flew as far as neighboring Goose Island, where the two little Plewniak boys slept. The power of the blast propelled one fragment 1,500 feet from the blast site. A 60-ton piece traveled 1,200 feet. But these incidences were rare – most of the debris fell inside the refinery, and that created a significant problem.

When General Manager of Manufacturing Jesse Ducommun arrived at the scene, one of the first things he noticed was streams of gasoline "gushing out of the ground." It was oil from the two neighboring cat cracking units. The explosion had launched a chunk of the hydroformer skyward, and when it came back down, the steel fragment sliced through the ground and cut through several four-inch, six-inch and eight-inch pipes buried two-and-a-half feet underground. Other pieces split steam lines, gas lines and air lines. "The roar and din in the area was tremendous," Ducommun said, "a high-pitched cacophony."[172]

Metal fragments hit the cat crackers. They also hit a vapor recovery unit. But the most serious problem inside the refinery was that some of the fragments pierced about 20 nearby oil storage tanks. The storage tanks were 80 to 100 feet in diameter and 30 to 40 feet high, each capable of holding a million gallons of oil. Seconds after impact, the tanks exploded into flames. Stieglitz Park residents were still dealing with the shock of a blast strong enough to knock some of their homes off their foundations. They were still in fear after seeing fragments of flying steel rain down on their neighborhood. Now, they could see an inferno in the refinery across the street. The roar of the flames was almost deafening.[173]

Lyle Gehrke, the shift fire marshal, was getting ready to leave his office inside the refinery at 6:12 a.m. When he heard the explosion, he looked out the window and saw a huge ball of fire to the south. In a few seconds, he saw another ball of fire appear even closer as a storage tank exploded. "Almost instantly," he said, "I knew there was nothing to do except call for help." He went to his phone, but it was out of service.

His other option was to sound the "big whistle" at the refinery's fire station. It was a signal to all members of the plant's seven-unit fire department to immediately report to duty. Everyone in Whiting-Robertsdale heard the blast. But just in case anyone was in doubt about the location, the whistle would make it clear. Everyone in the area could hear the whistle, and almost everyone knew it meant there was a problem at the refinery.[174]

With millions of barrels of highly flammable material flowing through the plant, Standard Oil was prepared for fires. Company Fire Marshal Horlbeck had a full-time crew of 13 men under his supervision. To back them up, he had about 300 refinery employees fully trained to battle fires. As additional backup, there were 300 more with less training but standing by and available to help. Standard Oil was prepared for a disaster.[175]

Jesse Ducommun was still near the rubble of the hydroformer when Plant Manager Arthur Endres arrived. Several assistants and a few superintendents were with him. They developed a plan to deal with the situation and dispatched messengers to put those plans into effect. But they soon saw that the job of fighting the fire was already well underway.

Only 10 minutes had passed from the time Frank Horlbeck abruptly woke up to the time he walked into the refinery fire station. When he arrived, "What will we do?" was the question that greeted him. His short answer was, "We're going to get in there and hem her in."[176]

The first step was to immediately shut down all refinery operations close to the fire. At the same time, they needed to shut down all lines running into and out of the blazing storage tanks, as well as those tanks that were near the fire. They had to pump oil out of some units and replace it with water. They had to remove hydrogen from other units and replace it with an inert gas. Assigned to those tasks were workers familiar with those parts of the refinery.[177]

There were at least three major parts to the early plan. First: "Don't feed the flames." The firefighters shut off the flow of oil to the sections of the refinery that were burning. Second: "Don't let the flames spread to adjacent structures." The firefighters poured streams of water onto anything close to the flames. Third: "Don't let the fire spread to more distant areas." Some storage tanks were spilt open by the flying debris, while others collapsed or boiled over from the intense heat of the fire. Oil gushed out of those ruptured storage tanks and onto the ground. That created rivers of oil, which flowed past walls of flames. The potential existed for those rivers to catch on fire and carry flames to all parts of the refinery and into Stieglitz Park. Sand dikes were the solution to containing the oil. The job of building the containment walls went to workers who were not busy shutting down operations or trained in firefighting.[178]

Some refinery employees who were at home, awakened from sleep by the blast, rushed to the plant to help. One of those was 61-year-old Walter Rhea, a resident of Whiting for over 40 years. As an assistant general foreman of the Light Oils Division, Rhea was familiar with the refinery's underground structure. He knew the location of the underground cutoff valves that controlled the flow of liquids into the storage tanks. After the explosion, Rhea left his home in the 1600 block of Cleveland Avenue and drove to the refinery.[179]

What happened after Walter arrived at the plant is not entirely clear. News reports said that Rhea had a heart attack as he walked from his car toward the fire. Richard Rhea, his grandson, has a different understanding. Richard was 17 at the time and lived in nearby Hammond. He spent a lot of time at his grandparents' Whiting home and remembered his grandfather as a strong, fit man, even at the age of 61. According to Richard, Walter Rhea arrived at the plant and quickly got to work on shutting off one of the valves leading to a storage tank. A neighboring tank exploded. That explosion, Richard said, pulled all the oxygen out of the air, causing Walter to suffocate. Whatever the cause, Walter Rhea died at the scene of the fire. Whiting physician Peter Stecy ruled it a heart attack.[180]

Even as he called for help by sounding the "big whistle," a feeling of hopelessness crept into the back of Shift Fire Marshal Lyle Gehrke's mind. This was nothing like anything he had ever experienced before. He "wondered how anyone could fight such a fire." Would more firefighters do much good?[181]

The sound of the big whistle was a call to all Standard Oil firefighters. As a 1948 article in the *Standard Torch,* a company magazine, described it: "Whether an employee is at home, shopping downtown in Whiting, or visiting friends in his off-hours, he is expected to respond to the alarm and to give whatever assistance he can." John Kark was at home at the time of the explosion. It was his day off. "Dad knew what had to be done without having to be called," said Janet Kark Tindall, his daughter. "Dad dressed and went out the door and on his way to the refinery in a matter of minutes, which was only a four-block walk or run." Kark was a company fire truck driver.[182]

In 1947, Horlbeck led an effort to beef up the refinery's firefighting. The plan was to make employees understand that "Firefighting is a part of everyone's job," as Jesse Ducommun put it. In 1954, 2,516 Whiting Refinery workers attended training in the techniques of fighting small fires. The idea of all the training programs was to familiarize employees with the equipment and give them more confidence in using it. "The men learn," Horlbeck said, "that if they use their equipment correctly, it will handle the fire."[183]

Employees not trained as firefighters were not expected to report when the big whistle sounded. But some supervisors inside the plant looked for any help they could get. Jack Whiting was a pipefitter at the plant, and this was his day off. Like many others, he wanted to get as close to the fire as he could to get a better view of what was happening. While he was standing at the edge of the plant in the Marktown area of East Chicago, one of his supervisors spotted him. "What are you doing here?" the supervisor asked. "I'm watching the fire," Whiting said. "Get your butt over to such and such place," was how Whiting described his supervisor's response. Whiting said he spent most of the next week inside the refinery, helping to contain the fire.[184]

First on the scene, of course, were those already inside the plant. The overnight shift was nearing its end when the hydroformer exploded. Now, everyone was needed to help contain the fire. Many had no idea what they should do. Some, like Steve Fusak, were in other parts of the refinery. He was at work in a lab located in the same building as the refinery's medical unit. When he heard the explosion, he ran outside. None of the men in his area knew what had happened or how serious it was. That changed when a man came toward the medical unit covered in soot, looking dazed.[185]

Twenty-five-year-old Bob Usselman was in a pickup truck collecting samples from various units and tanks at the time of the blast. Because of the early morning heat, the vehicle windows were wide open. Suddenly, a strong gust of wind shook the truck. He looked out the window and saw the blaze. His first reaction was to drive away from the fire, to protect himself. But then he realized he needed to help. He stopped his truck, turned it around, and headed toward the fire until he found someone who could tell him what he needed to do.[186]

Lawrence Broviak worked at the end of the refinery opposite the hydroformer. The explosion was so loud, and the ground shook so hard, that he was certain the propane plant next to him had blown up. Before long, someone handed him a shovel and told him to walk toward 129th Street. "I didn't know what the hell I was supposed to do with a shovel," he said. "So you go along and do what you're told to do." When he arrived at 129th Street, he saw piles of sand. He was now a part of the dike building crew, one of the armies of men protecting the refinery and the city from the rapidly spreading fire.[187]

The early stages of the company's efforts to contain the fire were in place. Firefighters moved in close to the flames, lugging large hoses into position. As flames filled the sky above their heads, supervisors guided the workers to close valves and shut off the flow of flammable substances. As burning rivers of oil flowed close by, hundreds of refinery workers built sand dikes.[188]

In the first hours after the explosion, the firefighting efforts felt chaotic. Fires were burning in multiple areas and men were trickling in one by one, trying to figure out where they needed to be. In those early moments, the priority was to get the firefighters into position quickly. They had to keep the huge flames from spreading.

Once all the firefighters were in place, Refinery Fire Chief Frank Horlbeck moved to the next phase of his strategy. He set up five control zones around the fire. Zone 1 was the No. 16 continuous pressure stills, with O.L. Hurley in charge. G.H. Jones was in charge of Zone 2, the No. 9 pipe still. Zone 3 was the Indiana Tank Field Pump House, with Dan Smith in charge. M.J. See was responsible for Zone 4, the Alkylation Unit. And Zone 5, the Fluid Catalytic Unit No. 600, had F. Cushing Smith in charge. All of those put in charge were supervisors from the Light Oils Division. Horlbeck chose them because they were most familiar with the areas at the heart of the fire. Each was given a truck equipped with a two-way radio. All phones in the fire area were out, so radio-equipped vehicles were also set up at key locations. They were the only means of communication between central command, located in Horlbeck's office, and the front lines of the firefighters.[189]

Outside the refinery, Whiting Fire Chief George Macko had the same priorities as Chief Horlbeck had inside. He needed to organize his fire department to deal with this emergency. Whiting had 18 firemen, and

Macko immediately knew that was not enough. He would need all the firefighters from neighboring communities who were willing to come, so he began contacting them.[190]

They responded. Firemen came from cities in Indiana: Hammond, East Chicago, Gary and Black Oak. They came from Chicago and its southern suburbs in Illinois: Blue Island, Oak Park, Oak Lawn, Columbus Manor, Midlothian, Grand View, Chicago Ridge, Harvey, Dalton, Riverdale, Chicago Heights, Dixie Garden and East Chicago Heights.[191]

Gary Mayor Peter Mandich headed to the scene. When he saw the extent of the fire, he called for all the fire equipment and men Gary could spare to come to the refinery. Gary Fire Chief Joseph Zale commanded his men at the scene. Gary's five engine companies and about 40 men reported for duty.[192]

Richard J. Daley, in his first months as mayor of Chicago, rushed to Whiting to see what aid his city might provide. "Give them whatever they need," he told his fire and police chiefs. Chicago firemen arrived with high-pressure units designed to throw water farther than any equipment Whiting had available. The Chicago police were on standby just in case they needed to move in.[193]

Macko assembled a crew of 289 firemen from Whiting and neighboring communities to assist Horlbeck's refinery workers to control and fight the fire. All of them faced a huge challenge. Within minutes of the hydroformer explosion, more than 17 acres of the plant were on fire. Despite the personnel and equipment on the scene, the fire burned out of control throughout the morning hours.[194]

George Murray, a reporter for the *Chicago American,* flew over Whiting in a plane chartered by the newspaper. It gave him and photographer Cliff Oliver a good view of the fire. The sight below brought to Murray's mind images of volcanoes such as Vesuvius or Mt. Etna, but he said this fire looked 10 to 20 times larger. Around its perimeter, he saw fire hoses aimed at the blaze. To him, "their streams looked infinitesimal and helpless" against the fire.[195]

The pilot of a TWA flight from New York to Midway Airport in Chicago became another spectator from aloft. He radioed the control tower at

Midway that dark smoke from the fire rose 6,000 feet above the ground, and that flames shot up to about 500 feet.[196]

The *Chicago Tribune* also had photographers taking photos from the sky. They were in a helicopter piloted by Peter Cranford of Chicago. His estimate was that the flames were leaping 1,100 feet into the air. He said the heat reaching the helicopter was "terrific."[197]

Chicago American reporter Murray said the flames "rose, bright orange, half a mile in the air." Once the plane he was in went under the cloud of smoke, "Our bright sunlight was blotted out and we flew in semi-darkness. But the fire was clearer to the eye." Photographer Cliff Oliver wanted to get as close to the fire as possible. Pilot Bob Winfield dropped the plane to 500 feet. "With our window open for photographs," Murray wrote, "we could feel the rising heat from the blazing lake of oil below."[198]

On the ground, 13-year-old George Timko looked up at the aircraft just as one of the refinery's oil storage tanks detonated. The flames reached toward the small plane, which made a quick maneuver to avoid their grasp. It may have been the plane reporter George Murray was in. Murray wrote that his tiny plane "rocked in the updraft" as an oil tank disappeared "in a hot blast of fire."[199]

Ray Sons, of the *Chicago Daily News*, was one of the first reporters to get close to the fire at ground level. "As I watched," he said, "great puffballs of flame shot 400 feet into the heavy air. Here was an inferno: great wild flames – thick smoke climbing 4,000 feet high – stench and shouting and sweat."[200]

Twenty-one-year-old Dennis Moore of Whiting was at Cedar Lake, enjoying a day of swimming and water skiing. In a little more than a month he would have to answer the military draft and report to duty. He saw the smoke and figured it was coming from a nearby town. He never imagined that he could see smoke rising from the refinery in Whiting, 21 miles away.[201]

Fires fascinated nine-year-old George Grenchik. His home on West Fred Street was about 1.1 miles from the blast. He ran from home to the corner of Indianapolis Boulevard so he could get a better look. With his father, he walked down the Boulevard and got as close as the police would allow. He saw balls of flame radiate into the sky as one oil storage tank after another exploded. "You could actually feel the heat coming down Indianapolis Boulevard," he said. "You'd see the fireball, and within a second or two you'd feel the heat." For the first time in his young life, he was not fascinated by fire. He was, at least as much as a nine-year-old boy might admit, a bit nervous and scared.[202]

Twenty-three-year-old Grace Kovach had no desire to get closer. She was a self-described "pantywaist when it comes to fires" who settled for occasionally looking out the window of her John Street home. From there, she could see others walking to the nearby intersection of Schrage Avenue to get a better look. Throughout the morning, she heard muffled, explosive sounds as the storage tanks blew up. When she looked outside, she saw a massive wall of fire behind the houses across the street from her.

At one point, the phone rang. It was her grandmother calling from Chicago, and Grandma was upset. She'd had trouble reaching Grace on the phone. "What is the matter with this phone company?" her grandmother complained. "Well, Grandmother," Grace said, "there's a big fire we're having here."

Suddenly the windows in Grace's house started to rattle. "I'm looking at these windows shaking, and I see this huge ball of fire the size of a house across the street rolling towards me. Rolling like it's rolling right over the roofs towards our house. I tell you, the sound of those windows rattling, the heat was so hot that I looked down on my arms and thought they were burning. It felt like they were burning just from the heat."[203]

Frank Vargo Jr. had evacuated with his family to his grandparents' home on John Street. He saw those same flames towering over Immaculate Conception, where he attended school. "This was a tall three-story brick structure. The flames seemed to leap a hundred feet or so over the top of our school."[204]

The heat was much more intense for the firefighters. By noon, even without the added heat of the fire, the temperature was 93. To make matters worse, the flames were still spreading. By 8:30 that morning, the fire area had increased to about 20 acres. Storage tanks continued to catch on fire and explode. Filled with oil, they ignited and produced huge clouds of smoke.[205]

About 70 oil storage tanks were damaged by the fire. One is seen in the center and another to the left in this photo, both located just a few yards east of Indianapolis Boulevard. "By Saturday afternoon," the Chicago Daily News reported, "60 tanks, each averaging about a million gallons of oil or gasoline, were blazing and scores of other tanks were in immediate danger." (Photo taken by Joseph Dudzik. Courtesy of Gina Vitucci.)

One of those tanks was close to Indianapolis Boulevard, U.S. Highways 12 and 20 – a route that was not only a main path to the refinery but a major route across the United States for traffic coming to and from Chicago. When the tank exploded, rivers of hot oil gushed toward the highway. "A burning swamp of oil spread like lava across Indianapolis Boulevard," was how one newspaper reporter described it. Between 126th and 129th Streets, Indianapolis Boulevard was on fire. The flowing oil didn't stop there; it continued west across the highway. On the other side was Stieglitz Park, and next door to that was another field of tanks. Fifty oil tanks were directly in the path of the oncoming river of hot oil crossing Indianapolis Boulevard.[206]

"If that field goes," Whiting Fire Department Lieutenant Norbert Duray said, "another 500 homes will be endangered." Explosions in that tank field were a threat to the houses to its south, in Stieglitz Park. They also threatened homes in neighboring Goose Island, just to the west of the tank field.[207]

Firefighters rushed to the scene. Indianapolis Boulevard had to be their line in the sand, a line they could not let the fire cross. Their battlefront was a half-mile stretch of the Boulevard, covered with hot, steaming, bubbling oil. Some of it reached the tank field. One storage tank caught on fire. But then the firefighters gained control. They kept the storage tank from exploding and put out the fire on Indianapolis Boulevard. They saved Stieglitz Park and Goose Island.[208]

Despite winning that battle, firefighters were still losing the war against the flames. By noon, the fire had spread to 42 acres. Whiting Fire Captain Joseph Kasper said the blaze was "out of control." In every direction, there was potential disaster. The flames had to be kept out of Stieglitz Park to the west. Firefighters had to keep them from spreading north and east into the refinery. Meanwhile, a couple of huge disasters loomed if they could not keep the flames from moving south.

To the south was the refinery of the Sinclair Oil Company, and a 200 foot tall tank, owned by the utility company, filled with natural gas. Those two sites were threatened not just by the flames, but by the rivers of oil flowing out of Standard's ruptured storage tanks. The oil was running into the waters of the Indiana Harbor Ship Canal. The canal allowed ships from Lake Michigan to drop off and pick up material from the steel mills and other heavy industries along its banks. Both the Sinclair Refinery and the giant tank filled with natural gas sat next to the canal.[209]

As oil flowed into the canal, there was a growing fear that the canal would catch on fire – a fire that could ignite the natural gas storage tank and spread to the Sinclair Refinery, which would make the firefighters' worst nightmare come true. If the flames reached that area, a Standard Oil official warned, "anything can happen." Blasts from Sinclair had the potential to demolish hundreds of homes in Whiting, East Chicago, and nearby Hammond. "Half of the town could go," a company official said. The city of Chicago sent the Victor Schlager, its fireboat, to the canal in case the water caught on fire.[210]

The priority of the firefighters was not to extinguish the fires. Their priority was to keep them contained. Even that seemed to be a losing battle in the early stages. Jesse Ducommun watched the firefighters try to enter the tank fields to contain individual fires. And he watched many of them driven back by flash fires as oil spilled out of the storage tanks and ran onto the ground. The intense heat made it almost impossible for firefighters to get close enough to put the fires out. What Ducommun saw convinced him that, at that time, the fire was "humanly impossible to extinguish."[211]

The insurmountable obstacle? The firefighters were not fighting "a fire," but were fighting a "multitude of fires." The men trying to contain the flowing rivers of oil were not building "a dike," but had to build a "series of dikes." The random flight of debris from the exploding hydroformer ignited one tank here, another tank there. The oil, once stored in those ruptured tanks, now flowed in many different directions.[212]

The Justak Trucking Company, located close to the refinery, received a call from Standard early in the day. The plant needed sand for building dikes. Justak delivered all the sand it could shovel. Other trucking companies also helped. Hundreds of small dump trucks raced into the flaming area carrying sand. *Chicago Daily News* reporter Ray Sons, called the truck drivers, "Heroes, all." He noted how they "backed virtually into the flames to drop loads of sand in hopes of encircling the flaming area."[213]

"Heroic" is a word usually bestowed to someone after confronting a life-threatening situation. That word probably does not come to mind at the time the person is actually in such a situation. For them, a feeling of fear would be understandable. Most likely, they are too busy dealing with the task at hand to allow them time to think about heroism.

For the firefighters, danger was everywhere. At any moment, a storage tank could explode. But there they stood, their hoses aimed at huge metal tanks each holding 600,000 to a million gallons of oil, trying desperately to keep the tanks from exploding. Working outside on a humid, 95-degree day was bad enough, but the fire caused the heat to rise "to almost unbearable intensity," according to Ray Sons of the *Chicago Daily News*. "Grim firefighters," he wrote, "drenched with hot oil ran wearily past us, looking for fresh clothes so they could return to the fight." A National Guardsman on the scene saw the firemen drenched in sweat from the intense heat. But he said they continued to work at keeping "the tanks as cool as they could by plying the water against the tops of them."[214]

There were more than 400 water hydrants in the refinery, and the pumps generally maintained 175 pounds of pressure. But so many streams of water aimed at storage tanks dropped that pressure to 70 pounds at the peak of the fire. Despite that, there was never a shortage of water. Yet, by the afternoon of August 27, with flames still shooting up into the sky, the fire was not under control.[215]

THE EVACUEES

Frank Vargo Sr. had packed up his golf clubs and was ready to go. He worked the day shift, Monday through Friday, at the Standard Oil Refinery. Saturday was his day to enjoy. With summer winding down, the opportunities to play a round of golf would soon be few. His golfing buddies arrived at his house on the 2700 block of Birch Avenue, in the Goose Island neighborhood, just a little before 6 a.m. Frank jumped in the back seat.

Frank's wife and two sons were still in bed when he left. But Frank made just enough noise to wake up six-year-old Frank Jr., who was in no hurry to get out of bed. Frank Sr., meanwhile, riding with his golf partners, took Birch Avenue south to 129th Street. They then turned left toward the intersection of 129th and Indianapolis Boulevard. They drove past Schrage Avenue, where just a couple of blocks north the Plewniak boys were sleeping at the time. They drove past the Stieglitz Park neighborhood where Dennis Hittle was on his bike delivering newspapers. They were just a couple of hundred feet from Al Plant, Thad Bogusz and the rest of the crew who were almost ready to bring the hydroformer back online. Then they turned south toward Wicker Park, their favorite golf course – about seven miles away in the neighboring town of Highland.

By 6:12 a.m., the car of golfers had traveled five miles south to the Woodmar section of Hammond. They heard a loud explosion. Frank turned around, and through the back window of the car, he could see smoke rising in the air. The golfers wondered what it was. One of them said it probably wasn't anything serious, so they kept driving toward the golf course.

Frank Jr., who was still trying to get back to sleep after his father's departure woke him up, jumped out of bed when he heard the explosion. He and his two-year-old brother, Rick, ran into the hallway. Anne Vargo, their mother, also fled to the hallway. All the knickknacks in a shadowbox that hung on the wall over her bed had been knocked off the shelf. Some hit, but did not injure, her.

The three looked out the window and saw a gigantic fireball. The hydroformer was just under a half-mile from their home, but to Frank Jr., it looked like the fire was in their backyard. They knew they had to leave. Like many women of that time, Anne did not drive. They ran to the front door to see if any of their neighbors could give them a ride to safety. Charlie and Marge Schweikert, the family right across the street, were loading up their car and their sons, Freddie and Roger. Anne yelled out to them, but because of the noise from the raging fire they did not hear her.

Anne turned around and calmly told her two boys to get dressed and ready to leave. A short time later, Jeff Wagner, Anne's brother, showed up at the house with a car. He whisked them away to safety on John Street, where Anne and Jeff's mother, Anna Wagner, lived.[216]

In those first minutes after the blast, similar stories played out in hundreds of homes in Stieglitz Park, Goose Island and other parts of Whiting-Robertsdale and neighboring East Chicago. The Moskalick family, a little over a half-mile away in the 2400 block of White Oak Avenue, wasted no time. Sonny, the oldest boy, was at summer camp. But parents Edward and Justine Moskalick still had seven other children to round up.

Edward quickly entered their bedrooms. "Kids, hurry, hurry…an explosion at Standard Oil. Go down the back stairs." Nine-year-old Mike was on the floor. The blast had knocked him out of bed and left him in a daze. But he soon understood what was going on. With his brother away at camp, he was now the oldest of the seven. He knew he had to help his parents get his younger siblings moving.

The window in the boys' bedroom faced east, toward the fire. The explosion had blown out the glass, and the Moskalicks could feel the intense heat from the flames. Edward told his family not to go out the front door. He was afraid of the heat and fire on the other side of it. Edward and Justine carried the youngest downstairs, 11-month-old

Steve. Soon the rest of the children, still in their nightclothes, made their way down the back stairs.

By that time, Edward had turned off the gas lines into the house and gotten the car ready. Within minutes, at a speed any fire drill organizer would admire, nine members of the Moskalick family were in that car and on their way to their grandparents' house in the 1400 block of 121st Street. They were, almost certainly, among the first to evacuate.[217]

While some made a quick decision to leave, others were not sure what to do – especially those living farther from the blast than Stieglitz Park or Goose Island. JoAnne Samila lived in East Chicago. Her neighborhood, in the vicinity of East Chicago Roosevelt High School, was not in the backyard of the refinery. But at just 1.9 miles away, the flames were still huge and frightening. Her neighbors talked about evacuating. But "Where are we going to go? How are we going to go?" she wondered.[218]

Even for some living closer to the fire, the decision to evacuate did not come easily. Eugene Crews was at work at the refinery, but his 25-year-old wife was home in the 2400 block of New York Avenue, about 0.6 miles from the blast. She wasn't sure what to do, either. She waited, worried and wondered all morning. About six hours after the explosion, "the house was beginning to get very hot." When she noticed that, she did not hesitate. "I didn't even take time to pack clothes."[219]

The Macielewicz family lived in the 2700 block of New York Avenue in the Goose Island neighborhood. The flames seemed to be coming toward their house, so they knew they needed to evacuate. As they drove out of town to safety, 16-year-old Patricia Macielewicz looked back. In the foreground, she saw "Bairstow Mountain" – so called because it was a huge pile of slag, or waste, which the Bairstow Company collected from the area steel mills. It was so high it resembled a mountain. Over the top of the "mountain," she saw smoke from the refinery fire rising high into the sky. She began to cry, fearing that when they returned their house might not be there.[220]

At 6:11 a.m., Stieglitz Park was quiet. Some may have started to wake as the sun rose, but most of the neighborhood was asleep. Two minutes later, it was a scene of near pandemonium. The massive blast woke everyone up. When they looked outside, they saw gigantic flames and billowing black smoke rising to the sky from less than a mile away. People ran to their windows, ran to their doors, ran outside to figure out what was happening.

The northern end of the Goose Island neighborhood is seen in the foreground of this photo. The hydroformer was located roughly at the far right end of the pillar of smoke that rose from the ground after the explosion. Most of the smoke, though, came from the oil storage tanks, which were located just to the north (to the left in this photo) of the hydroformer. (Photo courtesy of Betty Delinck.)

Julia Miller, who lived in the 2800 block of Schrage Avenue, was on the living room couch. "I thought a bomb had hit. The children started to scream. I became hysterical. I didn't know what I was doing. I ran into the street after grabbing one or two of my children. I had a baby buggy with me and I don't know where I got it." Her husband, Edward Miller, brought the other child and followed her outside. "We walked around without knowing what to do." Someone, she did not remember who, picked them up and took them to safety.[221]

Amidst all the panic, fear, and confusion, a reporter from the *Chicago Daily News* spotted a man standing calmly on a street corner staring ahead. He asked the man why he wasn't fleeing from the scene. "My house, my house," was all he could say as he sobbed. "It's gone."[222]

Many left home with almost nothing; others took the time to cart off what they could. John Antich lived in the 2900 block of Indianapolis Boulevard just 0.2 miles from the hydroformer site. He piled his belongings into a wheelbarrow and carted them off as he hurried away.[223]

No matter how close or how far they lived from the blast, some chose to evacuate as far away as they could from the refinery. Lynn Larsen and her family lived in the 2900 block of Berry Street, just across the street from Standard Oil in Stieglitz Park. Because it was so hot the morning of the explosion, they were sleeping on cots in the enclosed porch at the front of their house. A four-foot square chunk of steel from the hydroformer landed 10 to 15 feet from them, hitting the sidewalk and wooden gate in front of their house. That was enough to convince them to drive over eight miles to the safety of a hotel in the town of Highland. Others, like 11-year-old Shirley Pullo Christ and her family, stayed with friends about 10 miles away in Griffith. Their house was a comparatively safe 1.7 miles from the site.[224]

Stieglitz Park paperboy Dennis Hittle and his family felt that a distance of 1.7 miles was much more secure than their home in Stieglitz Park. That's how far they moved when they evacuated to the home of Dennis' aunt on Roosevelt Drive in Robertsdale. It's safe to assume that everyone who evacuated was looking to go someplace safe and comfortable. So many, if not most, sought out their families for help.[225]

"Anything that happened, any babies coming in our house, we always went to Grandma's," remembered Justine Moskalick Bircher. She was the oldest daughter in a family of nine who quickly left their Goose Island home after the blast.[226]

Joe and Frances Vanek grew up in Whiting, but after they married they moved into a home in North Hammond about two miles from the explosion. Friends had been over to the house Friday, the night before. It was birthday eve for both Joe and Frances. He was turning 27 on Saturday, August 27; she was turning 24. They didn't get to bed until 3:30 a.m. The blast woke Joe up, but Frances was so tired she slept through it. She did not sleep long. Just 20 minutes later, the telephone rang for the first time.[227]

Joe's family lived on Front Street and Center Street, near the northern end of the refinery. They wanted to be farther away from the fire. Could they come stay with Joe and Frances? Frances' family lived on Schrage Avenue, to the west of the refinery. They also wanted to know, could they come stay with Joe and Frances? In all, 15 people crowded into Joe and Frances' two-bedroom house. They slept in the bedrooms, on the floors, in the living room, and even in the kitchen. About the only thing Joe and Frances had in their basement at that time was a sofa. Some slept there, and some on the basement floor.[228]

A few of the relatives brought their pillows and blankets, and the women carried their purses. They'd had no time to take anything else, including food. Joe was a good eater, so Frances had food in the house for him, but they soon were sharing it with their relatives. Frances' brother was friendly with some taverns and restaurants in the Chicago neighborhood of Hegewisch, just across the Illinois state line. He brought back fruit, lunch meat, milk and a couple of bottles of wine.[229]

Most homes in Northwest Indiana were not large. Still, families made room to accommodate their evacuated relatives. Fifteen-year-old Bonnie Wilson Faulkner and her family moved into a tiny apartment in East Chicago with her mother's two sisters. They stayed three nights. During the day, Bonnie's parents took the children to Cedar Lake, 21 miles from Whiting, just to give their relatives a break from the tight living arrangements. Even from Cedar Lake, Bonnie and her family could see the large cloud of smoke from the refinery fire.[230]

For children, getting away was something of an adventure. Ten-year-old Ann Karin Gregorovich got to stay with relatives in South Chicago who had two girls close to her age. The girls camped out in the living room and just had fun. "We were away from the fire. We were safe, so we didn't worry about it," she remembered years later. "The older people, they were worried, but we as children, it was something exciting, you might say."[231]

For the older people, there was a lot of worry, as well as a feeling of helplessness. Joe and Frances Vanek's relatives could do little but eat, sleep, and talk. They spent many hours outside, watching the flames and the smoke rise into the sky just a couple of miles away. They also prayed. Were their homes destroyed? Was their property vandalized, their possessions looted? They didn't know if they would ever be able to go back home.[232]

Joseph Vanek woke up to a cloud of smoke on his "Golden Birthday," which occurs when someone's age matches the date of their birth. He turned 27 on August 27. It was also the 24th birthday of Frances Vanek, his wife. They lived about two miles from the refinery in the North Hammond neighborhood, but could easily see the refinery fire's huge column of smoke from their home. (Photo by Joseph Vanek. Courtesy of Frances Vanek.)

Fourteen-year-old Betty Small Delinck felt sorry for her Stieglitz Park relatives. A towering fire burned across the street from their evacuated home. Her relatives didn't know if they had a home to return to. "They had to leave everything," she said, "the memories and everything, and just go, not knowing if it was all going to go up in blazes or not."[233]

That uncertainty was why some, even those in nearby Stieglitz Park and Goose Island, were reluctant to leave. John Santay, a foreman at the Inland Steel Company, lived in the 2500 block of White Oak Avenue, less than 0.5 miles from the blast. He stayed in place inside his six-room house. "I've spent so much time and money on it…well, it hurts." After the hydroformer exploded, he told his wife, Margaret, "We won't leave." They did not leave until they heard the ongoing sound of exploding oil storage tanks. That's when John, Margaret and their three children

87

packed their clothing and the family's home movie equipment. They headed to his father's house in Hammond, several miles away.[234]

For the most part, those with families to protect left their homes. The ones who stayed, who refused to leave, were the older men. Bonnie Wilson Faulkner says those who did not want to evacuate her neighborhood on 121st Street were "the older Polish people." Nick Karin remembers a neighbor, Tony "Peggy" Shultz. He was a one-legged man who ran McClelland's grocery store on Schrage Avenue, which was close to the Plewniak house. "He didn't want to leave the neighborhood. They had to force him out."[235]

Thirty-three-year-old Ann Kiraly and her husband, Andrew, felt safe in their home on Davis Avenue. It was nearly 1.8 miles from the explosion. But Andrew's family lived closer, on Steiber Street. Andrew went to his family's home to talk to them. All of them agreed to leave and come to his house, except for his father. Thomas Kiraly, a 65-year-old who had come to America 47 years earlier and had built his life on the hard work he did as a laborer in the refinery, refused to go. He stayed behind, wetting down his house with a garden hose to keep the intense heat from burning it down. He slept on the front lawn to scare away potential looters.[236]

Sixty-four-year-old Steve Pasko, an immigrant from Slovakia, had also built his life as a laborer at the refinery. And he also refused to leave his house in the 1500 block of Fred Street, one mile from the explosion. Everyone else on his block evacuated, but he sat on his porch saying, "Nobody's going to take my building. I suffered too long to get it." His daughter, Ann Devoy, did not have time to deal with her father, but William Devoy, her husband, agreed to stay with the older man and make sure he was safe. "You have my permission," Ann told her husband, "to give my father a punch in the nose," if that was necessary to force him into a car and evacuate him in the event of impending danger.[237]

Jo Ann Dudzik Jancosek, just going into her junior year of high school, heard talk of evacuation on her block of Lakeview Avenue, about one mile from the blast site. Everyone was in an uproar, and she was worried. Her father, a policeman, was working. Her mother was sick. She felt she needed to take charge and get her elderly grandparents, who lived next door, to evacuate. Her grandfather refused. Her grandmother refused. She couldn't get them to change their minds.[238]

Frank Vargo Sr. kept an anxious eye to the sky while playing golf at Wicker Park. He worried that the smoke filling the sky to the north might be close to his home. His golfing buddies finally agreed to cut their game short and head back to Whiting. By the time they got back, Indianapolis Boulevard was closed to traffic. They were familiar with the area, so they cut over to Calumet Avenue and then turned back toward Frank's Goose Island home on Birch Avenue. By the time he got there, his family was gone. He gathered up a few things and pulled the car out of the garage. He headed to the one place he knew his family would be safe and waiting for him, at the home of his wife's mother.[239]

THE NURSE

It was the job of the Whiting city nurse to be concerned about the health of the community. She had to make sure the children learned to eat healthy, practice basic hygiene, brush their teeth, get their vaccinations. She had to help pregnant women understand what was best for their health and the health of the baby they would soon be bringing into the world. She had to keep a watchful eye on the elderly, particularly those living alone, to make sure they stayed as healthy and safe as possible. She had to protect the community from the spread of communicable diseases. All these responsibilities easily filled the time of Whiting City Nurse Ann Devoy. But on August 27, 1955, one more concern was added to her list.

Whiting City Nurse Ann Devoy. (Photo courtesy of Ann Devoy.)

The 32-year-old nurse was sleeping in her home in the 1500 block of Fred Street, just under one mile from the hydroformer. At 6:12 a.m. a blast, unlike any other she had ever heard, woke her up. "Standard Oil," is what she immediately said. Her husband, Bill, valued his sleep. "It's your imagination," he said. "Go back to bed. There's probably just a little..."

"No, no," Ann interrupted, "this is different."

She got out of bed, trying to figure out what had happened. Minutes later, still in her pajamas, her hair in rollers, there was a knock on the door. It was the police.

"Annie, the mayor said you got to come quick," the officer told her. "There's about 25 people sitting on the sidewalk in front of the city hall. They're urgently wanting you to come so that you could take the glass out of their feet."

She told them she would come right away, as soon as she got her hair out of rollers and put on her uniform.

"No!" the officer said. "We have to wait here and get you, and you have to get into the squad car and we're taking you. Put your nurse's uniform on over your pajamas and come on."

She hurriedly got ready and went, looking, in her words, "like the wrath of God."

When she arrived at Whiting City Hall, she went to her office. "Oh my God," she said to herself, "what do I do? I'm not geared for such first aid; I'm geared for children's stuff." She spent most workdays in the schools. The only medical supplies she had at city hall were bandages and a few other first aid items, just in case someone at city hall needed help. She had nothing to sterilize wounds. She also did not have much time to think about it. There were people outside with injuries, and they needed her help.[240]

The first person she saw was Pete Strezo, a 54-year-old gas station owner who lived on Ann Street in Stieglitz Park, 0.2 miles from the explosion. At first, his wife, Grace, thought the noise was thunder. Then the ceiling caved in, and plaster fell. "Thunder, hell," he said. 'Let's get out of here.'" He jumped out of bed and stepped on a piece of glass. But they needed to leave. Their two sons were away at summer camp. But their eight-year-old daughter, Marge, was home. The three of them ran outside. They saw the house next door, wrecked; the car parked next to the house flattened by a giant piece of metal. Pete and his family got their car out of the garage and left as quickly as they could.[241]

"Pete, I have to sterilize some instruments," Ann said after she examined his foot. "I don't want to be responsible for anything that happens."

"Ann. You know my wife. She only speaks Slovak. She's crying and screaming...'Don't go! Don't go! But I can't walk. I've got that glass in my foot."

"OK, Pete. Sit down. I'm going to wash my hands."

"No! Just run some alcohol on your hands."

She did as he asked. He lifted his leg, and she poured alcohol on his wound. Then she slowly pulled a piece of glass out of his foot. The glass was about five inches long.

"There might be other fragments in there," she told him, saying she needed to use a hemostat.

"No," he said, "let me do this my way." He jumped off the table, stomped his foot on the floor and declared, "It's fine." Then he kissed her hand, thanked her and quickly went back to his family.[242]

Glass did not hold up well to the hydrofomer explosion anywhere in the area. In the neighboring city of East Chicago, 55 stores had their windows shattered by the shock waves – 43 in the Indiana Harbor neighborhood alone, about 2.3 miles to the southeast. Nineteen stores on the Harbor's Michigan Avenue had their showroom windows broken to pieces. The blast shattered 12 more to the south, on Chicago Avenue in East Chicago.[243]

In Whiting, the explosion destroyed close to 150 plate glass windows in storefronts along 119th Street, Indianapolis Boulevard, Schrage Avenue and other locations. The shards of glass pierced merchandise in display windows, causing additional damage. *Hammond Times* reporter Fred Krecker said it looked like a tornado had hit Whiting's main street. "Merchants were making surveys trying to estimate damage to their merchandise in their display windows," he wrote. "Workmen all along the street were cleaning up the debris and boarding up gaping holes in their store fronts where once were plate glass windows. Merchandise in display windows was ripped, cut and ruined by the flying glass from the smashed plate glass."[244]

Virtually every window shattered in Standard Oil's four-story research building in the 2400 block of New York Avenue, 0.8 miles away. Plywood to cover broken windows was suddenly in demand.[245]

It was in Stieglitz Park, Goose Island and other residential areas where the broken glass created the greatest danger. City Nurse Ann Devoy realized something as she worked her way through the line of people needing help to get the glass out of their feet. She noticed that most of the injured were men.

"When the blast occurred, the glass from their houses imploded," she explained. "So the windows all shattered on the sleeping people and all over the floor. Well, who got up first to see what happened? The head of the household, the father. So most of them were men." And since most of them were in bed at 6:12 a.m., they were barefoot.[246]

At least 35 people waited their turn at city hall. Ann realized she needed two things: more help and a better place for people to go. She called the Whiting-Robertsdale chapter of the American Red Cross. "This is getting out of hand," she told them. The Red Cross, the organization founded in the previous century by Clara Barton, cousin of Herbert "Pop" Whiting's wife, got to work providing the help the city of Whiting needed.

Some of the people who escaped Stieglitz Park and Goose Island had no place to go. Two of those were Harvey and Beverly Hunter, who lived in the 1800 block of 128th Street in Stieglitz Park, just 100 yards from the explosion. The blast threw the couple out of bed and something hit Harvey on the head. It may have been one of the chunks of steel pipe that crashed through the ceiling. Maybe it was something that came off the windows and screens when they blew inward. Or perhaps it was the plaster that fell from the ceiling. Harvey, who worked as a crane operator at Inland Steel in the Indiana Harbor section of East Chicago, didn't have time to give it much thought. "I picked myself up off the floor and started looking for the children." The bed where Dennis, their 1½-year-old, slept was upside down. The baby was under it, covered with broken glass and plaster but not injured. Harvey and Beverly grabbed their son and their 2½-year-old daughter, Bonnie, and got out of the house in a hurry.

"We got into our station wagon and started down the alley," Harvey said, "but the way was blocked by a metal casting – it must have weighed 100 tons – that had been hurled there from the refinery. We turned back and got out the other end of the alley and finally got here."[247]

"Here" was the Whiting Community Center. Generations of Whiting-Robertsdale adults and children knew the Community Center well. It had gyms for basketball and gymnastics. It had an indoor track and swimming pool for exercise. Its ping-pong tables, pool tables, and bowling alley provided recreation. Its auditorium hosted plays and concerts. It also had social rooms, reading rooms and much more. The building was one of Whiting's most attractive. "The gentle slope of the Spanish-tile roof," historian Archibald McKinlay wrote, "surmounts walls of rough textured brick in varying shades of red, laid with cream-colored mortar joints."

The Community Center opened in 1923. Standard Oil donated $450,000 for its construction. John D. Rockefeller and his son, John D. Rockefeller Jr., kicked in another $150,000. It was a gift from the company and its owners to the people of Whiting. Now, the Red Cross and the city agreed that the Community Center was the best place to set up a shelter for those people.[248]

The Red Cross moved quickly. Within an hour of the explosion, Whiting Red Cross Chairman Alfred Ciesar set the emergency response into motion. Red Cross chapters in East Chicago and Hammond were on standby to provide first aid, food, clothing, shelter, and equipment. Practically every Red Cross chapter in a 25-mile radius volunteered assistance. Some of the Chicago hospitals offered to send doctors and nurses if needed. Dr. Harry Silvian took charge of getting doctors to come help, and Jeannie Haddad scheduled the nurses.[249]

The Community Center became the headquarters for the community's response to the disaster. It served as a place to treat those who needed medical attention and evacuees who needed somewhere to stay. It also served as a place to prepare food and drink for the firefighters and other emergency personnel at the scene of the fire. Plus, it was a central location for the public to get information, and for volunteers to offer their help.[250]

Ciesar estimated that 800 families left their homes because of the explosion and fire. Others estimated there were over a thousand who had to go, and one estimate put the number at 2,000. The consensus seems to be that anywhere from 1,500 to 2,000 people left their homes for safety. Most who left went to the homes of relatives or friends. A few chose to sleep outdoors, borrowing blankets from nearby homes and making a bed in the parks. But if someone came to the Community Center, the Red Cross found them a place to stay. Whiting-Robertsdale residents opened the doors of their homes to approximately 75 people who were in need of shelter. Another 125 remained inside the Community Center, including a handful of elderly individuals and five babies.[251]

Many of those who found shelter in the Community Center would have preferred staying with family. Frances and Edward Gajewski lived on 128th Street in Stieglitz Park, just a few yards from the explosion. When they evacuated, their first choice was to stay with Frances' parents, John and Mary Mucha. But her parents lived in the 2600 block of Schrage Avenue, just a little down the street from the Plewniak family, and they'd had to evacuate. Frances' next choice was her sister, Julia Miller, but she and her family also lived on Schrage Avenue and had had to evacuate. "All my relatives are here," Frances said, as she sat next to her sister on a cot in the Community Center. "We have no other place to go."[252]

For some, getting to the Community Center was not easy. The Community Center was about 1.5 miles from 128th Street and Schrage Avenue in the Goose Island neighborhood. In 1955, it was not unusual to find residents who did not own cars. "A lot of people had to walk," remembered Larry Jennings. "That was a pretty good walk from Goose Island over to there."[253]

JoAnne Samila said a neighbor in East Chicago was trying to figure out how to evacuate. The neighbor had two small boys and a baby, her husband was at work, and she had no car. She quickly devised a plan for walking to safety. JoAnne recalled, "She got herself some rope, and she said, 'If I have to, I'll just tie my two boys together, tie them around my waist, and carry the baby, and out we go.'" Fortunately, their neighborhood did not need to evacuate.[254]

Because the refinery explosion was early on a Saturday morning, many of the families at the Community Center rushed out of their homes wearing nothing but pajamas. Some were not wearing shoes or socks. When people in the community heard there was a need for clothing, donations poured in. Even Chicago residents like Pat Piper, who every Chicago Cubs baseball fan knew as the team's long-time public address announcer, showed up with bundles of clothing to donate. Local businesses donated shoes and clothing.[255]

There was also the matter of dealing with people with special needs. "When you have a city, you have people who are bedridden, you have children who are in bed with fevers," Devoy said. "So you have to provide for them." The Red Cross brought in cots, not only for the bedridden and ill, but for those who simply needed a bed to sleep on. The Boy Scouts and neighboring Inland Steel Company also provided cots. "I had children who had fevers, who had communicable diseases," Devoy said. "I got one-quarter of that place so that these children would be confined and we could keep the communicability down to a minimum."[256]

Cots were spread throughout much of the Community Center building. "We had cots all over the boys' gym. We had cots in the girls' gym. We had enough showers in the basement. We had enough toilets in the basement. We had enough toilets on the first floor," Devoy said. "I had doctors around the clock. I had everything. It was just a wonderful setup."[257]

Ciesar fielded calls from numerous businesses and organizations offering help. Sol Polk of Polk Brothers Central Appliances & Furniture offered the use of 45 of his delivery trucks to evacuate families. He said he could manage more vehicles from the furniture industry if necessary.[258]

Because of the enormity of the disaster, Disaster Specialist Robert Rollins arrived in Whiting from the American Red Cross headquarters. As the former director of field services in Indiana, he was familiar with the state.[259]

Volunteers also showed up at the Community Center. Members of the Red Cross chapter in Elkhart, Indiana, some 80 miles from Whiting, were on their way to the Indiana Dunes for a picnic and a relaxing day on the beach. Across the waters of Lake Michigan, they saw a huge column of smoke. When they found out what it was, they left their picnic baskets untouched and drove straight to Whiting. They donated their picnic food and offered their assistance. Offers of help came from all Red Cross chapters in northwest Indiana and many in Illinois.[260]

Women from the area volunteered to work in the Community Center's kitchen. Lillian Adams headed up a crew of volunteers preparing food and drink for those in the shelter, for the firefighters and for others at the scene of the blaze. "We had an assembly line making sandwiches," Beatrice Stawitcke remembered.[261]

Other local residents made food at home and brought it to the Community Center. Various "Women's Clubs" in the area volunteered to register people coming into the shelter and to run errands as needed. Doctors, nurses and other medical assistants arrived to offer help.[262]

Major W.A. MacKenzie of the Salvation Army in Chicago drove a mobile canteen filled with sandwiches, coffee, and milk onto the refinery grounds. He brought it to a stop just 300 feet from the fire. He wanted to get close so the firefighters could have easy access to the sandwiches, doughnuts, coffee, milk and water he had stocked inside his truck. Mrs. Major Boley Black of East Chicago and a half-dozen other Salvation Army volunteers took charge of the food and drink distribution.[263]

Even a passerby came in to volunteer. Ann Devoy said she was at her desk when a young man came up and told her he was on vacation, passing through on his way to Chicago. He saw the fire, saw people coming into the Community Center, and followed them inside. "Instead of going to Chicago," he asked her, "can I help you here?" She immediately put him to work, and he stayed until the evacuees began to leave. "Godspeed," she told him before he parted, and she thanked him for all he did for the people of Whiting. "I wouldn't have missed this for the world," he responded. "It was remarkable what I learned."[264]

Before sunrise, the Community Center had been set to open for another day of swimming, bowling, ping-pong, and other activities. By sunset, it had become a first aid facility, emergency kitchen, shelter for evacuees, and a communications center. Amazingly, it went "smoothly," the word used to describe the transformation by Fred Rader, the Community Center's 29-year-old men's athletic director. The people staying there, those who came in for medical help, and numerous volunteers – all of them, Rader said, were cooperating and doing everything they could to survive the blow they'd received from the explosion and fire. It impressed a reporter for the *Chicago Daily News*. Based on what he saw at the Community Center, "Whiting," he wrote, "was proving it can take it."[265]

THE NATIONAL GUARDSMAN

The windows rattled and the house shook. Nineteen-year-old Earl Yoho was in Hammond, more than six miles from the Whiting Refinery, but he still felt the explosion. Within hours, Earl would be on his way to the refinery and wouldn't come home for the next few days. About 30 years later, Earl would retire from the Indiana National Guard as a lieutenant colonel. But on August 27, 1955, he was only a few months past his graduation from Calumet Township High School.

Earl joined the National Guard while still in school. He was a private first class in Company C of the 113th Engineers. The night of August 26, he had returned home after a nice vacation, which included a visit with family in Ohio. When he felt the explosion, he turned on the radio to find out what had happened. A couple of hours later his phone rang. The call was from his company commander – Earl was to report immediately to the armory.[266]

Whiting Mayor Michael Blastick had asked for the National Guard's help. Usually, the governor would receive the request, but Indiana Governor George Craig was out of the state. Major General Harold Doherty, the commanding general of the Indiana National Guard, acted on his behalf. The governor later flew to the area from Indianapolis and declared a state of emergency in Whiting.[267]

Earl was one of 200 Guardsmen who arrived at the scene. They were under the command of Lieutenant Colonel Robert Stimson from nearby Gary. When they arrived, one of their first jobs was to set up roadblocks. The primary road that had to be closed was Indianapolis Boulevard, which was also U.S. 12 and U.S. 20. As major routes into Chicago from the east, they were two of the busiest routes in America.

Traffic piled up on Indianapolis Boulevard after the explosion. Emergency responders had problems getting through. Whiting police quickly moved in to reroute traffic. American Legion members and other volunteers arrived to help, but the job was too massive for them to handle on their own.

When the National Guard arrived, they sealed off a portion of Indianapolis Boulevard, shutting it down on the north at the spot where U.S. 12 and 20 (Indianapolis Boulevard) intersected U.S. 41 (Calumet Avenue). From that intersection, known as Five Points, all three U.S. routes continued west into Chicago. To the south, Guardsmen blocked off the Boulevard at Columbus Drive in East Chicago, 1.7 miles from the blast site. They closed the intersecting roads. Roadblocks set up near the Marktown neighborhood kept traffic from East Chicago away from the fire scene. The Civil Air Patrol sent planes over the area to spot developing traffic jams and relay that information to police on the ground. But although they effectively sealed off the disaster site, the blockades made it impossible to get in and out of Stieglitz Park.[268]

With massive fires burning and more explosions possible, Stieglitz Park was a dangerous place. But there was also concern about looters, and no one was more concerned about looting than Stieglitz Park's residents. Walking down a Stieglitz Park street, a passerby could see abandoned breakfast meals sitting on some kitchen tables. They were visible from the street because the explosion caused structural damage to some homes, which made it impossible for the owners of those homes to close their doors. The explosion also blew out windows, making it easy for a thief to crawl inside. The fire department had encouraged Stieglitz Park residents to open up their houses before they evacuated, though, because they were afraid that gas lines could rupture and that the buildup of gas in closed houses might lead to further explosions.[269]

As evacuees talked among themselves, concern about looting spread. John Santay, who had reluctantly left his house in the 2500 block of White Oak Avenue, spoke with other evacuees. Many of them expressed their fears of looting. "I have to protect my house," Santay explained after he returned to Goose Island to board up his windows and doors.[270]

Thanks to the street blockades, the likelihood of a suspicious person walking around Stieglitz Park was remote. The two-square mile area just north, west and south of the refinery was empty. "A strange after-effect of the explosion," a reporter for the *Chicago Daily News* wrote, "was the dead calm between 127th and 129th streets just west of Indianapolis Boulevard. The stillness seemed like that of a bombed-out town." For the Guardsmen, that stillness made their jobs easier. "Anybody we'd see that was not in uniform," Earl Yoho said, "we would quickly approach and find out what their business was and see if they should be there or not."[271]

Complicating the Guardsmen's job were people who did not want to leave or were slow to get out. Not long after the explosion, Standard Oil sent a few employees door to door in Stieglitz Park to check on residents. Steve Fusak was one of those. He started at the tavern at 129th and Indianapolis Boulevard, near where paperboy Dennis Hittle was on his bike at the moment of the explosion. No one was inside, but tables and chairs were upended, and broken bottles and glasses were on the floor. He continued on to the houses in Stieglitz Park. Some residents were still there and were not anxious to leave. "Some said, 'No, I want to stay.' They said 'There's nothing wrong.' I would tell them, 'Wait a minute, this is a real endangered area.'"[272]

Fusak was a 25-year-old refinery worker who did not have any authority to tell people to leave; National Guardsmen wearing uniforms and carrying rifles had more success. The Whiting police made most of the door-to-door checks. Police Chief James Mullaney had only 27 officers in his department. With roads to blockade, homes to evacuate, and concerns that the fire might spread to other parts of the city, he needed any help the city could get.[273]

Besides the National Guard, Governor Craig ordered 200 Indiana State Police officers to duty. With the help of other cities and counties, the policing effort in Whiting grew to a total of 12 police agencies. Captain Kenneth Kupcha also called in Civil Defense workers from Whiting and neighboring communities to help.[274]

Even before the National Guard arrived, the Whiting Police were getting help from the local American Legion. Less than an hour after the blast, 125 Legionnaires reported for duty. Each man wore a uniform and carried a sidearm, shotgun, or rifle. Some of the rifles had bayonets. Many of the men were in their twenties and thirties, recent veterans of World War II and Korea. With their wartime experience and training, they were ready, willing and able to help.[275]

Organizing the mobilization was Whiting Post 80 Commander Mike Benko, outgoing Commander George Harangody, and Whiting Post Adjutant Leo Mulva. They were able to get Legionnaires deputized and ready to stand guard in Stieglitz Park within minutes of the blast.

Reinforcements were also available. Ten miles away, in Gary, American Legion 1st District Commander Richard Kaplan was on the telephone. In less than a half-hour he made 12 calls, which put 1,300 men on alert in a dozen Northwest Indiana American Legion posts.

The Legion also made plans to house and feed up to 5,000 people displaced by the explosion and fire. If that wasn't going to be sufficient, Crown Point resident Alton Cochran, the state department commander of the Legion, told Kaplan, "Spend what you need and if we don't have enough, we'll get more." Cochran said he would call on American Legion posts in the 47 other states to help if Indiana's funds ran out.

In the early minutes and hours of the explosion and fire, the Legionnaires helped wherever needed. They assisted the police with traffic control, evacuations, and guarding the homes of evacuees. They put their lives at risk by laying fire hoses and assisting with the firefighting. Some used their own vehicles to transport the injured for medical help. Others carried gasoline to the fire engines and pumpers at the heart of the blaze. The American Legion Auxiliary also mobilized. They gathered clothing for the children who had evacuated wearing only their pajamas. The Auxiliary also worked at the Community Center, where they provided care for the evacuees and assisted in the kitchen.

The response and performance of his fellow Legionnaires impressed Kaplan. He gave credit to their military experience. Every one of them, he said, "knew how, and was willing, to follow orders in coping with the emergency."[276]

Above and beyond all the basic needs, motorcycles also were in demand – so other Whiting residents helped the police. When Joe Gray wasn't working his regular job at the Youngstown Sheet & Tube Tin Mill in East Chicago, he worked part-time at Molenaars Harley Davidson in Hammond. That job had connected him with some motorcycle cops in the area. He had a new motorcycle at the time of the explosion. When

Whiting policeman Don Parker asked to borrow his new bike for the emergency, Gray hesitated briefly. Over a week later, the policeman returned the Harley in good shape but covered with a coat of oil. The Illiana Lucky Wheels Motorcycle Club also furnished extra motorcycles to the Whiting police. Some of its members helped with traffic control.[277]

The Whiting police continued to knock on doors in Stieglitz Park. Some residents were still there when the National Guard arrived, most of them still reluctant to abandon their home and their belongings. The Guardsmen reassured them that no one would be in the neighborhood but the Guard. The reassurance made a difference. "Help yourself," some residents told the Guardsmen before leaving, telling them to feel free to take anything out of their refrigerators. "We're just happy to have you," Earl Yoho remembers some residents saying. A few said it was okay if Guardsmen wanted to stay in their houses during the evacuation period. Yoho said that none of the Guardsmen took them up on those offers.[278]

Once everyone evacuated, the Guard did not find many people wandering into the area. Lieutenant Colonel D.K. Stimson, commander of the 113th Battalion, said they did question or turn back "50 to 60 sightseers." Many of those turned out to be residents of the evacuated area. They hovered along the edges of their neighborhood, anxious and worried about their homes. Donna Writt was 13 years old at the time and lived safely away from the fire in North Hammond. Some evacuees took shelter in her neighborhood. Sixty years later, she remembered the sight of those evacuees pacing the streets of her neighborhood all night long, fearing what had happened to their homes. One Guardsmen did spot a man who refused to give his name or produce any identification until pressured into doing so. But in the end, there were no arrests. There was not a single confirmed report of looting in Stieglitz Park or in any other part of Whiting-Robertsdale.[279]

The Whiting Police and National Guard were soon dealing with another concern, though. Oil from the ruptured storage tanks was flowing into the sewers. "The oil was feared to be spreading through the sewers that vein the city of 10,000," the *Chicago Daily News* reported. "This could spread the havoc throughout the area." Whiting Fire Chief George Macko later said he was less concerned with the fire inside the refinery than he was with the danger posed by an underground river of oil running through the city.[280]

One of the biggest fears was of exploding manhole covers. It was reported that a woman was driving in Goose Island near the south end of Schrage Avenue when a manhole cover blew into the sky right in front of her. Nine-year-old Kay Gregorovich Rosinski lived in the 600 block of 118th Street. That was a comfortable distance from the fire, but too far away to get a good view of it. Her older sister and a friend wanted a better look. Kay rode along. They parked the family's 1953 Studebaker at the south end of New York Avenue, got out of the car and walked down the street. Just as they passed a manhole cover, it went "Poom!" Kay remembered, gesturing to show it shooting upwards. "And then they were all popping like tiddlywinks," as more of the heavy metal manhole covers soared several feet into the sky.[281]

City workers poured sand over manhole covers to keep the flames from shooting out. But there was a growing fear of new, and more severe, sewer explosions. People needed to be alerted to the dangers. Cars and trucks with huge speakers mounted on top were put into use to spread the word. One car traveled up and down the Whiting city streets with four speakers on top. The voice from the speakers warned people to stay away from manhole covers, because if there were an explosion in the sewers, the thick metal plates could shoot into the air and become deadly.

"Don't put any cigarettes down the sewers," was a message 37-year-old Doris Wickhorst heard from the panel trucks. A casual toss of a cigarette, even a few miles from the refinery, could result in a catastrophe. So the city issued a smoking ban and ordered people not to strike a match. The speaker trucks also warned people not to operate any electrical device that might give off a spark. Some businesses closed, since it was better to be safe than to accidentally ignite the gas flowing in the sewers outside their front doors.[282]

It was also feared that many evacuees had left home with small flames still burning in their gas water heaters. For a 12-year-old like Larry Jennings, the warnings were frightening. "We thought the whole city was going to go up," he said.[283]

City, police, and fire department officials debated whether they should evacuate more homes. Stieglitz Park was almost empty of people. Many had left Goose Island. Now, it appeared likely that the rest of Goose Island should be evacuated, as well as neighborhoods along the west side of the refinery.

Earl Yoho and the other National Guardsmen on duty patrolled the neighborhoods around the clock. Most worked 12- to 18-hour shifts, sleeping when they could. The Guard's command post was in tents at Todd Park in East Chicago, just south of the refinery fire site. There were a few cots under the tents. The Guardsmen slept there or on the ground. They settled in for what looked like a long deployment.[284]

THE SPECTATORS

Fourteen years before the 1955 explosion, another blast at the Standard Oil Refinery woke the people of Whiting. This one was at 5:50 a.m. on September 24, 1941. Just as they did in 1955, people streamed out of their homes to see what had happened. An estimated crowd of one thousand gathered on the railroad tracks between the refinery and Lake Michigan. Suddenly, the wind shifted, and flames ignited a storage tank close to the spectators. When it went up in flames, the crowd ran for their lives.[285]

Human nature did not change between 1941 and 1955. Curiosity was still part of our makeup. While residents of Stieglitz Park and Goose Island tried to get far away from the fire in August 1955, "thousands of curious," according to the *Chicago Daily News*, tried to get as close as they could. They "poured into the area," the newspaper said, "adding to the confusion."[286]

Twenty-year-old Bob Babbitt was one of the curious. He got on his bike after the initial explosion and pedaled to Stieglitz Park. He saw houses damaged and cars flattened by the flying debris, until the police saw him – and told him to leave. Taxi driver Donald DeLong was in his cab on Main Street in neighboring Indiana Harbor when he heard the blast. He headed straight to Stieglitz Park. At 129th and Indianapolis Boulevard, he got his first glimpse of the aftermath. He could see some of the victims, standing along the streets, looking stunned. When the police spotted DeLong, they told him to leave.[287]

Fifteen-year-old Geraldine Schultz and her family lived in East Chicago. The initial blast knocked her mother off a kitchen chair. Her father nearly fell off the toilet. Geraldine awakened when her bed started to shake. Once they realized what had happened, they got in their car and drove as close to the refinery as possible – close enough to see the damage to Stieglitz Park – but the scorching heat of the fire convinced them it was too dangerous to get any closer.[288]

Betty and Clarence Gehrke lived on Davis Avenue, more than 1.5 miles from the explosion. The blast blew their front door open. They ran upstairs to look out the window and saw smoke, so they jumped in their car and headed toward the fire. They parked their vehicle and walked past the Schrage Avenue house where Ricky Plewniak had been killed just a short time earlier. They walked on to Stieglitz Park, where they saw a grocery store flattened by the flying debris. Strewn over the ground were the pads the grocer used to write down credit purchases. When the police saw the Gehrkes, they were told to leave the area. Since Clarence worked at Standard Oil's Administration & Engineering Building on New York Avenue, they went there and climbed to the 10th floor for a different view of the fire.[289]

The family of 12-year-old Nick Karin evacuated their home in the 2700 block of Schrage Avenue. They didn't know what to do next, so they drove to Whiting Park on the city's Lake Michigan lakefront to figure it out. As they sat in their car, they saw fishermen on boats, congregated near the shoreline to get a better look.[290]

Dennis Hittle, the Stieglitz Park paperboy, started his day just a few hundred feet from the blast. Now he was near Wolf Lake, a relatively safe 1.6 miles away, sitting on the branch of a tree that he and his cousins had climbed to watch the fire.[291]

Within seconds of the blast, Elaine Gehring said almost everyone in 1700 block of Davis Avenue was outside, still wearing pajamas and housecoats. They could see the smoke rising from 1.8 miles away, but the tops of the neighborhood houses partially blocked their view. After they got dressed, some of them walked to the George Rogers Clark High School football field, about a half-mile closer to the fire. The bleachers gave them a clearer view. High school football fields became popular spots for watching the blaze. The Clark football field afforded a good view from the west. From the south, 1.5 miles away, the bleachers at East Chicago Roosevelt's football field provided JoAnne Samila with her vantage point. Her husband brought his home movie camera along to get shots of the fire.[292]

Spectators got as close as they could and climbed as high as they could to get better views of the refinery fire. (Photo courtesy of Dennis Hittle.)

Many grabbed their cameras before they left their houses. Five-year-old Dennis Fech watched as his older brother rushed outside with the family's movie camera. Even priests wanted a closer look. Monsignor Stanley Zjawinsky of St. Adalbert's Church recruited parishioner Joe Dudzik to come along. Joe loved photography and was able to get some close-up shots of the damage and fire.[293]

The fire was so massive that many did not have to leave their homes or neighborhoods to watch it. The initial blast tossed five-year-old Maurice Campbell out of bed. He later used a pair of binoculars to watch the fire from the second-floor balcony of a neighbor's home in East Chicago.[294]

Residents in the Marktown neighborhood had an excellent view of the fire from the comfort of their homes. "In those days," Jim Hoelzel remembered, "people sitting on their front porch - that was part of social interaction." His aunts and uncles from other parts of East Chicago came to Marktown to join his family on the front porch. They watched the fire and socialized for hours. "And, of course, you'd see suddenly the gigantic ball of flame go up and…Yeah! There goes another tank!"[295]

Although cars could not get into the city, Whiting and Robertsdale residents knew the side streets. Some drove as close as they could, parked their cars, and walked to get even closer. Others simply walked from home. They congregated at police barricades, many at the barricade by the A&W Root Beer drive-in at Indianapolis Boulevard and Schrage Avenue, about a half-mile from the blast site. Police struggled to keep the sightseers on the sidewalks. Trucks carrying sand for dike building rushed past the crowds. Trucks, supplying firefighters with food and water on this humid, 90-degree-plus day, had to get through. Ironically, as millions of gallons of gasoline burned, trucks carrying gasoline were a priority. Fire trucks needed fuel to operate. After hours of firefighting, many of them were running out of gas.[296]

By 4 p.m., nearly 10 hours after the explosion, the fire was still fiercely burning. Yet, even with many oil storage tanks bursting all around them, heroic acts of bravery by the firefighters slowed the spread of the conflagration. Vapors escaped from a seal atop one tank and ignited. Firefighters climbed onto the tank, dangerously close to the blaze, to extinguish it with foam. There were signs of progress in getting the fire under control. By late afternoon, the company felt comfortable enough to let 10 reporters and photographers onto the plant site so they could get a closer look at the firefighting.[297]

The newsmen saw firefighters stand just feet away from highly flammable storage tanks. The firemen drenched the tanks in water, hoping to keep them cool enough that they would not explode. One tank, in particular, worried them. It contained three million gallons of naphtha, a highly flammable liquid used in the hydroforming process. Four volunteer firemen from Black Oak, a neighborhood just southwest of Gary, were just feet from the tank, manning the fire hoses. The group of reporters and photographers approached the area. *Chicago American* reporter Emil Bartos and photographer Howard Borvig stepped off the loading platform of a building close to the naphtha tank. Only a fire truck stood between *Gary Post-Tribune* reporter George Lindberg and the naphtha tank.[298]

Suddenly, they heard a "swoosh." Flames shot out from the naphtha tank. Three million gallons of the highly flammable gas burst into flames and blew the tank open. A ball of fire, 400 feet in diameter and reaching a half-mile into the sky, shot from the tank. The heat was tremendous.[299]

Lindberg watched as flaming oil spewed across Indianapolis Boulevard. He and others near him scurried for cover. "But the heat was so intense," he said, "that we had to drop to the ground every few seconds to cool off before getting up again."[300]

The four volunteer firemen from Black Oak were among those closest to the blast. "We couldn't have been more than 100 feet from her," said 44-year-old Sam Ordean, the Black Oak Volunteer Fire Department chief at the time. "More like 75," corrected his brother, 34-year-old Nick Ordean. Robert Jennings, one of the four, said, "the tank rose up and quivered before it let go." That gave them just enough time to drop their hoses and run to a 12-foot protective firewall 200 feet away. "The closer I got to that wall, the farther away it seemed, "said Sam. "I guess I was the most nimble. I sailed over that wall," said 24-year-old Doyle Miller, the youngest of the crew. The intense heat burned a raincoat off his back.[301]

At her mother's house in Hammond, six miles from the naphtha tank, Louise Macko saw smoke rising ever higher in the sky. What she didn't know was that a driver had dropped off Whiting Fire Chief George Macko, her husband, close to the naphtha tank just seconds before it exploded. Macko turned back toward his car immediately, but the driver was already gone. "I ran and ran," he said. "I ran across the Boulevard, but the more I ran, the more I was being burned by the trailing naphtha vapors – right through my raincoat." He jumped over firewalls. He was exhausted; he felt like he had died. "But I had to keep going. Finally, I crawled through a hole in a fence, and wound up in a medical hut that had been set up on Schrage Avenue." He had third-degree burns on his shoulders and both upper arms.[302]

Everyone close to the blast ran for cover. Reporter George Lindberg ran several blocks until he got to his car. Two injured men had gotten there before him and were trying to get it started so they could get medical care. Lindberg had burns on his arms and upper body.

Minutes before the naphtha tank exploded, 18-year-old Larry McClelland was sitting outside South Side Grade School, located in the Goose Island neighborhood less than a half-mile from the tank. It was a good spot for neighborhood residents to gather and watch the fires. Several sat on the lawn, others on the steps of the school – a mix of younger and older people from the neighborhood. Mrs. Pokraka was with them, in her late fifties, only about five feet tall and on the heavy side.

Tony "Peggy" Shultz was also there. He ran the candy store on Schrage Avenue owned by Larry's cousin. Neighborhood kids best remembered him for taking forever to prepare an ice cream cone. "It would melt by time he got it to you," Larry complained. He was indeed a slow mover, and called "Peggy" because of his wooden leg. A train accident had cut off his leg years earlier.

John "Shinney" Fritz was there. He was still recovering from an accident he'd had about a year-and-a-half earlier. Shinney had fallen off the scaffold while painting a storage tank at the refinery. He broke both legs and damaged a hip in the fall. Even with therapy, doctors told him he would barely be able to walk. Robert McClelland, Larry's 49-year-old cousin, was another one of those present. He had nearly died two years earlier after a heart attack and was now limited in what he could do.

They were all outside, in front of the school, within yards of the naphtha tank. They watched the column of fire from the blast shoot hundreds of feet into the sky. "Our mouths were frozen wide open," Larry said. As if the sight of the giant flames wasn't enough to strike them with awe, they also felt a strange sensation as the fire sucked the oxygen from around them. The air was blowing so fast that dirt, paper, garbage cans, and pieces of wood catapulted past them in the direction of the fire.

Then, after a short time, the giant column of fire dropped. It moved ominously closer to the ground. "It looked like it was going to land on us," Larry said. "You could feel the temperature start to get hotter and hotter." Somebody in the crowd outside South Side School yelled, "Let's get the hell out of here," and everyone took off running.

Larry was only 18 and was working that summer at the Youngstown Steel plant in East Chicago. Every day he worked, he walked two miles to work and two miles back. He'd also just graduated that spring from high school, where he ran track and cross country. He was in good physical condition, and as he and others ran west toward George Lake he was among those at the front of the pack. Others in the lead were friends who were around his age. Larry later figured he ran 100 yards in 9.0 seconds, a full second-and-a-half better than he ran it in high school.

As he fled, he looked back to see if he was outrunning the fire. But what caught his eye, after he took note of the position of the flames, was the sight of Mrs. Pokraka, Tony "Peggy" Shultz, John "Shinney" Fritz and Robert McClelland. Despite the short height and heavy weight of one, the wooden leg of another, the recovery from two broken legs and the damaged hip of the third, and the recent recovery from a severe heart attack of the fourth, all were just 20 to 50 feet behind.[303]

Anyone close to the naphtha blast had to retreat. The heat was severe. But some valiantly rushed toward the flames to help. Bud Bardowski, the head of Gary's Civil Defense unit, went into the area immediately to see if everyone was out. He then rushed the victims to the hospital in his emergency vehicle. Two Gary motorcycle police officers, Cliff Graham and Robert Miller, also rode their three-wheel cycles toward the blast area to see if anyone needed help. They spotted six men trapped behind a steel fence. The policemen rammed the fence with their bikes to create a hole through which the men were able to crawl and escape the burning gasoline and oil. Graham came away with painful burns to his hand.[304]

The naphtha tank explosion caused the number of injuries to grow, and most of the injured were firefighters. Forty-four-year-old East Chicago Fire Captain Samuel Ross suffered burns on his face. He was also treated for smoke inhalation. Twenty-seven-year-old James Ford, a Blue Island fireman, received burns on his back and arms.[305]

The heat of the naphtha fire was so severe that several people outside the refinery received burns. Lou Klein, the director of the East Chicago Department of Community Relations, was near 129th and Indianapolis

Boulevard delivering milk to the firefighters when the blast of heat burned both his arms. East Chicago Police Chief Anthony Majewski and Whiting City Engineer Stephen Manich were directing evacuations across the street in Stieglitz Park and Goose Island. They were both seriously burned on the face and body.[306]

It wasn't necessary to be close to the naphtha fire to feel its burn. Lawrence Broviak was in the plant when the tank blew up. He ran across a viaduct that went over Indianapolis Boulevard from the refinery to a parking lot on the other side. He continued running through Stieglitz Park and on to Goose Island. "I ended up on the other side of Schrage Avenue in somebody's backyard. I don't think there was anybody who passed me up," he said. The entire time he was running, he could feel the intense warmth licking at his heels.[307]

Tom Marciniak was near St. Adalbert's Church, a mile from the site. "I felt this heat on the back of my neck," he said. "It's like 95 degrees out, and you could feel extra heat on the back of your neck. I looked around, and there's this great big fireball right above my head, practically. And the heat from that thing is just spectacular."[308]

It was hot even before the naphtha tank went up. In the 10 hours after the hydroformer exploded, dozens of oil storage tanks ignited and burned. The sky was already ablaze with a wall of flames. On top of that, it was over 90 degrees and humid – one more hot day during one of the hottest summers on record in northwest Indiana and the Chicago area. Lawns were already brown from the lack of rain and day after day of 90-degree-plus weather.

While the flames burned, eight-year-old Bill Haddad and his friend Phil Kokandy played on the porch of Phil's house in the 2600 block of Birch Avenue, just a half-mile from the hydroformer site. Suddenly, the front lawn of the Kokandy house was set alight. It was spontaneous combustion from the scorching heat of the refinery blaze. "We couldn't believe what we were seeing," Haddad said. The boys ran inside to tell Phil's father, and Sam Kokandy ran out and extinguished the fire with a garden hose.[309]

Temperatures were already in the 90s on the August day in 1955 when the hydroformer exploded and set numerous oil storage tanks on fire. The heat of those fires was intense, especially for the firefighters who battled the blaze. (Photo courtesy of Betty Delinck.)

Just a few blocks away, Joseph Tomera was at his Goose Island home on Schrage Avenue. He was a truck driver at Standard but had the day off. After the hydroformer explosion he evacuated his family, but then returned to hose down the roof of his garage to cool it from the heat of the fire. He was pouring water on the roof when the naphtha tank exploded. He ran as fast as he could toward White Oak Avenue, fearing that the heat and flames would overtake him.[310]

On Indianapolis Boulevard, where the police had set up barricades to keep the spectators from getting too close to the refinery, a crowd of people ran for safety when the naphtha tank exploded. "Don't panic! Don't panic!" a policeman shouted, as dozens of onlookers fled in terror. Mary Ann Stofcik Dominiak, 16 at the time, was one of them. It looked to her like the flames from the blast were in the backyard of the house across the street and that they were rising above the house. She could feel the extreme heat on her face. So, along with her cousin Dolores, she quickly turned and ran. Dolores had injured her ankle and was walking with a limp before the blast. But once they witnessed the explosion, Mary Ann said, "both of us took off like jackrabbits down the alley."

It was the initial shock of seeing the huge ball of flame and feeling the heat that scared the two teenage girls. "That was my life-and-death experience," Mary Ann said years later, the memories of that day still very clear in her mind. "I thought I was going to die."[311]

So did George Timko. He was walking near 126th and Schrage, about 0.4 miles from the initial hydroformer explosion site. To him, the flame from the naphtha tank explosion "looked like it was going up to the sun. It just never stopped." The heat was unreal. He said it was like the sun was falling. He ran as hard as he could to get home. He saw a pile of freshly clipped branches that someone had laid in the alley after cutting their shrubs. "I literally dove into those bushes because the heat was so bad." He echoed Mary Ann, "I thought I was going to die."[312]

The heat was also felt south of the blast site. Timko said his aunt and uncle were on Indianapolis Boulevard in East Chicago when the tank exploded. People ran to escape the heat, and his aunt and uncle told him that paint blistered on some of the cars.[313]

Seventeen-year-old Dave Sharp was walking from his home in the 1700 block of Sheridan Avenue with some family members and a few neighborhood girls to get a better look at the fire. When the naphtha tank exploded, they whirled around to escape the heat. The boys outran the girls, but stopped to catch their breath and wait for the girls to catch up. When the girls reached the boys, they all turned to see the devastation. "Look at your legs!" one of the boys shouted. The legs of the girls, who were wearing shorts, were so red from the heat of the fire that it looked like they'd baked in the sun all day at the beach.[314]

The naphtha explosion created a new wave of evacuations. Those who had felt safe after surviving the hydroformer blast began to rethink their situations. Before the tank went up in flames, Evelyn Kortokrax looked at the dark smoke in the sky and asked her husband, "Should we worry?" Everett Kortokrax responded, "No, things look okay yet." She was outside hanging newly washed diapers on the laundry line when the naphtha tank exploded. Everett bolted out of the house. "Forget those diapers, put them in the basket. We're going to my mother's."[315]

Susan Brown was a nine-year-old in Marktown in 1955. Her family wasn't worried after the hydroformer blew up and the storage tanks caught on fire. "Looks like Standard's at it again," her father said. "It's probably more bark than bite." They carried on with their Saturday. Susan's father and brother went to get haircuts and run errands; her mother washed clothes. But Susan worried, especially when a sound truck came through and a voice told residents to evacuate. "Ma," Susan pleaded, "he said we've got to leave. Now! Marktown's gonna be flattened!" Her mother told her to calm down. But when the naphtha tank exploded, Susan said her mother "lost her ladylike composure," and said, "Pack your clothes. We're leaving, even if we have to walk!"[316]

For the Vargo family, the naphtha explosion meant evacuating for the third time. The first had been when Frank Vargo Sr. was on his way to Wicker Park to play golf at the time of the initial hydroformer explosion. His wife, Anne Wagner Vargo, evacuated their Birch Avenue house with their two sons and went to John Street in Whiting, where Anne's mother, her sister Mary Novotny, and Mary's family all lived. The Birch Avenue home was less than a half-mile from the hydroformer site, while the John Street home was just over a mile away. But shortly after Frank rejoined his family, the police told people on John Street to evacuate. This second evacuation sent the Vargos, the Novotnys, and Grandmother Wagner to LaPorte Avenue, about 1.5 miles from the refinery fire. Another sister, Mitzi Fischer, lived there with her husband, George. When the naphtha tank exploded, even LaPorte Avenue did not seem safe. So the Vargo, Novotny, and Fischer families, along with Grandma Wagner, evacuated the third time to the home of a brother, Chuck Wagner. He lived with his family near downtown Hammond, about 4.5 miles away, and fortunately had enough room for everyone.[317]

Standard Oil took pride in its readiness to deal with fires. In 1917, there was an average of nearly two lost-time accidents per day in the refinery. They viewed accidents as "just one of those things." In 1918, Whiting became the first oil refinery in the world to establish a safety department. From that point, the number of accidents dropped. By 1952, 1953 and 1954 the Whiting Refinery had one of the best safety records in America and had received the National Safety Council award. It was probably on its way to another award in 1955. At the time of the explosion, it was averaging just 0.84 disabling injuries per million man hours worked. "Until the fire," Chairman of the Board Robert Wilson told the Kiwanis Club of Evansville, Indiana, "Whiting this year had been having an almost unbelievable safety record. There had been less than one lost-time accident for every one million man hours worked there."[318]

Standard Oil had a well-trained team of firefighters. It had the equipment and the infrastructure to deal with an emergency. It had over 400 hydrants in a high-pressure, looped-water system. It had 11 stationary pumps, which maintained 175 pounds of pressure. It had 51 turret nozzles located in key spots. It also had seven fire trucks, 44 hose carts, and nearly 80,000 feet of fire hose. It even had a team of over 100 canaries, constantly on guard.[319]

Canaries are extremely sensitive to gas. A slight whiff of hydrogen sulfide can kill one of these birds. The highly toxic gas is also fatal to humans, but canaries succumb to the fumes early enough to give people time to respond to the danger. Standard brought its first canaries on board in 1944, when the company began processing high-sulfur West Texas crude oil. Whiting was the only Standard Oil refinery to employ canaries. Almost all the members of the canary crew were female. The reason was pure corporate economics – male canaries sing, which means they are in higher demand among pet owners, increasing their cost. In an average year, the Whiting Refinery would lose about 125 birds. Most losses were due to natural reasons. Thus, it was better for the bottom line to lose the less expensive females than the singing males.

The canaries received excellent care. Maria Surdukowich was one of the refinery workers assigned to work with them. She helped feed the birds about 400 pounds of seed a year. She also helped trim their claws, change the water in their cages, and keep the cages clean. Maria did not look like a typical refinery worker as she pedaled her bicycle across the refinery. The big basket attached to her bike contained the seed and supplies Maria needed to care for the birds.

The canaries were strategically positioned around the refinery, wherever the threat of hydrogen sulfide existed. They were in small cages in very visible locations. Workers needed to see them to be sure the air was safe. Because they were highly visible, the birds were also popular. The employees in one of the plant's control rooms painted their canary colleague's cage. Occasionally they opened the cage door to let her exercise. One group of workers remodeled their canary's cage. They gave her a bigger and better bath than the standard issue birdbath. One employee even brought in a male canary from home to give the female some companionship.[320]

Steve Fusak had hoped to go home as his shift at the refinery drew to a close on the morning of August 27, 1955. The explosion changed his plans. As the fire raged, a storage tank close to him exploded. He ran. He headed toward the refinery's two giant cat crackers. "The first thing I looked at," he said, "I looked at where the canary was...no canary!"

Maybe she died in the line of duty. Maybe another refinery worker saw her inside her cage, opened the gate, and encouraged her to evacuate. Or, maybe she flew off and stopped for a moment to become one of the spectators watching the fire, before moving on to a new life.[321]

THE BOY AT SUMMER CAMP

By August 27, summer was winding down. Within two weeks, schools would be back in session. Jim Sandrick's family lived about 1.7 miles from the hydroformer site, but on August 27, Jim was 95 miles away. He was enjoying his last days of summer at a Catholic Youth Organization camp at Our Lady of the Lake Seminary on Lake Wawasee near Syracuse, Indiana. It was time to go home, and his parents were driving over to pick him up.

As the scheduled pickup time approached, Jim was called into the seminary office. "There was an explosion at Standard Oil," a priest told him. "Your parents will not be able to pick you up." Information was scarce. Were they safe? Was his family alive? Jim didn't know, and no one was able to find the answers. He tried calling, but the phone lines were down. His parents were dead, he thought. They had to be. That terrible fear ran through the mind of the grade-school boy. He called his aunts, his uncles, anyone he could think of. None of the calls went through.

A priest at the camp offered to take him on a train back to Whiting. As they got closer to the train station in Gary, they could see black smoke filling the sky to the west. The sight made him feel even more sure that his parents and sister were all gone. The priest tried to comfort him. "If your parents are gone," he said, "it was God's will. Hopefully, they didn't suffer."

When the train arrived in Gary, Jim went straight to the phone booth. He finally got through to some family friends. It was only then that he heard the news: His family was alive; everyone was all right. The friends drove to Gary to pick him up and take him home.[322]

Fear and anxiety affected many Whiting residents. Just minutes before the explosion, Thomas Jurbala drove past the hydroformer on his way to his job in East Chicago. When he got to work, he raced into his office to call home, worried about his family's safety. But the phone lines were

119

jammed and his call would not go through. His wife Anna was at home, pacing the floor with the phone in her hand. She was just as worried about her husband's safety. She feared that he'd been driving past the hydroformer at the exact moment it exploded. But her phone calls to him could not get through, either. With no phone service, Thomas tried driving back home, but by that time all roads into Whiting were blocked. It was hours before he found out his family was safe and they were sure he was still alive.[323]

Many Whiting residents who were not at home and out-of-town family and friends experienced great fear and frustration. Friends and relatives tried calling the Gehring family. Their son, away in Iowa, finally got through after repeated attempts to see if they were safe. But the relatives of Doris Wickhorst called over and over without success. As their concerns grew, they called other family members to see if they could reach her.

Barb Poppen, a student nurse at St. Mary Mercy Hospital in Gary, heard the explosion and ran to the windows to see a huge black cloud rising in the direction of Whiting. Her fear intensified when she called her parents and could not get through. When she finally reached them, her father's humor quickly put her at ease. "Funniest thing," he said, "I was in the bathroom getting ready to go to work, and the darn thing blew me off the pot!"[324]

The initial blast damaged telephone cables, affecting virtually every phone in the refinery. The blast and fires that followed also damaged phone cables serving parts of the city. In all, 12,000 phones lost service in some areas of Whiting, Robertsdale and neighboring East Chicago.[325]

Illinois Bell Telephone rushed 100 repairmen into the area. Many repairs were needed close to the heart of the massive blaze, which firefighters were still trying to contain. Despite the danger, repairmen from Illinois Bell erected new telephone poles to replace those damaged by the blast. Ignoring the heat of the nearby fire, they climbed poles to reattach phone wires that had become disconnected.[326]

Phone company repairmen also went to work inside the refinery. They laid emergency lines to Standard's lab and hospital, as well as other key sites. Illinois Bell brought in 10 mobile radio units for firemen and police to use. Two other local companies also pitched in. The Inland Steel Company brought in two additional radio units and Northern Indiana Public Service Company (NIPSCO), the public utility company, supplied five more mobile units.[327]

Illinois Bell also brought two trailers to the city. One was an emergency unit, which they parked in front of their office in the 1800 block of Indianapolis Boulevard. They equipped that unit with a teletype, radar service, and a paging system, as well as emergency radios and regular telephones. They parked the other trailer outside the Community Center so evacuees would have a place to make phone calls.[328]

On top of the problems caused by the phone line damage, Illinois Bell faced an additional challenge. Jesse Ducommun was one of many who experienced it. Standard Oil's general manager of manufacturing went to his home phone just seconds after the initial blast. The phone was not dead, but because so many people were using their phones, he was unable to get a connection. Callers overwhelmed the phone system. In the 12 hours that followed the blast, 45,000 phone calls came through the Whiting switchboards. In 1955, telephone operators had to manually connect each call.[329]

The Illinois Bell office in Whiting had 25 telephone operator stations. Within a half-hour after the blast, all 25 were in use. Operators continued to work through the day. Forty additional operators went on duty at the East Chicago telephone exchange. Most volunteered to come in, including Mary Jenkins. She worked all night at the Gary exchange and went right to East Chicago to help out.[330]

With phone service down, the Lake County Civil Defense Unit set up a radio base station in East Chicago to help direct firefighters. Amateur radio operators also helped out. About 20 of them worked 48 consecutive hours, passing along information to people around the world. They positioned themselves as close to the scene as possible. Twenty-five-year-old Jack Theodore, a ham radio operator from Gary, parked so close to the refinery that heat from the fire singed the paint of his vehicle. Jim Hoelzel, a boy living in Marktown at the time, said an uncle's friend parked his car nearby at 129th and Dickey Road and gave a minute-by-minute ham radio account of what he was seeing. It would be more than a half-century later before instant communication via social media became common, but the ham radio operators of the day provided a similar service to their followers. Via radios set up in their cars, they watched what happened and broadcast it instantaneously to other amateur radio operators around the world, who responded with comments and questions of their own.[331]

Television had the ability to show dramatic footage of the fire, but TV news was in its infancy in 1955. The technology for a television station to report live from the scene of an event, or even to shoot videotape, was more than a decade away. Television news used film cameras in 1955. Chicago television news crews had to rush the film back to the station and have someone process it before it could go on the air.[332]

1955 was the year that America crossed the 50 percent mark in the percentage of homes with TV sets. But television had limited news programming in 1955. Nationally, NBC's "Camel News Caravan," anchored by John Cameron Swayze, CBS's "Douglas Edwards with the

News," and ABC's "John Charles Daly and the News" were the extent of the network newscasts, and each was just 15 minutes in length.

Chicago's television stations did their best with the technological constraints of the time. They interrupted regular programming to give updates. Film footage was broadcast as it became available. Reporters interviewed firefighters and others on the scene. Eight-year-old Cheryl Macko watched from her grandmother's house in Hammond as WBBM-TV reporter Hugh Hill interviewed her father, Whiting Fire Chief George Macko. Hill had worked in radio in Hammond before going to Chicago.[333]

Numerous young television reporters received valuable experience covering the Whiting Refinery fire. William Obermiller, later to serve 36 years as Whiting's City Judge, worked as the refinery's community relations director. That job made him the primary contact between the news media and Standard Oil during the fire. He recalled working with East Chicago native Frank Reynolds, a Chicago TV reporter at the time. Reynolds would later become the main anchor of ABC "World News Tonight" in the late 1960s and into 1970, and again from 1978 until his death in 1983. Besides growing up and attending high school locally at Bishop Noll in Hammond, Reynolds worked at WJOB radio in Hammond before moving on to television in Chicago. Another Chicago television reporter who covered the refinery fire was John Chancellor. His coverage of the fire caught the attention of NBC News executives. It helped launch a career that took him to the main anchor desk of the "NBC Nightly News" from 1970 to 1982.[334]

Obermiller and Standard Oil set up a media center in the company's Industrial Relations Building on Front Street, at the northern end of the refinery. The company planned to have one office where all reporters could receive updates on what was happening inside the plant. Phones were set up to allow reporters to get their stories to their news organizations. The company stocked the room with coffee and sandwiches to keep the reporters nourished. But the fire soon knocked out the phone service at Front Street. All media operations had to shift to the Administration and Engineering Building on New York Avenue, just west of the refinery.[335]

In those days, newsreels preceded the main feature at many movie theaters. The newsreels reported on a series of current news events. The dramatic footage of flames rising high in the sky made for compelling viewing at movie houses in the days following the explosion. National news magazines also ran stories and photos from Whiting, and soldiers serving overseas read about it in *Stars & Stripes*.[336]

Radio was a major source of news in 1955. Locally, WJOB in Hammond was the primary radio source for Whiting news. Richard Joyce, in his early 20s in 1955, was a part-time employee there while going to school at Purdue University's Calumet Campus in Hammond. The station had a license that allowed it to broadcast only during the daylight hours. So at 5 a.m., Joyce reported to work and turned on the transmitter. He was the only person in the station at that time of day on the weekend. He was not an on-air personality. His job was to start the station's broadcast day by playing pre-recorded programming.

The station was 4.6 miles from the hydroformer. Joyce was inside a windowless concrete block building when he heard the blast at 6:12 a.m. Still, it wasn't until the station's telephone started ringing off the hook that he knew something big had happened. He finally stopped answering the phone, and for the first and only time in his life, he turned on the microphone and went live on the air. "Any WJOB employee who is listening," he broadcast, "please immediately come to the station." The station's sportscaster was the first to arrive and gathered enough information to go on the air with reports.[337]

Earl Yoho, the young National Guardsman who would soon report to duty at the refinery, found out about the explosion at his home in Hammond while listening to WJOB. The Vargo family, who had evacuated their Goose Island home and moved three more times to find a safer place, listened to WJOB on a big radio on the porch of a relative's La Porte Avenue home in Whiting.[338]

News coverage was extensive. "It seemed like there were helicopters overhead 24/7," said Elaine Gehring. Newspapers provided most of the Whiting disaster coverage. Chicago had four major newspapers: the *Chicago Tribune, Chicago Sun-Times, Chicago Daily News* and *Chicago American*. All four sent reporters and photographers to the scene. More locally, the *Hammond Times* and *Gary Post-Tribune* gave the disaster full coverage. So did the weekly Whiting newspaper, the *Times-Graphic*. Reports from the Associated Press and United Press International spread the story across the country and around the world. Whiting became the news capital of the United States. Saturday newspapers across America covered the story with dramatic photographs and lengthy stories.[339]

The story caught the attention of people far and wide. "Oil Refinery Shocks Indiana City," the page one headline read in *The Lethbridge Herald* in Alberta, Canada. Haydar Gork, the ambassador of Turkey to the United States, sent his sympathy to the people of Whiting. J.A. Chieze of Martigues, France, who had visited the refinery earlier in the year, wrote a letter to the company. He said he enjoyed his visit and felt the community's pain. "I...send you," he wrote, "my heartfelt condolences asking you to convey them to the families concerned." The American Legion Post in South Chicago started a relief fund. It kicked in $100 of its own money to get the fund started. Belgian-born artist Marcel Cockx, living in Muskegon, Michigan, drove immediately to Whiting when he heard about the explosion. He painted a picture of the fire, which he displayed for the first time at the 1956 Tulip Festival in Holland, Michigan.[340]

But it was out-of-town Whiting residents, family, and friends who had the most interest in the story. Fred Behrens, a 20-year-old soldier stationed at a missile base in New Jersey, walked into his barracks after "chow." That was when he heard a TV report broadcasting the news that his hometown of Whiting was on fire. He tried calling home, but like summer camper Jim Sandrick, he was unable to get a phone connection. It was two days before he was able to get through and find out that his family was safe.[341]

Ray Gajewski, stationed at Fort Knox in Kentucky, was preparing for reveille when he heard the news over a radio at a fellow soldier's footlocker. He stopped dead in his tracks, but realized he had to get into formation. Afterward, he asked his company commander if he could go home. He got a 10-day leave to return to Whiting. As he approached Chicago, the Eastern Airlines pilot announced to the passengers that he would bank the plane "a little to the right so you could see the Standard Oil fire."[342]

Many rushed home after hearing about the explosion. Unable to reach anyone in Whiting by phone, the sight of smoke rising in the direction of Whiting made drivers' journeys tense as they inched closer. Sonny Moskalick was at a Boy Scout camp at Starved Rock in Illinois as his parents and seven younger brothers and sisters hurriedly evacuated their Goose Island home. Scout leader George Oprisko immediately brought the Whiting Boy Scouts home. Even at a distance, they could see the red sky as they drove from the west. They did not know whether Whiting was gone, if their families were safe, or if they still had a house to live in. Oprisko took them to the Community Center, where Red Cross volunteers helped him track down the family of each boy.[343]

Joseph Sotak and Joe McKennan, two labor leaders at the refinery, were on union business in Wood River, Illinois that day. Standard Oil had another refinery in Wood River. Someone knocked on Sotak's motel room door and said, "Mr. Sotak, you've got a telephone call downstairs." It was his wife. "Joe, you better come home," she said. "Whiting's on fire." He figured she was exaggerating, and told her so. "No," she said, "they had a big explosion." The two men immediately caught a train from Alton to Chicago, and then a South Shore commuter train from Chicago to Northwest Indiana. As they rode the South Shore, Sotak realized for certain that his wife had not been exaggerating. "We could see that inferno from there."[344]

Newspaper headlines heightened the anxiety felt by some who were out of town. In those days, many newspapers came out in the morning. Others published their editions in the afternoon to give readers updated news at the end of the workday. By Saturday afternoon, hours after the blast, newspaper stories began appearing. Some painted a frightening picture for out-of-town families and friends. "City Imperiled as Blasts Fire Big Indiana Oil Refinery; 1,400 Flee, 2 Die," read the headline in the New York Times. "Thousands Fleeing City; Fire May Rage for Days," was another headline – while another declared it was "Like End of the World."

Relatives of Betty Small Delinck lived near Effingham in southern Illinois. "We heard Whiting was blown off the map," they said, when they were able to get through with their phone call. Dale Seliger, 20 years old at the time, had relatives in Nevada and Utah. News reports led them to believe a massive fire had engulfed much of Whiting and destroyed the city.[345]

Rose Lubeck owned a small plane and had taken off for St. Louis the day before the fire. As she prepared to return home on Saturday, a worker at the airport in St. Louis asked about her destination. She told him she was from Whiting. He told her that Whiting had been evacuated. Not knowing what to expect, she flew toward home. She could clearly see the huge, black pillar of smoke over the city. It got larger as she approached the area and landed her plane in nearby Dyer, Indiana. She reached her family home near 121st and New York Avenue, a mile from the blast site, just as her family was evacuating.[346]

Rosemary Kraly was in Livingston, Montana, visiting relatives with her parents and her children, Jim and Cindy. Her dad wanted to top off his western visit with a 10-gallon Stetson hat, so she took him into town to buy one. On the car radio, they caught just a fragment of a story about Whiting. It surprised Rosemary. "Nobody knows about Whiting," she said. "They don't even know where Indiana is when you're out in Montana." She pieced together enough information to conclude that Standard must have blown up. "They're saying Whiting, Indiana. Sure as God the Standard had blown up and there we are; we don't know beans about it. I figured my house was leveled…the whole bit. Instead of going on to a couple of other places, we headed for home."[347]

Within the city, there was intense anxiety over the safety of those battling the fire. Standard Oil made an effort to put those minds at ease. "I didn't hear from Bob all day," said Betty Herakovich. Her husband worked at the refinery on Saturdays. "Around midnight, a man [who worked at the plant] came by the house and told me that Bob would be home soon." Her son, Robert Herakovich Jr., remembers Standard Oil trucks coming down 119th Street in Robertsdale, "almost stopping door to door and providing verbal reports on the status of our loved ones."[348]

Standard Oil also used its telephone operators to reach families. Ann Marie Kaminsky had heard rumors that her husband, Ed, an assistant fire marshal at the refinery, was injured. A woman from the plant called later in the day and said, "Ann, Ed did hurt his ankle, but he's OK," putting her mind at ease. A company phone operator also called the family of Stanley Kazmierczak and said he was fine. His wife expressed gratitude to the operators for "the comfort they gave me when I was desperate in not knowing what to expect."[349]

An early phone call from Standard Oil brought little relief to the family of 63-year-old William Cinotto. They knew he worked right next to the hydroformer, and when the first call came in from Standard Oil, they were told he was missing and that a search was underway. His 23-year-old daughter, Doris, decided not to wait for the next call. She and some of her cousins walked from the family's Atchison Avenue home to the refinery. The police stopped them, saying it was too dangerous to get closer, even after Doris told them her father was missing. It was more than 12 hours after the blast that they received a call saying he was safe. To protect himself from the flying debris and flames, William had crawled under some heavy machinery and stayed there until he felt it was safe to come out.[350]

The uncertainty about the safety of loved ones impacted not just the wives of men working at the fire, but also their children. Eight-year-old Bill Haddad's father was not scheduled to work that day, but he was called in for fire duty. "I would not see him for three days," Haddad said years later, "and I recall the real fear of losing him." Then his mother, a registered nurse, went to help at the Community Center. She made arrangements with the neighbors to watch her children. "This was quickly becoming more than I cared to deal with as an eight-year-old, and I was genuinely scared."[351]

Seven-year-old Lynn Larsen and her parents had evacuated their Stieglitz Park home just across the street from the refinery. But her father, a security guard at the plant, had to go into work. "I was scared to death," she said, "that there was going to be another explosion; that my dad would get injured or killed. I'm sure my mom was thinking the same thing. I was terrified. I was just so afraid that he was not going to come home."[352]

Janet Kark Tindall later remembered the fear she felt after her father, John Kark, went into the plant that morning to help fight the fire. "The only thing that I was worried about was my dad." She had no idea at the time what a close call he'd experienced. A storage tank exploded as he was driving a truck past it. The force of the explosion rolled the vehicle over, but his injuries were actually caused by the heat of the fire. He received significant burns on his ears and the back of his neck. "We hadn't seen him all day, and we didn't know where he was until he came back from the hospital with his ears all bandaged up and his neck all bandaged up."[353]

Many children naturally feared for their own safety, as well as their loved ones'. "It was the first time in my life," Barry Klemm remembered, "when I personally knew that I could be in danger." He knew it from the tone of his mother's voice as she told him, "You cannot leave the yard. I must be able to see you at all times." From that, he said, "I knew, boy, this is dangerous." Her words grew stronger in his mind as he stood in his blue jeans in his family's backyard and watched a series of storage tanks explode. Even if his mother had allowed it, he was certain: "I don't want to leave the yard."[354]

THE BRIDE

In Hammond on the morning of August 27, 1955, Pat McArty Mazanek was busy. If her house shook from the power of the blast, which went off about five miles away, she didn't notice. Even though she was getting ready to go to Whiting, she didn't know the city was dealing with a major emergency. When the driver arrived to pick her up, his first words to her were, "You are not getting married today." He then told her about the refinery explosion. "I'm in my gown," she responded. "I'm getting married today." She was 18.

Patricia McArty Mazanek

The wedding was to take place at Immaculate Conception Church, just a mile from the hydroformer site. The fire blocked the route between Pat's home and the church. "If you insist on going," the driver told her, "I know some back roads into Whiting."

Just minutes before heading to the nearby church, Joe Mazanek, soon to be Pat's husband, was in his tuxedo sweeping glass off the sidewalk in front of his family's grocery store. The plate glass at the front of the store shattered. Glass fell onto the sidewalk and on the oranges, apples, and other grocery items in the window display.

As the guests and members of the wedding party arrived, a sky full of smoke and flame formed the backdrop. One of Pat's bridesmaids lived close to the blast site and needed to evacuate before she could drive to the wedding. In her car were belongings from her vacated home, including a pet bird in its cage. The best man arrived in his tuxedo but left immediately after the wedding to fight the fire. He came back later in the day for the reception.[355]

Just like newly married Joe and Pat Mazanek, life went on for many in Whiting on August 27. Even with billowing black smoke in the sky, six-year-old Bob Hanchar watched as his mother did what she always did for her growing family: hang diapers on the backyard laundry line. She was hardly atypical. Saturday was laundry day for many women. Elizabeth Herakovich watched the smoke rise over the trees near her house and would occasionally see red flames in the sky while she hung the clothes out to dry.[356]

Like many teenagers, Jo Ann Dudzik Jancosek did not understand adults. The fire completely captured her attention, and she could not figure out why it wasn't the same with her father. She watched him casually walk to the big metal container in the alley where he burned his trash every Saturday. "I remember standing at that bedroom window saying, 'What kind of man burns the week's garbage while that great big fire is going on?' But he took his time to burn the garbage." Teenager Mary Ann Stofcik Dominiak was equally puzzled about her uncle. After evacuating his family from Birch Avenue in Goose Island, he told them "I'm going back. I got a job to do." The job was to use his day off to paint his house. "I'm thinking, painting?" Mary Ann said. "In the midst of all this commotion?"[357]

Life went on in a memorable way for the family of Albert and Mary Hernandez. The initial explosion knocked Mary from her bed. An hour later, they rushed her from her Main Street home in Indiana Harbor to nearby St. Catherine's Hospital. Three minutes after admission to the hospital, the 45-year-old gave birth to a boy. Hospital records said "explosion shock" induced labor. It was a memorable birth for her, even though this was her 16th child.[358]

For many, Saturday was a regular workday, but for some, getting to work was difficult. Twenty-five-year-old Ina Kizziah lived on the 4900 block of Indianapolis Boulevard in East Chicago. She worked at a restaurant on the 2000 block of the Boulevard in Whiting. Standard Oil truck drivers frequently stopped there for coffee. Getting past the roadblocks and the fire was difficult for Ina, and the fire prevented her truck driver customers from hauling fuel that day. So she never made it into work. For 20-year-old Dale Seliger and his father, it was a different matter. They owned an electrical contracting business on Indianapolis Boulevard. Even though the explosion cracked some shop windows, there was no other damage to the building. They didn't need to pass the refinery to get from home to their shop, so they headed out, as planned, to work on a job outside Whiting. Another young worker took his job seriously and went beyond the call of duty. Even though most residents evacuated the homes on his Goose Island newspaper route, he dutifully delivered the Sunday papers to the porch of each house.[359]

The Mazaneks were not the only couple to wed that day. John and Jeanne Ruman married in Sacred Heart Church in Whiting. "There were explosions during Mass," Jeanne remembered. "After Mass, we looked in that direction and could see flames shooting up in the air." And as far away as Hobart, 15 miles from the fire, Don and Joyce Coleman looked up at the black sky after marrying that morning.[360]

Where there are weddings, there are people who work to make them happen. The Mazaneks had their reception at St. John the Baptist Church's Panel Room, which had enough space for dancing. Joe had his own band, the Blue Tones, which performed at many weddings. But he hired Hal Morris and his band to play while he, Pat and their guests danced into the evening as the fire continued to burn. The reception guests were still afraid the city might explode, "but they were ready for a wedding," Pat said. "Those good old Slovaks wanted to have a little dance. And the band played on."

The women who worked in the Panel Room showed up to cook for the wedding, as planned. They prepared the typical "CBS" menu – chicken, beef, and sausage – for 400. Whiting Bakery made a wedding cake. It was baked, iced and delivered on time for the reception.

Two hundred to 250 attended the Mazanek wedding, but thanks to the fire, another 200 could not. The leftover food was taken to the Community Center and served to evacuees, firefighters, and other emergency workers. Other groups also donated food to those involved in the fire. The Glen Park Post of the American Legion had its installation banquet scheduled that night in Gary. They canceled so its members could be available to help with the emergency, and they sent the banquet food to the fire scene. The American Legion Post in Merrillville sent a truckload of corn on the cob to feed the emergency crews.[361]

The weddings also meant florists had to work. Howard and Beatrice Stawitcke operated the Whiting Flower Shop on 119th Street in Whiting. They were at their shop when the hydroformer explosion sent a blast of air pressure sweeping through the building. "You could feel yourself rising," Beatrice said. "It almost threw me in the air." They tried to figure out what was happening, but nonetheless, they had to keep working – they had three weddings that day. Despite the roadblocks set up by the police and National Guard, they delivered all three sets of flowers on time.[362]

"The choir for the church came," Pat Mazanek said. "A lot of people just went ahead and lived their life as if Whiting wasn't on fire."

Along with the weddings, there were also funerals. Fifty-three-year-old Frank Bonchik had died just a few days earlier. "They didn't postpone anything. We went on," said Teresa Zebracki, his daughter. "The church had the Mass. We went to the cemetery. They even had the luncheon, because the cooks prepared everything…but when you walked out of the hall and looked down the street it was…oh my God…it looked like an inferno."[363]

Many who had planned on a late summer day of fun went ahead with those plans despite the huge fire burning within miles of their homes. Out on Lake Michigan, sailboats dotted the lake as curiosity seekers drifted close to the shore. They wanted a better look at the source of the smoke they could see from miles away. Dennis Zelenke had an even better view. The boy who never missed a chance to swim was in the waters of the lake, watching the smoke and flames. "If you faced in the direction of the flames," he said, "you could feel the intense heat." Being in the water cooled it down a bit.[364]

While life went on for many in Whiting, the fire was never-ending for the firefighters as they continued to risk their lives to bring it under control. Storage tanks continued to explode. One eyewitness said, "It was as if someone had gone around with a giant match touching it here and there, starting fires everywhere in the tanks to the north."[365]

Containing the fire and keeping it away from other oil storage tanks was important because of the damage each explosion could cause. Every storage tank explosion created "flashing blasts of flames and floods of burning oil."[366]

The explosions also created more flying debris that could puncture other tanks or seriously injure firefighters. Thirteen-year-old George Timko climbed a ladder onto the roof of a neighbor's garage to watch the fire. The explosions reminded him of science fiction hero Flash Gordon. The force of the blast would sometimes send the round-shaped tops of the storage tanks skyward, making them look like flying saucers. But to the firefighters, they were a frightening and significant threat to their lives.[367]

For 14-year-old Betty Small Delinck, standing on Calumet Avenue watching the fire with her friends, every time a tank exploded the sight was impressive. Flames would shoot into the sky, smoke would billow up, and they could feel the heat from each blast. About 1.5 miles from the heart of the fire, what they saw, heard and felt mesmerized them. But for the firefighters, just feet away from those blasts, every storage tank explosion put their lives in jeopardy.[368]

Firefighters explored every reasonable idea to avoid those explosions. Some suggested that they fire bullets into the lower part of some storage tanks – better to deal with oil flowing out of a punctured tank than run the risk of an overheated tank boiling over and exploding. The other side of that argument was that the puncture caused by the bullet might trigger its own explosion. According to a report from the *Chicago Sun-Times*, that actually happened when a bullet pierced one tank. Flames shot 500 feet into the air. The firefighters were, however, able to contain that fire.[369]

By late afternoon, despite the explosion of the naphtha tank, the flowing oil that set Indianapolis Boulevard on fire, and the explosion of several other storage tanks, the firefighters saw signs of hope. By 7:30 p.m., Lieutenant Norbert Duray of the Whiting Fire Department told a news reporter that firefighters were making progress. "The fire is not exactly under control," he said, "but we don't consider it a disaster situation at the moment." And at 9:15 p.m., Whiting Fire Chief George Macko said, "We have it confined, and we'll be okay unless the wind comes up or shifts."[370]

Although city fire officials assumed an optimistic tone, Standard Oil officials were reluctant to go that far. Into the evening hours, all Plant Manager Arthur Endres would say was that the fire was no longer spreading. He would not say that it was under control. Shortly before midnight, Standard Oil Fire Chief Frank Horlbeck said that while the flames had been "contained," it would be "12 or 13 hours" longer before they might be under control.[371]

As August 27, 1955, drew to a close, many were still affected by what was going on, even though they were not directly affected by the fire. For almost everyone in the area, the smoke and flames were a constant reminder. Horse racing fans at Washington Park in Homewood, Illinois, could see the flames from the grandstand 15 miles away as the horses crossed the finish line. Farm households living in the flatlands that make up most of northern Indiana could see the orange glow of the fire in the nighttime sky. Nine-year-old Verne Seehausen, who lived on a farm 16 miles away near Dyer, Indiana, climbed a corncrib that night to get a better view. He and his siblings could tell when another storage tank had exploded just by watching the eerie glare rise in the blackness. Ten-year-old Mike Ramey looked out the window of his family's farmhouse into the darkness of the night. He could see the unearthly illumination in the sky all the way from Gillam Township in Jasper County, Indiana, 51 miles from Whiting.[372]

The massive cloud of smoke from the fire filled the sky. "It wasn't like a regular fire, when you see a fire and it's just smoking," remembered Leilani Suchanuk. "This was billowing and rolling, and it seemed the more we looked at it, the more intense it got." Although it was a cloudless summer day, the city of Gary, eight miles to the southeast, was overcast from the clouds of smoke blowing from the refinery. In Valparaiso, 25 miles southeast, some people left home with umbrellas, thinking that the dark skies meant rain was on the way.[373]

Those closer to the fire found it difficult not to think about it. For many, there was the added worry of their fathers, sons, or brothers battling the flames. Monsignor Stanley Zjawinsky of St. Adalbert Church held a special church service in the middle of the day to pray for them.[374]

The fire even affected those who tried not to dwell on it. The George Grenchik family decided the fire was not going to ruin their day. They went ahead with plans to visit Brookfield Zoo in Chicago, yet they could not ignore the cloud of smoke they saw on their drive back home. They also had to deal with police roadblocks as they tried to get back into town. Pat and Joe Mazanek did their best to enjoy their wedding. When they left the church, they wanted to ride through town and blow their car horn, like young newlyweds often did at the time. But with so many people in Whiting living in fear, the police told them the sound of horns blowing might cause unnecessary panic. They spent their wedding night in Chicago. They took with them the important papers Joe's parents didn't want to leave behind after evacuating their home. Joe and Pat spent much of the evening listening to the news on the radio, worrying about family and friends as the fires continued to burn.[375]

The day ended as it had started for the firefighters. It had become evident earlier in the afternoon that the fire would burn through the night. Standard Fire Chief Horlbeck arranged schedules to set up three shifts of firefighting, and sent some men home in the afternoon so they could return rested and relieve those on duty. He saw no alternative to around-the-clock firefighting.[376]

THE GARDENER

Seventy-three-year-old Charles Fizer was born in Slovakia and came to the United States at the age of 22. Six years later, he arrived in Whiting. He worked in the steel mills and bought a home in the 1800 block of 129th Street in Stieglitz Park. He and his wife raised six children in that home. Most Slovak immigrants were poor when they came to Whiting, emigrating from villages where they lived a rural life. In the early 20th century, to own a piece of property – to have a house you could call your own – was something many young Slovak immigrants couldn't even imagine in the old country. For some of them, this was their American dream.

"He was very proud of this, that he owned the property, coming from Europe," said JoAnne Samila, wife of one of Charlie's nephews. "He had this little vegetable garden and everything, and he was content to stay there for the rest of his life." For Charlie, his garden, his little piece of land was what he wanted in life. "This dream place was probably the size of a postage stamp," JoAnne said, "but it was his home."[377]

Less than a mile from Charlie's home, firefighters were still at work as Whiting woke up on August 28, the day after the explosion. Thirty tanks were still on fire more than 24 hours after the initial blast. Most of the fires, though, were gradually dying out. The situation was better, but no one was willing to declare that the end was at hand. "The fire is contained," was the official word, "but we won't say it is under control yet."[378]

In about six hours, caution turned to optimism. At 11:40 a.m., 29½ hours after the fire had begun, Plant Manager Arthur Endres was willing to say the fire was under control. By the next morning, 48 hours after the hydroformer explosion, firefighters had reduced the fire area to two large storage tanks. They considered the possibility of the fire spreading to be remote. Keeping it from spreading was still the firefighters' priority, because the plan was to allow the fire to burn itself out. Rebuilding the refinery rose to the top of management's minds. They considered it safer to continue letting the oil burn away, rather than have it remain a hazard that work crews had to deal with when rebuilding began.[379]

The report that the fire was under control was good news for many of the evacuated residents. At 10 a.m. on Monday, August 29, Whiting Mayor Michael Blastick declared, "Things are beginning to return to normal." He announced that, except for residents of Stieglitz Park, all evacuees could return home. That included everyone in the Goose Island neighborhood.[380]

Sound trucks again drove through the city, but this time they announced the good news that some residents could return home. It didn't take long before families began to pour back into the area, most by automobile, but some on foot. The city had small trucks on standby to help anyone who needed to haul items back home. By nightfall, residents reoccupied about two-thirds of the evacuated homes outside Stieglitz Park.[381]

The return home was delayed only slightly by police blockades. Whiting Police Chief James Mullaney was still guarding against looters. Those with identification could get back in, but police accompanied those without identification to their homes. If they wanted to return, they had to do one of two things: give the police a complete description of the interior of their homes, or be "viewed by their neighbors and cleared." There were no reports of problems.[382]

"It's wonderful to get back," said Natalie Crews, who lived with her husband in the 2400 block of New York Avenue, "even though we'll have to board up the windows to live here until we can get repairs." If the evacuees sustained any damage at all, for the most part it was the kind Andrew and Ellen Blasko returned to. They lived in the 2700 block of New York Avenue and found many of their windows broken.[383]

But even if there was no damage to a house, the fire still burned at the refinery and served as a constant reminder of the dangers. The Vargo family was back home in the 2700 block of Birch Avenue. Tuesday, August 30, was Frank Vargo Jr.'s seventh birthday. The family had a small birthday party for him, just some cake and ice cream. That evening, he looked out the same window where just three days earlier he'd seen nothing but smoke and fire before his family evacuated. This time, there were only occasional orange flames shooting into the air.[384]

The Timko family spent part of their first day back throwing out almost everything in their refrigerator. The electricity had been out since the initial explosion. Thirteen-year-old George Timko stayed home while his parents went to the Parkview Grocery Store in Robertsdale to restock their food supply. When he heard another explosion, he nervously looked out the window of their home in the 2500 block of New York Avenue. "Here we go again," he thought. It turned out to be nothing serious, but it was enough to spook him – for at least a moment – as it probably did many others.[385]

City officials met to talk about Stieglitz Park. Dr. Peter Stecy, director of the Lake County Board of Health, pointed out that the sewers were not yet clear of flammable material. It was, according to Whiting Public Works Commissioner John Stanish, like "living on a powder keg." The city officials decided to keep the citywide smoking ban in effect. They also decided that no one from Stieglitz Park should return home until the city flushed the sewers.[386]

Some of them didn't want to wait. When the city announced that Goose Island residents could return, some Stieglitz Park residents tried to go back home. The police and National Guard politely turned them back. Many of those residents roamed along the edge of Stieglitz Park, trying to get a look at their neighborhood. What they saw looked like a bombed-out ghost town, with only National Guardsmen walking the streets. The scene reminded some of the battle-scarred European cities they had seen in photos at the end of the Second World War, just a decade earlier.[387]

Over the next two days, city inspectors and crews from NIPSCO, the gas and electric company, went door to door in Stieglitz Park. They made sure there were no gas leaks and that the homes were fit for habitation. By the morning of Wednesday, August 31, all but 30 houses had passed the inspection. The houses that did not pass were those that had taken the brunt of the explosion and were unlikely ever to be fit for habitation. By Thursday, September 1 – five days after the blast – the inspections were complete. Everyone who had a house that was still habitable could return.[388]

Gary Post-Tribune reporter George Lindberg said, "The hearts and spirits of the evacuees were high as they dribbled back to the desolate scene caused by the weekend of horror." But while some were anxious to get back home, others seemed reluctant.[389]

When John Springer returned to his house, just across the street from the refinery in the 2800 block of Indianapolis Boulevard, the devastation shocked him. To keep the house from catching on fire, firefighters had drenched it with water, which seeped through the explosion-damaged roof of the house and all its broken windows. The inside of his house was a muddy mess. Glass was embedded in the floors and walls. The house was uninhabitable.[390]

These houses on Indianapolis Boulevard, directly across the street from the refinery, did not suffer major damage from the metal debris that struck other buildings in Stieglitz Park. Still, glass was shattered in all Stieglitz Park homes, in most the walls and ceilings were cracked, many had structural damage, and some had water damage from firefighters hosing the houses down to keep them from catching on fire. (Photo by Joseph Dudzik. Courtesy of Gina Vitucci.)

"There are some who will not move back to homes completely destroyed by the blast," Lindberg wrote. "Others will move back but may not live there much longer. A few who refuse to give up their familiar home sites will try to live out their lives there."[391]

Seventy-three-year-old Charles Fizer was one of those who wanted to live out his life in Stieglitz Park. But as he looked around the neighborhood, it was a depressing sight. Just a few blocks away, 14-year-old paperboy Dennis Hittle returned to his home. Every window was broken, plaster was cracked, and ceiling lamps were lying in pieces on the floors. Broken glass was everywhere. A piece of steel about 15 feet long projected from the side of the front porch on the house just to the north. Other pieces were embedded in the side and back of a house to the east. Their little neighborhood grocery store was flattened. A huge piece of metal, possibly the side of an oil storage tank, sat on top of the building – just a few doors down the street from Charlie Fizer's garden.

Stieglitz Park would never be the same. A reporter for the *Chicago Daily News* described it as "a rubble-strewn ghost town – silent, eerie, awesome." On the morning of August 27, it resembled a man struck down by a heart attack: It was still alive, but everyone knew there was almost no hope of recovery. Standard Oil offered Charlie a fair price for his property. He accepted the offer. He gave up the home where he'd raised his family; where he had a little garden that he loved to tend. He gave up his dream and moved away. Two months later, he died. "The family story goes," said JoAnne Samila, "that he died of a broken heart."[392]

THE CHAIRMAN OF THE BOARD

In the Standard Oil corporate hierarchy, they didn't get much higher than Robert E. Wilson. A graduate of the Massachusetts Institute of Technology (MIT), the many awards he received for his work as a chemical engineer showed that he was one of the best. The 89 patents in his name and the 70 or more technical papers he wrote made him a leading authority on cracking, motor fuels and lubricants. During his lifetime, Wilson received 10 or 12 honorary degrees, but earned only a master's degree at MIT. However, despite the absence of a doctorate, he insisted on being called "Doctor" Wilson.[393]

Wilson joined the company in 1922 after serving in the First World War as a major in the Chemical Warfare Service. His skills won him attention and promotions. In 1944, Standard Oil's board of directors needed someone to replace the retiring Edward Seubert as president, chairman of the board, and chief executive officer (CEO). Instead of choosing one person to assume all three titles, the board named Alonzo Peake president and Wilson the new CEO and chairman.

When the hydroformer exploded, Dr. Wilson was in Pennsylvania. Soon after he learned of the explosion at the company's Whiting Refinery, he boarded a plane to come to the scene. He was in Whiting within the first 24 hours and met with the refinery's local management team. "Even while the fire was at its height," said Jesse Ducommun, the general manager of manufacturing at the refinery, "it was determined that the company would expedite payment of claims."

By Sunday morning, newspapers were printing a statement from Dr. Wilson: "The company will act quickly to compensate families of the dead and the injured and to repair the damage caused by the fire in the community of Whiting, as well as in the plant."[394]

Local management moved quickly to develop a plan and implement it. By Monday morning, the first business day after the explosion, they opened an office for those who had damage claims in the Standard Oil

Administration and Engineering Building, located on New York Avenue in Goose Island. "In our prompt settlement of claims we were, of course, seeking to alleviate public concern as well as to quickly compensate for damages," Jesse Ducommun said.[395]

As a preliminary guide for arriving at fair settlements, the company looked at a map. On that map, they labeled neighborhoods closest to the hydroformer as "disaster areas." Those a little further out were labeled "fringe areas." The company started with the presumption that those who lived in a disaster area had suffered the heaviest damage to their home and belongings. "Final settlements, of course, depended upon the merit of individual claims, not the neighborhood in which the damage occurred," said Superintendent of Industrial Relations Joseph Sullivan. But "by referring to these areas we could tell from a claimant's address the approximate extent of damages involved."[396]

The office opened at 8 a.m. and did not close until 9 p.m. on its first day. Twenty interviewers were on hand, taking information from applicants. By the end of that day, about 90 claims were filed. Most were for minor damage, such as broken windows. The person making a claim would come in, fill out a form, talk to a claims settler, and might have the claim settled on the spot. At least 15 claims were resolved on the first day.[397]

Justine Moskalick walked to the claims office with her eight children following behind. "Mom did the paperwork," said her daughter, Justine Moskalick Bircher, "and they wrote a check immediately, as many times as we walked down there." The day before the explosion, the family had taken their new Ford station wagon to the A&P grocery store on 119th Street and loaded it up with groceries. When the blast knocked out the electricity, they lost everything in their refrigerator. Standard reimbursed them for all of it, as well as for their broken windows. There were cracks on the walls inside their home, the tar paper siding on the outside had melted from the heat of the fire, and there was damage to the roof. Edward Moskalick gradually made the repairs to his house with some help from relatives, but Standard Oil paid for all the materials.[398]

The company also paid for injuries, even minor ones. Marge Milligan cut her finger on a broken window on the door of her grocery store in the 1700 block of Indianapolis Boulevard. The company quickly paid her $25 for the glass and her cut.[399]

The company encouraged people to bring an appraisal of the damages to speed the process along. Some people brought along a professional claims adjuster to advise them. Most came on their own, and most received reimbursement on the spot. If a claim seemed excessive, the company had 10 investigators on duty to go to the houses.[400]

The claims were not restricted to Whiting and Robertsdale. There were several claims in Indiana Harbor, within two miles of the blast, most for broken windows. There were, however, a few attempts made to take advantage of Standard Oil's willingness to settle small claims quickly. Someone in Harvey, Illinois, nine miles in a straight line from the hydroformer blast, filed a claim for a cracked mirror. Someone in Crown Point, 18 miles to the south, said they suffered a broken window and other minor damage. The company rejected both claims.[401]

By quickly settling claims, Standard avoided dealing with numerous insurance companies filing on behalf of residents. But in some cases, especially in the case of renters, people did not have insurance on their personal belongings. Joseph Benish lived in the 2800 block of Indianapolis Boulevard, just across the street from the hydroformer. The back of his rental home collapsed, his furniture beneath it. With no insurance, he gladly accepted Standard's compensation offer.[402]

The peak day for claims came on Wednesday, August 31, when 171 claims were filed and settled. The office on New York Avenue remained open for 12 days, handling nearly 1,900 claims, and resolving nearly 1,500 of those in that time. The claims were mostly small, for items such as personal property damage and minor physical injuries. In total, they cost the company about $265,000.[403]

As business at the claims office slowed and came to a close, so did other operations connected to the fire. That brought relief to families of the National Guardsmen who were on duty. Newlywed Martha Thompson was just one of many family members worried about the safety of a loved one on patrol in a highly dangerous area. When she hadn't heard from her husband for two days, she drove to the refinery to see if he was okay.

She was relieved when most of the 200 National Guardsmen returned home by the Monday after the explosion. Only 80 remained on duty. By Tuesday, most of the national news media had left town. By Wednesday, all those who took shelter at the Community Center had either returned home or moved in with friends and relatives. The Community Center shelter ceased its operations. On Thursday, the rest of the National Guardsmen went home.[404]

Still on duty were the firefighters, but in smaller numbers. In the first days of the fire, several thousand men fought the blaze. As it came under control, the number of firefighters dwindled to about 50 per shift. The firemen who came from surrounding communities left the day after the explosion. The Standard Oil firemen continued to battle the blaze inside the refinery. Standard Oil Fire Chief Frank Horlbeck breathed a sigh of relief when the others left. Although the outside fire departments had many experienced, professional firefighters, Horlbeck worried about their safety inside the refinery. "They weren't trained to handle anything in there," he said. "Actually," he added, "nobody was trained to handle that one."[405]

Whiting Fire Chief George Macko finally was able to rejoin his family after two days without sleep. He could not return to his Stieglitz Park house, so he went to the house in Hammond to which his family had evacuated. He was exhausted and filthy from two days of intense firefighting, and he was in pain. His upper arms had several layers of gauze and bandages to cover the third-degree burns he'd received when the naphtha tank exploded. His wife, Louise, helped him wash up and got him comfortable in bed, putting pillows under his badly burned arms to help him sleep. At best he slept two hours. A phone call woke him up. He hung up, got dressed, went back to the scene and was not able to return for several more days.[406]

Some refinery workers practically lived at the plant for days as the fire raged on. The initial blast knocked 38-year-old Joseph Nemeth to the ground and covered him with debris. It shredded some of his clothing and left him with several burns. But for the next three days and nights he stayed at the plant, sleeping there when the opportunity permitted, helping to fight the fire.[407]

The fire was under control by noon on Sunday, 30 hours after the explosion. But it was far from extinguished. By noon on Monday, two large oil tanks and 10 smaller ones were still burning. Firefighters feared that the gentle five to 10-mile-per-hour winds might increase in strength or change direction. The winds had been favorable throughout the fire, blowing the smoke toward Lake Michigan and away from most residential areas, and away from the oil tanks to the southwest.[408]

Late on Monday, a storm moved in, and a heavy rain fell on Whiting. Although rain can have an impact on some types of fires, it proved to be more of a problem than a help in this case. "It just added a little more water to the millions of gallons already standing in the area," one of the company firefighters said. "Water is no good in putting out an oil fire."

The rain also caused problems for Whiting's sewers. The sudden rush of stormwater caused water to build up in the sewers. As the water levels rose in the sewer system, the oil that had poured into the sewers from the refinery oozed out of manhole covers and onto city streets, particularly White Oak Avenue in the Goose Island neighborhood. The thundershowers also washed oil and water off of the refinery grounds and onto Indianapolis Boulevard. It gave the road an oily coating about six inches thick. Crews went to work the next morning, dumping sand on the roads to make the oil removal easier. Whiting Police Chief James Mullaney said it might be a couple of weeks before all streets were fully cleaned.[409]

The rain did help in one way. It brought the 90-degree temperatures down a little, making working conditions a bit better for the firefighters. By Tuesday, there was still heavy smoke pouring from the burning oil storage tanks. But according to company officials, the fire remained under control and was merely burning itself out. Firefighters focused most of their attention on the flames that threatened a large propane storage tank. Firefighting crews sprayed constant streams of water on the tank.[410]

On Wednesday, "stubborn isolated fires" continued to draw the attention of firefighters. But Company Fire Chief Frank Horlbeck said his crews were now engaged in "mopping up" operations. Two small storage tanks were still smoldering and periodically blazed up. Some of the

300 firefighters still on duty kept watch to make sure the tanks did not get out of control. Other firefighters focused their attention on a tank containing high-grade diesel fuel.[411]

The fires burned throughout the week. On Thursday, the blaze was down to two tanks, one of which gave off yellow oil vapor fumes. On Friday, it was down to one 30,000-gallon tank. It continued to burn through Saturday, one week after the explosion that started the fires. Horlbeck had his crew pour 16,000 pounds of foamite on the tank to speed up the burning. The tank rekindled, shooting 50-foot high flames upward and belching out clouds of black smoke.[412]

The firefighters said the fire and smoke were not dangerous. Still, the sight was dramatic for motorists traveling on newly reopened Indianapolis Boulevard. Earlier in the week, after the pavement fire on Indianapolis Boulevard, workmen had been faced with a difficult cleanup job. The oil was up to two inches thick. It took them over 18 hours to sop it up. They used the blotter technique: Apply sand; soak up the oil; scrape off the sand; repeat as often as necessary.[413]

The road reopened in time for the Labor Day weekend, and thousands of cars returned to Indianapolis Boulevard. Not surprisingly, almost every one of them slowed down as they passed the refinery on one side of the street and Stieglitz Park on the other. Passengers tried to get a good look at the flames, the smoke, and the damage. Plant security guards and Whiting police patrolled the edges of the refinery to make sure no one stopped or parked their car. Whiting Police Chief James Mullaney pleaded with drivers via newspapers and radio, asking them to avoid the Boulevard. Still, bumper-to-bumper traffic jammed Indianapolis Boulevard from 121st to 129th Streets.[414]

Compounding the traffic problem was the daily rush of employees going to work. Tens of thousands worked at businesses within two or three miles of the Standard refinery, including the large Sinclair Refinery, Inland Steel, and Youngstown Sheet & Tube. Traffic surged when shifts at each of those plants changed. "It's a bad traffic problem and the large number of sightseers aren't helping," Whiting Mayor Michael Blastick said. "I'd appreciate it if people would stay out of the area for a few days."[415]

Traffic also jammed the side streets as some drivers searched for alternate routes to bypass the area. With the main roads closed or packed with traffic, even large trucks worked their way down side streets that were not built to handle their loads. The heavy truck traffic caused pavement and sewer damage on 117th, Center, and Front Streets. Whiting Police put restrictions on traffic over those streets to divert most of it back to jam-packed U.S. 41, Calumet Avenue.[416]

By mid-afternoon on Saturday, the foamite had done its job, extinguishing the flames on the last burning storage tank. But suddenly, the sides of the tank caved in – spilling more fuel onto the ground and restarting the fire. Fifty firemen battled the flames, but it wasn't until the next day, Sunday, September 4, that the fire was out for good. "The last remnants were quenched at 11 a.m.," said Arthur Endres, the plant manager. The fires had burned for eight days, four hours, and about 45 minutes after the hydroformer blast that ignited them.[417]

Now, all attention shifted to the aftermath. One of the most immediate problems was Stieglitz Park. In the days following the fire, Standard found temporary homes for those unable to move back and who had no place else to stay. On Thursday, just five days after the explosion, Standard announced that it would buy some of the homes in Stieglitz Park, "at prices the company regards as reasonable," in the words of Plant Manager Arthur Endres. But the offer was only to those living north of 129th Street, in the section of Stieglitz Park directly across the street from where the hydroformer had stood – the part hardest hit by the explosion.[418]

It did not take long for some of those residents to accept Standard's offer. When the explosion occurred, Nancy Bratcher was feeding her dog in the basement of their home in the 1800 block of 128th Street. She felt the house lift off the ground. The Bratchers were happy to sell. "Yes, I sold my home," said Isaac Bratcher, whose two-story gray shingled house was severely damaged, "and I think I got a fair price."[419]

Like the Bratchers, many were anxious to move because they no longer felt safe. The last time Marge Strezo Zubay was in her family's home in the 1800 block of Ann Street was just before they'd hurriedly evacuated. Their house was not severely damaged, but her father decided they were

148

moving, and that was that. They stayed with a relative for about four months before they found a house to purchase.[420]

While many of those living north of 129th Street in Stieglitz Park responded positively to the interest of Standard Oil in their property, many of those living south of 129th responded in anger to Standard's lack of interest in their property. On the Friday following the explosion, the day after Standard announced its intention to buy houses north of 129th Street, about 100 residents living south of 129th gathered at the small park located on May Street, less than a block south of 129th.

"I want Standard to buy me out at a fair price," said Alma Sankoff, who lived in the 2900 block of Berry Avenue. "I've lived here 53 years. That's enough." Stella Stavitzke, who lived across the street from her, echoed that feeling. The explosion had knocked her house off its foundation. One man yelled out that he wanted to sign a petition to demand that Standard buy them out.

Some said they no longer felt safe in Stieglitz Park. Others argued that their homes had lost significant value. Who would move to Stieglitz Park after the explosion and fire? Frank Murzyn, who lived in the 2900 block of Louisa Street and was a candidate for city council in that part of the city, presided at the meeting. He asked for volunteers to circulate petitions asking Standard to buy all the Stieglitz Park homes. Eli Madura, Julius Kish, Donald Flint, James Palmer, Walter Zurawski, Mary Clingerman, Margaret Turner, Anna Hittle and Mary Dudzik agreed to help.[421]

It took Standard Oil little time to respond. The next day, Plant Manager Arthur Endres said the company was also willing to buy houses south of 129th, "if they are reasonably priced." In all, Standard offered to buy about 165 Stieglitz Park houses. The company had no plans for the area, Endres said, but the property would be of value to industries. "If people want out of this area this is giving them a fair opportunity to do so." Within days, Standard claimed it was making substantial progress in its Stieglitz Park real estate buying.[422]

Even after the last flames died out, some people were dealing with injuries suffered in the blast and fire. The estimated number of injuries varied. Standard Oil put it at 382. Their number included 23 refinery workers who lost time on the job. Nine of those lost-time injuries came from the explosion; 11 from the firefighting. Three more got hurt during the cleanup operations after the fire.

Besides the 23 refinery workers, Standard Oil counted 359 non-employee injuries. Eight of those injuries required hospitalization. The others included 211 non-employees who received first aid within the refinery. The company reported that about 140 others received treatment at hospitals and first aid stations.[423]

But Standard Oil's numbers differ from other estimates. Newspaper reports put the number of injured due to the explosion (just the hydroformer explosion and not the subsequent fire and tank explosions), between 32 and 56. The *Chicago American* reported the higher number, saying that most of the injured went to St. Catherine's Hospital in East Chicago. The *New York Times* reported 40 injuries caused by the blast. It said that nine Whiting residents, "injured by flying debris," were still hospitalized into the evening on the first day.[424]

The fires and explosions that followed the hydroformer blast led to at least 80 injuries, according to the *Gary Post-Tribune*. Its count came from local hospitals and the Whiting Clinic. Edward Ranzal of the *New York Times* reported that 12 persons received burns from the naphtha tank explosion.[425]

Whiting Mayor Michael Blastick said that if minor injuries caused by the initial blast were included, the count would be in the hundreds. The Red Cross treated 70 to 120 people for injuries at the Community Center. The vast majority of those were Whiting residents who suffered cuts and lacerations caused by broken glass. Many others never went for help, and instead treated their own injuries.[426]

Does Standard's count of 382 injured include any or all of these? The company never gave details of how it arrived at its numbers, so we don't know. The figure also seems to undercount the number of injuries to its employees. While 23 lost time on the job, how many refinery employees received injuries that did not result in lost time at work? The company did not say. So, while there is no accurate count of the number of injured, Standard's estimate of 382 is a starting point but is almost certainly low.

As might be expected, firefighters suffered the most fire-related injuries. Both the Gary and Black Oak Fire Departments were hard-hit. Gary firemen Albert Krol, Jack Kerlin, Gerald Mulloy, William Martinez, Joe Honzel and David Cahill, were all treated for second- and third-degree burns at Mercy Hospital in Gary. The Black Oak Volunteer Fire Department suffered even more on a percentage basis. Four of its five volunteers on the scene were burned or overcome by smoke. Firefighter Doyle Miller spent 19 hours in the hospital and missed two days of work from the effects of smoke inhalation. Sam and Nick Ordean and Raymond Ragsdale suffered burns from the explosion of the naphtha tank. Only Bob Jennings returned to Black Oak without an injury.[427]

The storage tank explosions also took their toll on the reporters who were covering the fire. George Lindberg of the *Gary Post-Tribune* received burns. Joe Kordick, a photographer for the *Chicago Sun-Times,* was focusing his camera on two huge storage tanks when, "They blew up in a big ball of fire," he later said. Kordick received burns on his arms.[428]

For those inside the refinery, burns accounted for most of the injuries. For those outside the refinery, it was cuts from broken glass. People overcome by smoke, heat stroke, and shock also received treatment at area hospitals. The entire Benish family, from parents Joseph and Elizabeth to their five children, ranging in age from three to 14, received treatment at St. Catherine's Hospital for cuts and shock. They lived in the 2800 block of Indianapolis Boulevard, directly across the street from the hydroformer.[429]

Among the most seriously injured were two Standard employees, Jack Kosarko and Jess Abraham. Kosarko, 23, a resident of Chicago, was initially listed in critical condition after he fractured his skull. Abraham, 62, who lived in the 1400 block of 119th Street in Whiting, fell while he was trying to run from an exploding tank. He broke an arm, shattering his elbow.[430]

Possibly there were others like Julia Springer, who didn't even know she was injured. She lived across the street from the refinery in the 1800 block of Indianapolis Boulevard. When the hydroformer exploded, the house blew off its foundation. Every window in the house imploded, sending glass flying everywhere. On their way to the Community Center, John Springer noticed blood on the leg of his six-year-old daughter, Priscilla Springer. A nurse at the Community Center took care of that injury with a bandage while Julia brushed pieces of glass out of her daughter's hair. That appeared to be the extent of the family's injuries. But over time, Julia often complained of a pain in her leg. X-rays showed nothing, but the pain persisted. Years later, a doctor found a thin shard of glass in her leg – a souvenir from August 27, 1955.[431]

George Timko remembers a neighbor who worked at the refinery. The man came home after the blast, sat down in his living room and watched cartoons on television. His wife said he never watched cartoons and barely watched television. "He was in shock," Timko said. "He must have been blown through a cyclone fence, because the imprint of the cyclone fence was on his face, his chest, his arms."[432]

Every Stieglitz Park family was in turmoil, not knowing where they would live in the months ahead. Many had burns, cuts, and other injuries. But none suffered more than the Plewniak family.

Two days after the explosion that killed three-year-old Ricky and severed the leg of eight-year-old Ron, the parents of the two boys returned to their damaged home. Frank and Joan Plewniak had spent the weekend with relatives in nearby Indiana Harbor. On Monday they went to the Whiting Police station and asked if they could get back into their Goose Island home to pick up clothes and other belongings. Whiting Police Captain John Kopcha accompanied them.

When Frank and Joan arrived, several neighbors waved from a distance. The couple walked along a gangway between houses. Joan looked up at the hole in the side of their home. "Why couldn't it have fallen in the gangway here?" she asked. "Why did it have to go into the room of my babies?"

Inside the house for the first time since tragedy struck their family, neither one said much. On the floor amidst the rubble, Joan spotted a teddy bear. It was the same one that Ricky held in his hand in the family photo taken the previous Christmas. It was the one he had in bed with him as a large piece of metal ripped through the walls of his bedroom. Joan picked up the teddy bear and clutched it closely.

They spent about 15 minutes inside the house collecting belongings. When they came out, a neighbor was outside. She threw her arms around Joan, hugging her while shrieking, "I'm sorry. So sorry." Joan wept and then thanked the woman before she and Frank walked down the street to her mother's house. This would be their temporary home.[433]

Ricky Plewniak on his third birthday in June 1955. (Photo courtesy of Ronald Plewniak)

That night, a wake was held at Kosior Chapel on Indianapolis Boulevard, just over a mile from the blast site. There were 45 floral arrangements, including one from Standard Oil. Ron was not able to attend his brother's wake and funeral. He was still hospitalized, recovering from his injuries. But 900 to 1,000 people did come to the funeral chapel to offer their condolences. Ricky was in a white suit, his hands folded with his teddy bear beneath them.

The next day, Tuesday, August 30, was the funeral service. A children's choir sang the Mass of the Angels, a Catholic funeral service for little children. The service was held at St. Adalbert's Church as the refinery fire continued to burn just a mile away. The church was filled. "We know Richard is happy in Heaven as we bid him good-bye today," said Father Stanley Zjawinsky, the pastor. "He is sleeping the peaceful sleep of eternity."[434]

THE DUCK WASHERS

Three-year-old Betsy Boone was having fun. She stood next to the bathtub in her family's Michigan City house and watched a duck splashing around in the soapy suds. Another little neighbor boy brought a duck into his house. His mother agreed to help him carry it to the bathtub. When the boy brought a second duck inside, she drew the line. She didn't want the house to be "oily from top to bottom."[435]

Both children lived in the Dunes area of Indiana, the sandy mountains along Lake Michigan's southern shore. The Dunes are about 25 miles east of the Whiting Refinery, in a straight line across the southern tip of the lake. On a day in late November, close to Thanksgiving and almost three months after the refinery explosion, ducks covered in oil began to appear on the beaches of the Dunes.

Most came ashore on a 12-mile stretch along the beaches of Gary, Dune Acres, and Michigan City. Some residents took the birds into their homes. The Ross family of Ogden Dunes washed several horned grebes and filled their child's playpen with the freshly cleaned birds. Conservation groups also mobilized. Women from the Save the Dunes Council took ducks home to wash off the oil, or they took them to Thelma Jane Maffitt in Gary. She turned her home into a bird hospital, encouraging others to bring in any oil-covered creature. Members of the Izaak Walton League collected the birds from her and cared for them until they could be released. Chicago's Brookfield Zoo added some of the ducks to its collection. Still, all these efforts helped only a fraction of the ducks. The Humane Society helped others by hiring a crop duster to drop feed to the oil-covered ducks stranded on beaches.[436]

A Save the Dunes Council spokesperson sent out instructions to the public on how to help oil-covered ducks recover. Karl Plath said people should wash them gently in warm water with a mild detergent, such as dishwashing liquid. After rinsing, the ducks should thoroughly dry. Repeat the process as long as oil remained. Duck washers should keep the birds for at least five days, giving them time to preen themselves and allow their feathers to get back into shape.[437]

Although many seemed to know what to do, no one knew for sure why this had happened. They knew there was a huge oil slick on Lake Michigan. It was two inches thick, 50 feet wide, several miles long and of a heavy oil. One early guess was that it had come from a Lake Michigan tanker that somehow sprang a leak. A second guess was that a ship's crew had released the oil after washing out the onboard fuel tanks. Either way, intentional discharge of oil into the Great Lakes was against federal law.[438]

Days later, the "heavy, thick gumbo of oil," as described by Henry Michiels, showed up on the shores of Chicago. Michiels was park district harbor captain at the city's Belmont Harbor. Ice usually covers much of the water off North Avenue in the early days of Chicago's cold weather season. But in 1955, there was a large circle of water off the shore of North Avenue that didn't freeze because of the oil slick. The oil coated several miles of shoreline to the north of Belmont Harbor.[439]

The Coast Guard had jurisdiction over Lake Michigan's waters. It took samples of the oil and handed them over to the Army Corps of Engineers for analysis. The Corps of Engineers started its own investigation. Maybe, a third guess said, it had come from an oil cargo ship bound for the steel mills of Northwest Indiana or Chicago. The Corps examined dockage reports from all lake terminals in the Chicago area. When the analysis was complete, it was announced that this was "heavy residual industrial fuel oil," also called "Bunker C" or "Number 6" fuel oil - the type of oil used to fuel ships, but also for other possible purposes. Maybe, a fourth guess said, this had come from an oil refinery.[440]

The oil slick had not dissipated by Christmas. It wasn't until the new year that the Corps of Engineers released its findings. The oil spill, which trapped thousands of ducks and killed hundreds more, had come from Whiting. It was "accidentally released" during the refinery fire in August.[441]

Although the refinery explosion was an accident, the diversion of oil into the waterways was not exactly accidental. The objective of the sand dikes built inside the plant was to divert oil to the sewers, to get it out of the area and prevent it from igniting. "Crude oil and naphtha from ruptured tanks flowed onto the surface of the Indiana Harbor Ship Canal," reported the *Calumet News*, days after the fire died out. The Canal flowed into Lake Michigan. There was enough oil in the canal that the Chicago Fire Department sent its fireboat, the Victor Schlager, just in case its waters caught on fire. In 1955, however, federal clean water laws were so weak that Standard Oil faced few consequences for what happened.[442]

Water pollution was a growing concern throughout the first half of the 20th century. Even so, Congress did nothing until 1948 when industrial and urban growth made it impossible to ignore. The Federal Water Pollution Control Act of 1948 was the nation's first major legislation to deal with the problem. But the new law had problems of its own. It conferred most of its enforcement power to the states, many of which were neither equipped nor inclined to deal with environmental matters. Its enforcement mechanism was cumbersome. And in 1955, it was the law of the land dealing with water pollution.[443]

The explosion affected the air as well as the water. JoAnne Samila was accustomed to the smells of the refinery and other industries. From her home in East Chicago, she knew that if she smelled the refinery, she needed to put sweaters on her kids if they were playing outside. The refinery odor meant the wind was coming from the north. In the days after the fire, she said, "We smelled Whiting stronger than we ever did."[444]

"The smell of burning oil permeated the air," wrote a *Chicago American* reporter, observing from an airplane far above the flames and smoke. "You could taste it." Phone calls swamped the Chicago police and fire departments on the day the Whiting fire was officially declared to be out. People's Gas, Light and Coke Company – and even the *Chicago Tribune* – also received numerous calls, coming from thousands of Chicagoans living between 46th and 67th Streets who reported a gas odor. It was not a leak, the gas company said. The Weather Bureau, however, offered an explanation. A momentary shift in the wind from southwest to southeast had carried fumes from the Whiting fire into the city.[445]

Plants also were affected by the explosion and fire. The Vargo family felt relieved to see that there was no serious damage to their Goose Island home. But in their backyard, every flower and shrub they had was either dead or badly wilted from the heat of the blaze. The Timko family, also in Goose Island, had a large maple tree in their yard. Although the tree looked fine after the fire, a man inspecting the impact of the blast told them it was going to die. He said the tree had absorbed the impact of the explosion, possibly saving a building across the street from severe damage. In a couple of days, some of the leaves crinkled up, and in a few more days so did the leaves on the other side. Standard Oil paid the family for the loss of their tree.[446]

Animals also suffered from the blast and fires. Twelve miles away, the hydroformer explosion shook the stables at Washington Park Racetrack. The horses became unmanageable for a time afterward.[447]

Some families lost their pets as a result of the explosion and fire. George Turner was a taxi driver who lived in the 1800 block of 130th Street in Stieglitz Park. He fled with his family after windows shattered and plaster fell from the ceiling after the blast. They were able to take one of their two dogs, but the other ran off. Betty Small Delinck went searching for Sandy, her aunt's dog, who was the father of Betty's puppy, Lassie. Since whenever anyone needed anything related to the fire, they went to the Community Center, Betty went there with a leash in hand – hoping she'd find Sandy and bring him home. He was not at the Community Center. He took off after the explosion and was not seen again.[448]

The news was not all sad for Stieglitz Park pet lovers. Lynn Larsen had a black cat, naturally named Blackie, which usually spent its time outside. After the blast, the family put Blackie inside the house when they evacuated. Her father, who worked at the refinery during the fire, went to the house every day to feed the cat. Blackie was still there when the family returned.[449]

The Tokoly family had to leave behind their family dog, Penny. They let her loose in the hope that she could manage on her own as they went to Dyer to stay with relatives. Despite the hope of three-year-old John Tokoly and his older brother, Sammy, Penny was gone when they returned. A short time later, however, an Indiana National Guard truck arrived in Goose Island. The Guardsmen opened its doors and let loose the stray dogs they'd collected while patrolling the neighborhood. Once the doors opened, it was a dog stampede. Penny broke from the pack and headed straight to the Tokoly home. She was as safe, sound and happy in her reunion as John and Sammy were when they saw her coming home.[450]

THE BREAD AND BUTTER

Viewed from the road, the metal pipes and structures, the Flare Stacks topped with raging flames, the rows of storage tanks, and the occasional strange smells in the air are imposing. They either fascinate someone who sees the Whiting Refinery for the first time – or make the person want to get away as quickly as possible. Two days after the hydroformer explosion, the *Chicago Daily News* compared the refinery's skyline to "a tableland of domes and mesas as fantastic as the natural landscape of southern Utah." While some may not have had as strong an imagination as the newspaper writer, many shared the feelings expressed in the next lines:

> But, these far-spread masses are no inert sandstone. Each of them is a potential volcano containing volatile liquids, their flammability and explosiveness redoubled and refined by technology. Almost everyone who has traveled that way must have wondered uneasily: What would happen...? [451]

"It does make you really think," said George Timko. Yet like many Whiting residents, he explained, "It's like somebody says to you, 'I've been living next to these railroad tracks all my life. What trains?' You know? You get used to it."[452]

If you lived near the refinery, you got used to the sounds. "We never had to look at the clocks. When you heard the whistles blowing, changing shifts," laughed JoAnne Samila, "you knew the kids would be coming home from school and you'd better be home." For some in Whiting, the whistles not only substituted for clocks, but also served as messages that you could learn to decode. "We sort of lived with the whistles blowing even when we were in Immaculate Conception School," Janet Tindall said. "I would always know if there was a fire in my Dad's part of the refinery because we would listen to the beeping: Beep...Beep...Beep... And then it would be a pause."[453]

If you lived near the refinery, you got used to the smells, or tried to. Larry Jennings remembered what it was like to drive on the north end of the refinery, close to Lake Michigan. "You would get to a certain area over there that…you had to take a deep breath, and hold that for about five minutes until you got to Front Street before you could really breathe."[454]

The refinery workers had to make an extra effort to get used to the environmental dangers. John Marcisz worked on the sludge coker at the acid works from 1935 until Standard shut it down in 1955. "That was a terrible place, black, smoke, dust," he recalled. "We walked in dust that deep. Just fine dust like those guys going on the moon. Three or four inches…Them fumes out of the stacks; the fumes were real black like from a train years and years back. Black, and it was acidy and [it spread] all over the place."[455]

Ed Tokarz also had a job in the acid works. It required him to walk on top of the tanks. On his first day, a veteran stillman told him to "watch which way the wind blows, and go the opposite way when you come on the tank." Tokarz said one foreman went up there but was not "well versed on that stuff." The foreman passed out. "We had to get him down…acid fumes, they were strong. Man! Take your breath away."[456]

The acid recovery process, wrote Edward Nichols in his 1943 novel based on the Whiting Refinery, "gave off the sulfur stink, which was the worst of smells." According to Nichols, "the process made more than stink. Its fumes stung the eyes, the nose, throat, and any other exposed skin. They ate into clothes, and the acid that soaked the ground could go through ordinary shoe soles in a week."[457]

If you wanted to swim in the waters of Lake Michigan at Whiting Park, you got used to the scum. "I remember going to Lake Michigan and as far as you would walk in and come out there'd be a line on your body, [you'd] swim with globs of stuff," said Jim Sandrick. "Standard Oil used to dump things in the lake," Betty Gehrke said. "You'd go swimming one day, and the water would just be green and purple, the oil floating on top of it. You'd just make a path and swim under or swim out to a clear place."[458]

These problems were not new in the 1950s. As the *Lake County News* reported in 1906, "...the lake bottom in the vicinity of the Standard is in a particularly filthy condition, it being next to an impossibility for the occasional bather to make much headway in the black rubbery mess which secrets itself on the lake bottom."[459]

For many generations, you got used to all this because your life depended on it. "That was my source of living," Clarence Gehrke said. He said that whenever he drove down Standard Avenue, "we had to close our car windows because of the acid fumes hitting your skin and stinging it." Yet it was one of his pet peeves to hear people gripe about the foul-smelling air. "That was my source of living. I should put up with it and be happy that air was there. They don't consider," he said about the gripers, "that's where their bread and butter is coming from."[460]

"It would hurt your eyes sometimes," said George Brown, who was 83 years old when asked in 1990 about the pollution in earlier years. "But you still wouldn't mind it. It was your bread and butter, what the heck. You've got to give something to get something, [as] they used to say."[461]

And many Whiting residents felt they got something from Standard Oil. "I think Whiting is always grateful to Standard Oil," said Dennis Zelenke. "I think they're grateful because it paid a lot of bills, gave us a beautiful school system. We had wonderful teachers. We had great city services...We never paid for water through the 1950s." People in the '50s, he said, "were just glad to be employed. It was a relief after the war experiences, you know, to have a job, to have a family, to have a home." For all of that, they could put up with the negatives. "There's pollution, there's danger," Zelenke says, "but what was more important was putting food on the table, clothes on your back, and a roof over your head."[462]

Tom Marciniak remembers his Uncle Joey, a pipefitter. "He would tell this story about sitting in the control room of the cat crackers one day, and some guy said it smells like gasoline in here. My Uncle Joey looked at him and said, 'What the hell do you think this is? A bakery?'" And that's the nature of an oil refinery," Tom says. "You can never make the darn thing completely safe."[463]

And if you lived in Whiting, you knew that – because you knew someone who worked in the refinery and they would tell you that accidents happened. Residents got used to the danger because they had faith. They knew those accidents would not harm them. They knew Standard Oil had a good safety record. They also knew it had its own fire department that would handle whatever came up. "I felt like things were under control," Mary Ann Stofcik Dominiak said. "Because it seemed like whenever there were fires at Standard Oil, everything was taken care of right away. They just had a way of doing things like that. Making things safe again."[464]

"When I worked at the University of Chicago," Betty Gehrke said, "[fellow employees] couldn't understand why I would live anywhere near the Standard Oil Company for fear of an explosion. But there had never been anything serious until the fire of '55."[465]

And then, things changed.

The explosion in 1955 destroyed a neighborhood. It caused damage throughout the community. Many feared for their lives and feared their lives would change. The refinery explosion and fires tarnished the feeling of security in Whiting-Robertsdale.

After the explosion, "I think we were more wary that something could happen," said Pat Mazanek. "I do think people felt differently, that the unthinkable could happen." That fear led some to move away. "I don't think our parents trusted to live here," said Brenda Wilson Felton. The explosion convinced her family to move out of Whiting. Yet, although the sense of security may have become tarnished, it wasn't destroyed. Some who had the most reason to fear another explosion chose to stay, including the Plewniak family.[466]

After Ricky's funeral, Frank and Joan Plewniak still had eight-year-old Ron to worry about. For the most part, the news was good. A week after the explosion sent debris crashing into his bedroom, St. Catherine's Hospital listed his condition as "good." When the doctors said he needed transfusions, among those who stepped forward to donate blood were four Standard employees: Milan Dudas, Sam Pampalone, Norman Turpin and Cornelius Soeurt. As he continued his hospital stay and continued to improve, the Standard Oil Employees Athletic Association sent him a selection of fishing equipment and tackle box. They received a thank you note from Ron. "I am feeling tip-top," he told them.[467]

Ron was still in the hospital as his fourth grade school year began, but Standard Oil provided a tutor to help him keep up with his classmates. The company also paid for his medical care, as well as for the repairs to the family's badly damaged house. Frank did not want to move back. After losing one son and having another lose his leg in the blast, he did not feel certain he could keep his family safe in their Schrage Avenue house. But for Joan, moving elsewhere meant moving away from her family. She'd grown up on that block of Schrage Avenue. Her parents lived down the street. Her sisters and their husbands and children lived down the street as well. Almost everyone who was important in her life was right there. At a time when she was recovering from a horrible tragedy, the people who could best help her get through it were there on Schrage Avenue.[468]

The family was also there for Ron, when he was finally able to come home and adjust to life without the use of one leg. It was also where his friends were. At first, until his amputation healed, he had to get by with crutches. Then, he was fitted with an artificial leg. Besides learning to adjust to the new prosthetic, he had to adjust to the stares. "People try not to stare or look, but curiosity gets the best of them," Ron said years later. "It's a little strange, but you get used to that."[469]

Nowhere could stares be more numerous than at school. Ron Gaspar was a year younger. He remembers when Ron returned to St. Adalbert School after his release from the hospital. "His mother would pull up in front, and he would get out," he said. "He had to move around on crutches, so we would help him get into school." Ron Gaspar also helped by carrying his books. "It was a little difficult" for Ron Plewniak, because the school had no elevator, and getting around required walking up and down three flights of stairs.[470]

With the prosthetic, Ron learned to adjust. "I was able to walk around and look, appear, more normal," he said. "From then on it was fine. I just started to develop and live with that." He adjusted well. By the time he was old enough to attend Whiting High School he had blended in well with his classmates. Justine Moskalick Bircher didn't think much about his limp. She barely noticed it. She knew, from growing up just a few blocks away, that one boy had died and his brother lost a leg in the refinery explosion. She didn't know it was Ron until she asked him why he had a limp.[471]

With the help of three brothers-in-law and his father-in-law, Frank Plewniak rebuilt the house on Schrage Avenue. One thing he didn't do was talk much about the tragedy his family experienced. "It was like his experiences with World War II," Ron said. "He came back, and he didn't talk." But no one else in the family spent much time talking about it, either. "Everybody knew it was a very emotionally charged subject… didn't know whether the person was ready for it. It was more…where do we go from here? That's what's more important, where we do go from here and what's to be done."[472]

Frank and Joan had two more children, both sons: Alan was born in 1957; Mark in 1959. They also had to settle matters with Standard Oil. The family could not find an attorney in Whiting who was willing to represent them in court against the city's major employer. The family eventually hired Chicago attorney John J. Kennelly. He would go on to become one of the nation's leading lawyers on behalf of airline disaster victims. Kennelly filed a $700,000 damage suit against Standard Oil in Chicago's Cook County Circuit Court. The suit charged the company with negligence in connection with the explosion. In the end, Frank and Joan Plewniak received a $20,000 settlement for the death of Ricky, a $5,000 settlement for the damage caused by the 700-pound metal pipe from the hydroformer that crashed into their house, and a $150,000 settlement to compensate Ron for the loss of his leg. At the time, it was the largest settlement ever reached in the United States for the loss of a leg below the knee.[473]

Ron was unable to play sports at Whiting High School, but Athletic Director Peter Kovachic brought him on as equipment manager for the football and swimming teams. After graduating in 1965, he continued his schooling at Purdue University in West Lafayette. There, he obtained an electrical engineering degree. After 30 years at Inland Steel as an electrical engineer, he retired. Then he began another career with Crown ESA, a company that specialized in electrical engineering projects within the steel industry. In 1970, Ron married Debbie Kosior, who passed away in 2008.[474]

Joan Plewniak had two more sons after the refinery explosion took Ricky's life. Alan, born in 1957, is on the right. Mark, born in 1959, is on Joan's lap. Ron Plewniak, who survived the explosion but lost his leg because of it, is on the left in this 1959 photo. (Photo courtesy of Ronald Plewniak.)

His relationship with Standard Oil ended with the court settlement. But rumors circulated throughout Whiting that because of his injury, Standard would give him a job for life. Already employed at Inland, Ron decided to see if there was any truth to the rumors. "Just out of curiosity," he said, "I went to interview there." He was not offered the job.

For some years, Ron carried on one unofficial connection with Standard. The wife of one of the company's top executives started writing him letters while he was recovering from his injury. She also sent him postcards from wherever she and her husband traveled. He would write her back in an exchange that lasted for years. "It was a nice thing," he said. "She didn't have to do that, especially after everything was resolved with [Standard]."[475]

Frank Plewniak died in 1986 at the age of 64. Joan continued living in the Schrage Avenue house where she'd experienced so much happiness – and one horrible morning of tragedy. "She had every right after that to go on with her life being depressed and sad, but she didn't," Ron said about his mother. "She was always a happy, cheerful woman…She was wonderful for people to be around. She made the best of her life after that." One of her longtime wishes was to use some of the Standard Oil settlement money to donate a seeing-eye dog. Her sons helped her make that happen late in her life.[476]

Joan Plewniak passed away in 2014 at the age of 93. After her death, her family discovered a stuffed animal in one of her bedroom drawers. They guessed that it once belonged to Ricky and that she always kept it close as one way of remembering the three-year boy she lost in 1955. She died on August 25, just two days before the 59th anniversary of the refinery explosion.[477]

THE BOND

Even with a huge oil refinery nearby, most Whiting residents never worried. But the explosion and fire tainted that sense of security. It was the first substantial bit of erosion to appear in the bond between the company and the community. Stieglitz Park was first to feel the effects. Like refugees forced to leave their homes, the damage caused by the explosion uprooted Stieglitz Park residents and sent them searching for new places to live.

Most Stieglitz Park homeowners quickly accepted Standard Oil's offer to buy their properties. Within just two weeks of the explosion, 90 percent of property owners north of 129th Street and 50 percent south of 129th had agreed to sell to Standard Oil.[478]

"We were given the option to move the house or leave it," remembers Dennis Hittle, the neighborhood paperboy back in 1955. "Although some of our neighbors chose to move their houses, we chose to leave ours because the additions to it and the stucco exterior probably wouldn't survive the move."[479]

One of those who opted to move his house was Whiting Fire Chief George Macko. "It was an absolutely amazing sight to see our home in Stieglitz Park being placed on this large platform with enormously big wheels under," recalls Cheryl Macko Rosen, the oldest of the fire chief's children. Movers lifted their house off the ground at 3049 Berry Street in Stieglitz Park. They then moved it slowly down Indianapolis Boulevard behind a police escort. It caught on some telephone wires on the way, but made it in one piece to a small lot at 1610 La Porte Avenue.[480]

George Gajewski owned two homes in Stieglitz Park. When Standard offered to buy his property, he refused until they agreed to two conditions. They had to sell one of the other houses in Stieglitz Park to him, and they had to move it to a new location. They reached an agreement to sell him the house at 3012 Indianapolis Boulevard and move it a few blocks to 2840 Schrage Avenue. George's son, Raymond, moved there after finishing his military service and getting married.[481]

Only a handful chose to move their houses. Most sold their homes to Standard. There were different opinions on whether the company paid a fair price. Eleanor Kincheloe said her parents left angry, feeling they had no choice but to sell, and that they didn't get paid a good price for their home.[482]

The Kubacki family, which owned Kubacki & Son Grocery in Stieglitz Park, filed a half-million-dollar lawsuit against the company. They claimed that by buying up houses in Stieglitz Park, the company was causing financial harm to their business. But they eventually gave in and sold their property to Standard Oil. On the other side of the coin, Orlie Ferris, the owner of Ferris Garage in the 1800 block of 129th Street, was happy with the way Standard treated him. "There were no arguments over anything," he said. The company paid for the damage to his garage, for his loss of business, and a bent tool box. It even allowed him to temporarily rebuild his business on 129th Street before he could move it to its new home on White Oak Avenue.[483]

One year after the explosion, the company still had not completed the purchase of 40 of the roughly 180 houses. Gradually, residents of those properties gave in or their families sold the properties after they passed away. Standard had a negotiating advantage in Stieglitz Park because it was in no hurry to buy. It also isolated the holdouts. Every time Standard purchased a house, it tore the house down and left the lot empty. With each new purchase, every remaining house was more isolated.

The streets were still there: Grace Street, Ann Street, May Street, Louisa Avenue, Berry Avenue, and 128th, 129th, 130th and 131st Streets. "You saw some of the street signs, you saw the street pattern," Gayle Faulkner Kosalko remembered, "but you didn't see the houses anymore." Larry Jennings recalled the home of a classmate in Stieglitz Park. The classmate's family was among the last to sell to Standard. "You could come down the Boulevard, and you could look over, and you see that one little house sitting probably one hundred yards off, all by itself, no grass, no dirt, no trees, no nothing over there…just a little house sitting there." Francis and Louis Mason were the last to sell. They owned two lots that they finally vacated in 1973. "Stieglitz Park was gone. Everything gone," reminisced Betty Small Delinck, who spent much time there visiting relatives. "Nobody could go back and live there. That was sad."[484]

One of Andrew Jefchak's characters in his *Out of Stieglitz Park* novel spoke for the neighborhood residents who walked away angry. "Everybody who lives in Stieglitz Park," the character said, "their whole life is changed because of this, caused by a goddamn company that put an experimental monster right across from their houses – a stone's throw from houses with people in them."[485]

In the days following the hydroformer explosion, Standard Oil said it planned to build oil storage tanks on the land that had been Stieglitz Park. Some Whiting residents objected. Mary Kaine told the Whiting Plan Commission that a tank field at Stieglitz Park would put the tanks within yards of houses on Schrage Avenue in Goose Island. She encouraged the city to use the land for a city park or to build housing on it. City Engineer Leroy Young disagreed. He argued that there were more suitable places for housing in Whiting. He also said the city should encourage Standard "to build more industry in the city to increase our tax base." Not long after the final property sold, the land that was once Stieglitz Park – on the west side of Indianapolis Boulevard, just north and south of 129th Street – became an oil storage tank field.[486]

The loss of Stieglitz Park changed Whiting, if for no other reason than the fact that 180 homes were gone. Some said Whiting's population decline in the years that followed was directly due to the loss of those homes. In fact, though, Whiting's population decline started well before the 1950s. The city reached its population peak in the 1930 census with 10,880 people. The population dropped by 5.3 percent in that decade, and fell another 6.2 percent in the 1940s. By 1950, there were 9,669 individuals in the city. The elimination of an entire neighborhood certainly contributed to the 15.8 percent drop in the city's population during the 1950s. But it was not the only reason for Whiting's slide in population, which continued in the decades that followed. By 2010, Whiting's population stood at only 4,997.[487]

When asked how Whiting had changed over the years, Jim Etter, born in 1927, cited the number of people who moved out in his lifetime

- particularly those who wanted to start a family. "There was no place for them to buy in Whiting because Whiting could get no bigger, it was completely surrounded... and so the children that grew up there, very, very few of them ever stayed. They moved out to St. John, to Cedar Lake." Geography set limits on Whiting, hemming in the city: Lake Michigan on its northern border; Hammond on the west; East Chicago on its eastern side; Hammond and East Chicago from the south. And of the 1,100 acres of land within Whiting, industry occupied 52 percent. There was no room for growth.[488]

"Younger people, particularly those forming new families and looking for separate accommodations," said a Purdue Calumet Development Foundation study in 1958, "are leaving the community because they are unable to obtain suitable accommodation in the area."[489]

Leo Kus was renting an apartment on Schrage Avenue, across from the Globe Roofing Company. As his family grew, he wanted to build a house in Whiting. "I went all around Whiting. All the lots that were there were held by people that wanted to have their own children build on. So I couldn't buy. In fact, I had one I was going to buy...he asked for an enormous price but I was desperate, I wanted to buy it. So I decided I was going to buy and I came in there to complete the agreement, and he backed out. He says 'No, I don't want to. I'm going to save it for my children.'" Kus gave up on Whiting, temporarily rented in Hammond, and then bought land in a new subdivision in Griffith.[490]

"As we grew up," Justine Moskalick Bircher recalled, "we found that so many of our friends that we had, that we went to kindergarten with, had disappeared from town."[491]

The lack of room to grow wasn't the only problem Whiting faced in 1955. The world was changing. With the completion of the Indiana Toll Road in 1956, Whiting-Robertsdale had its first connection to the Interstate Highway System. Interstates helped fuel an already growing appetite for cars. Before 1955, many Standard employees walked to work. Their homes were just blocks from the refinery gates. "When I worked there," said John Marcisz, who'd been employed in the refinery as far back as the 1930s, "they had 9,000 employees. They used to walk on 121st Street because that used to be the main gate...Boy! You'd think it was like going to a football game or baseball game, just loaded with people walking in the morning, coming home at 4:40 in the evening."[492]

Cars were more popular; roads were better built. Now, workers could live farther away and commute to the refinery. Their new communities were appealing. In Whiting, many houses were just a few feet from neighboring homes. In newer communities, homeowners had space around their homes and backyards where children could play. They also had garages where they could park more than one car.

Among those who moved out of Whiting-Robertsdale in the years after the 1955 fire were many of the refinery's management-level employees. "In the older days, all the big shots that ran Standard Oil or the banks, they all lived north of 119th in those big houses on Oliver," Helen Dudzik said in 1991. "Now... the big shots all left. They went to other cities." Jim Sandrick said that when he was growing up in Whiting, the fathers of many of his friends were engineers and chemists. "The refinery managers lived here. Everybody lived here. But then sometime in the late '50s, early '60s, they opened up the door and the people, the doctors and lawyers, they all moved out to Munster." For local businesses, the decline in the city's population meant a drop in sales. Fewer residents with the higher salaries and disposable income that managers earned also meant a decrease in revenue for local merchants.[493]

But the loss of the executives was more than just an economic blow. It played a role in the weakening of the strong bond that existed between the city and company before the explosion. Living in the same community, "You really get to know each other beyond the workplace," said James Snee, a past president of Hormel Foods Corporation. The Hormel plant in Austin, Minnesota, is as central to the economy of that city as the refinery was to Whiting. Austin is a city of 25,000 people. Hormel's headquarters is in Austin, and nearly all of its top executives live there. "Their kids go to the same schools as the kids whose parents work in the factory, and they often pray in the same churches," said an article in *Fortune* magazine in 2016. "For me, personally," Snee said, "I think there is incredible value in that. You know who the individuals are, you know how they work, and you know what it takes to get things done." That's the kind of bond Standard Oil executives had with the people of Whiting before 1955. In the years after the fire, it changed.[494]

The loss of Stieglitz Park played a role in Whiting's population decline. The lack of room for growth played a role. Outside factors like the building of better highways had an impact. But perhaps the biggest reason for the shrinking population was the decline in employment at the Whiting Refinery. There were about 7,000 workers at the Whiting Refinery in 1955. Sixty years later, the number was down to about 1,800 – a decline that began shortly after the 1955 fire.

"Nobody lost employment at the refinery because of the fire," the company's employee magazine stated in October 1955. They also did not lose their jobs in the months that followed, because there was a lot of cleanup and rebuilding to do. Although the fire burned in just one-tenth of the refinery, it effectively shut down the entire operation. Plant manager Arthur Endres met with key personnel the day after the fire to draw up plans to bring it back online as soon as possible. The next day, Board Chairman Robert Wilson said publicly that Standard would rebuild. He said the refinery might even be back in operation in two weeks.[495]

Company firefighters still battled the flames on the Monday after the explosion. But when other refinery workers showed up for work that day, many of them started the cleanup. "We stayed away from the fire," said Robert Herakovich, one of those employees. They tore down damaged structures and cleared the land of debris so that rebuilding could begin. Men who regularly worked skilled or technical jobs joined everyone else in wielding shovels, driving bulldozers and removing debris.[496]

There was plenty of rubble, including railcars and railroad tracks. The heat of the fire was so strong that it melted steel. "It was unreal to see nothing left of the tank cars but the wheels," Joe Gray said. "The tracks were all curled up like spaghetti." The melted rail cars looked more like wax than steel to George Grenchik. National Guardsman Earl Yoho said the rails, "were bent and deformed. Just in terrible shape, even under the cars themselves. It was just a mangled mass of steel."[497]

Gary Post-Tribune reporter George Lindberg said the destruction he saw when he reentered the refinery several days after the initial explosion, "was reminiscent of sights ordinarily seen only in wartime when such magnificent installations are purposely attacked to cripple an enemy."[498]

Forty-seven of the refinery's 1,680 acres sustained damage. Within that area, workers had to remove the wreckage of 70 oil storage tanks destroyed by the fire. They also had to clear up miscellaneous debris. "Burned-through fire hoses lay in a tangled pile at the side of one of the many sand dikes hastily thrown up against the flooding oil released by ruptured tanks," Lindberg wrote. "All through the fire area, hundreds of electric and telephone wires hung uselessly. One of the metal hats worn by plant employees was placed atop a pile of planks; its top center melted through from the heat."[499]

Workers dismantled temporary firewalls along Indianapolis Boulevard, built in the early days of the fire to keep the flames from spreading to Stieglitz Park. Railroad tracks needed repair. The tracks that connected to rail lines outside the plant were a top priority. Pipelines were tested and replaced. Utilities, telephone lines, and power lines needed repair. Some of the water lines and water tanks for firefighting needed replacement. So did some of the fire trucks and equipment. Workers had to collect damaged pipes, valves and vessels of all sorts and cart them off. Some were salvaged; most were scrapped. To get the plant back into operation, workers had to recondition several key operating units.[500]

Yet despite the complete shutdown of the refinery in the days following the fire, there was no significant impact on Standard Oil. "Although we have lost millions of gallons of crude oil and finished products," the company said in a statement out of its Chicago office, "we have an adequate supply of gasoline and other products for our customers' immediate needs. The products are in storage at various terminals and bulk plants that can supply Chicago." An estimated 42 million gallons of crude oil and gasoline burned in the fire.[501]

Frank O. Prior, who took over as president of Standard Oil in 1955, said the loss in Whiting was only two percent of the company's product supply. He made the statement in a full-page newspaper ad and during a Chicago television weather report broadcast that Standard Oil sponsored. "We are fortunate," Prior said, "that our product pipelines can bring products into this area from other refineries."[502]

Soon after the explosion, Standard Oil's other Midwest refineries – located in Sugar Creek, Neodesha, Mandan and Wood River – began full-scale operation to process as much oil as possible. The way they responded, said Assistant General Manager of Supply and Transportation John Boatwright, was "marvelous testimony to the ability to bring unused capacity to bear." In addition, the fire had not reached the south tank farm at Whiting, and all its tanks were full. The company also had other terminals scattered throughout the Midwest with available inventory. Other refineries, including those of competitors, filled some of Standard's supply as well.[503]

But some areas did experience fuel shortages in the wake of the fire. In parts of Wisconsin, there was "an acute shortage of both gasoline and fuel oil." The Standard Oil fire and the lack of production in Whiting, "is being felt," the *Sheboygan Press* reported in January of 1956. As a result of the shortage, consumers saw a half-cent increase in a gallon of home fuel oil.[504]

One of Standard's first decisions after the explosion was to sharply cut back its crude oil purchases. Oil producers in West Texas, New Mexico, Wyoming, parts of Colorado, North and South Dakota, Iowa, Minnesota, Illinois and southern Indiana felt the impact. There were reports of a producer in Colorado having trouble meeting his bank loans due to Standard's decision to cut off purchases. Barge transportation rates on the Mississippi River spiked to their highest levels since 1918. The Whiting Refinery fire was blamed. The fire also received blame for prices at the gas pump going up five cents a gallon in 11 states along the East Coast.[505]

It was a temporary setback for most, since the cleanup in Whiting was going well. The refinery typically processed 195,000 barrels of crude oil a day. It produced a little more than 200,000 a day on August 26, the day before the explosion. By September 9, within management's two-week target, limited production resumed. By the end of September, production was back to 50 percent of capacity. By November 20, just 85 days after the start of the fire, it was back to its pre-fire levels.[506]

The disaster also had little impact on Standard Oil's finances in 1955. "The third quarter showed a good gain in earnings despite substantial losses from the explosion and fire in Whiting," the *New York Times* reported late that year. The company reported consolidated earnings of nearly $103 million for the first nine months of the year. That was an increase of 26.2 percent over those of a year earlier. In its annual report for 1955, Standard gave itself glowing reviews. "Our company prospered in 1955. Our net earnings were the highest in our history, showing a 34 percent gain over the year before…our total 1955 dividends were the highest in our history."[507]

One action the company took before the explosion helped it significantly. Early in 1955, Standard changed its insurance coverage, "to include its refineries and larger terminals under the catastrophe, fire and extended coverage insurance that had been carried on parent company properties since 1951." The change proved to be a tremendous cost savings for the company. The explosion and fire resulted in $19.7 million in damage to the refinery. That cost included damage to property, such as the hydroformer itself. It also included the loss of product such as the oil and other stock consumed by the fires. Until 1955, the company had carried a $500,000 deductible. Its new policy lowered the annual premium the company paid and raised the deductible to one million. The bottom line was that Standard Oil had to pay one million dollars to cover its losses. Its new insurance policy covered the other $18.7 million.[508]

In one way, the Whiting Refinery fire of 1955 was similar to the Great Chicago Fire of 1871. Chicago lost numerous old wooden buildings in that fire. The modern structures built to replace them helped accelerate Chicago's development into a major city at a time when the American Midwest was rapidly growing. The Whiting Refinery fire destroyed numerous older structures within the refinery. It gave the company an opportunity to modernize the Whiting Refinery at a time when the oil industry was rapidly growing. "The prospects for our Company are good," the annual report for Standard said after the fire. "We are in a real growth industry, and our modernization and expansion program has equipped us to take advantage of opportunities and to deal with problems as they arise."[509]

"They were talking about modernizing way before the fire. They were saying we got to modernize because things are not up to par," said Leo Kus, who worked as a pipefitter at the refinery. "What that explosion did," said Lawrence Broviak, who also worked at the refinery, "was knock down a lot of the stuff that they were going to tear down anyway.

So it just escalated everything." Tom Marciniak was a Whiting resident at the time of the fire. He later became an engineer and spent a little time working at the Whiting Refinery on a project late in his career. He said the fire "was sort of like industrial/urban renewal for Standard Oil because the place changed dramatically after that."[510]

In the year that followed the fire, the company went on a building spree. "New units put into operation since the fire," the company magazine said, "are a 60,000 barrel-a-day crude oil distillation plant, a dewaxing unit which removes wax from 4,150 barrels of motor oil daily, and a plant to produce high-grade benzene, toluene, and xylene." The company also announced plans for other improvements.

"Let's put it this way," George Timko said, "[the fire] sure made a mess of that whole refinery. Then after that, they started cleaning up and redoing things. A lot of people lost jobs."[511]

"They did away with the...pressure stills in their modernization," Clarence Gehrke remembered. And, he said, "[they] built better and more modern methods of refining crude oil into gasoline." Those changes, in turn, allowed them to reduce the workforce. Before the modernization, "they had to have what they called a stillman and then they had a stillman helper and then they had maintenance workers. They'd have this outfit for every unit." With each new unit built, the workforce declined. "'Cause when they eliminated that, why, they didn't need them all."[512]

"Before 1955," Whiting resident Grace Kovach said sixty years later, "there were eight men on a shift, three shifts a day. Of course, now there's only one because of the new technology."[513]

The size of the workforce remained steady in the years immediately after the fire. But, "We had a lot of layoffs in '58 and '59 and '60," recalled Joseph Sotak. He served as president of the union, as well as in other union posts during his employment at the refinery, from 1939 to 1980. Most of those, Sotak said, came about because of the company's profitability improvement program.[514]

"I'm a businessman," said Frank O. Prior, now chairman of Standard's board of directors, in 1959. "I'm going to talk about profits." But what he primarily talked about in a guest column in the *Chicago Tribune* was Standard Oil's lack of profits. Manufacturing companies, he said, "earn about 12 percent annually on invested capital." In 1958, Standard Oil, he claimed, had a rate of return of only 4.6 percent. "So when our refinery and corporation executives talk about the need for Standard Oil to increase its profitability, they aren't speaking idly. Rather, they're hitting at the one thing that must be done if we are to maintain our position in the oil industry."[515]

"At one time there were 9,000 employees," Sotak said. But the profitability improvement program, he realized, had a different objective: "The goal was to cut it down to 1,500."[516]

"I was working in the acid works," said Ed Tokarz, "jumping back and forth from the asphalting separators, and then they decided to shut the asphalting plant down. If a company doesn't make 200 percent or better, they shut the thing down. So they shut it down, and I was out of a job."[517]

For some workers, even those who were not let go, the layoffs weakened the loyalty they felt toward the company. Add to that the desire of many residents, including refinery workers, to move to communities farther out from Whiting. Add to that a population down by about half of what it was in 1950, and a refinery workforce down from about 7,000 in 1955 to about 1,800 in 2010. What you get are fewer people with a personal connection to the refinery.

Getting back to the kind of bond that once existed is probably impossible. The world, corporate economics, the Whiting Refinery and so much more changed in the decades after the fire of 1955 that it's not surprising the relationship between the company and the people of the city changed. That change was reflected in the opinions of 83-year-old George Brown. Brown lived in Whiting when the strong bond existed, and he appreciated what the refinery did for the city. "They spent millions and millions of dollars on this city freely without being solicited or bullied into it or anything," he said. But he also lived long enough to see the changes that came after 1955. "Do you think that's still the case?" interviewer David Dabertin asked in 1990. "No," Brown replied. "I don't think so."[518]

But as long as there is a refinery in Whiting, the company and the people of the city will remain intertwined. The refinery is a major part of the city's identity. Some cities choose the arrival of their first settlers as the year the city was born. Many pick the year they were incorporated as a city as their year of birth. Whiting, however, chooses neither. Whiting has always celebrated 1889 as the year of its birth, the year Standard Oil settled in Whiting. If any other evidence is needed to show how close the bond is, consider the nickname of the Whiting High School sports teams. They are the Whiting Oilers.

Six decades after the refinery explosion of 1955, the refinery was still the heart of the community. Even when it changed from Standard Oil to Amoco Oil and then to British Petroleum (BP), the bond remained. It may have become weaker than it was in generations past, but it still existed. "When BP hiccups, we feel it," said Whiting Mayor Joe Stahura in 2006. At one time, he said, the refinery contributed 75 percent of the city's property tax revenue. By 2006 it was down to 55 percent – a smaller number, but still significant.[519]

Millions of dollars in added tax revenue from a BP expansion project in 2013 gave Whiting enough funds to help finance the National Mascot Hall of Fame, a project designed to attract visitors and more revenue to the city. BP also funded projects benefiting Whiting, Northwest Indiana and the Chicago area. In 2015, for instance, it donated a million dollars to the Student Conservation Association for environmental projects in Chicago and Northwest Indiana.[520]

Even though fewer people in Whiting work in the refinery than in years past, many still rely on it for employment. The 2013 expansion project, which brought added tax revenue to Whiting, provided $1.7 billion in wages for local union construction workers. "The refinery accounts for nearly five percent of the manufacturing jobs in Northwest Indiana," said a 2016 article by Joseph Pete in *The Times*. And according to Micah Pollak, an assistant professor of economics at Indiana University Northwest, "they pay extremely well, about 40 percent better than the national average." That same year, the refinery paid its workers an estimated $130 million in wages.[521]

Although they're fewer in number, the people who rely on the refinery for jobs remain as strongly loyal to the company as the Standard Oil workers of the early 20th century. A group of environmental protestors found that out in 2016. A march by protesters worked its way down Front Street, past the home of Sylvia Corpus Stewart. They were walking to bring attention to the impact of fossil fuels on the environment. Sylvia stood outside with her two daughters. They held signs in support of BP. She said she had family who worked at the refinery. When one of the protestors tried to engage her in conversation, a reporter for *The Times* said Corpus Stewart told the woman to "get off my property."[522]

Post-Tribune columnist Jerry Davich said he understood where Corpus Stewart was coming from. "The woman said she has relatives who work inside the BP refinery. Those family members depend on BP paychecks. End of debate. I understand this stance." There was a time when many people in Whiting felt that way. They were willing, as Davich put it, "to cap our health and environment concerns for the trade-off of steady money and putting food on the table for our families." Some outsiders don't get this, Davich said. When they come to Northwest Indiana they "instinctively frog-jump out of here. They immediately see, feel and smell the stench of industrialization and they act accordingly." But, he wrote, "All of us know that living in this industrial park we call Northwest Indiana may endanger our health to some degree. We look the other way and whistle through the cemetery of fears."[523]

Even without the fire of 1955, the refinery would have cut its workforce. Manufacturers' need to achieve profitability goals would have required such an action. Even without the fire, Stieglitz Park probably would not have survived in the long run. Generations that grew up after 1955 would have found it too close to the refinery, and the old houses would have suffered from neglect and eventually been torn down. The fire of 1955 did not cause these changes in Whiting and the refinery, but it accelerated them - making them happen sooner than they would have happened had the explosion never occurred.

"THE FIRE OF '55"

If you measure disasters by number of deaths, the 1955 Whiting Refinery explosion and fire doesn't rank anywhere close to the top of the list. Even at the Whiting Refinery, there were other disasters that killed more people. On the Fourth of July in 1921, a 30-foot long still with an eight-foot diameter and made of a half-inch of steel blew up without warning. Inspectors had looked it over just 12 hours earlier and found no defect. Eight men were working near the still. Four died instantly, and the other four died in Chicago hospitals. The number of injured was 27.

The explosion occurred at 8:15 a.m., just after a shift change. The sound of the blast woke up the entire town. Hundreds of women ran to the refinery to find out if their husbands, fathers, sons or brothers were safe, but the company had a policy. Only workmen could enter the plant. The women, the security guards insisted, had to stand outside the gate. With no other way to find out what was happening, many of them screamed to any man they saw inside the plant, pleading for information about their loved ones. Unable to get answers, some of the women followed the ambulances that left the facility, hoping to find out who was getting carried away. Some went to the morgue if they failed to locate their relative. Three bodies were at Hayden's Morgue, two others at Owens'. Some of the bodies were so badly burned that identification was almost impossible. Half of a shoe, which still clung to his foot, was how they identified one man. A blackened ring, still on his finger, was how they identified another. For others, pieces of clothing served as clues for identification.[524]

Many of those who experienced the 1955 explosion and fire also remembered what happened in1941 and 1946. An explosion at the north end of the refinery killed John Yager on September 24, 1941. Twenty received injuries. The heat of the fire that followed, melted railroad tracks. That forced the New York Central's famous passenger train, the 20th Century Limited, to reroute onto a track through Hammond. At the time, some who remembered the 1921 fire said the 1941 fire was the worst in Whiting's history – surpassing the 1921 fire in terms of scope and intensity.[525]

No one died in the 1946 fire. The nine injuries were only scratches and bruises. But the fire was spectacular to watch. It was also frightening to experience for the 5,000 spectators who gathered for a closer look. The conflagration took place in the barrel house, located near Front Street and Standard Avenue. An electrical short sparked the blaze. As the name implies, Standard stored barrels of oil in the barrel house before shipping them out to buyers. Flames from the fire were a hundred feet high and the sky was filled with dense, black smoke. But the most spectacular sights occurred when the flames reached some of the barrels and sent them rocketing upward. One flew a quarter-mile. It landed 10 feet from a railroad freight house, sending 20 workers inside scurrying for safety. Another flew toward a group of spectators. It missed them, but landed on an active water hose manned by the Whiting Fire Department. The barrel split the hose open, saturating the firemen. Another fell close to a fire truck.[526]

There were numerous explosions and fires in the refinery before 1955. There were also a number of explosions after, including one just 15 days after August 27, 1955. That fire started in a filter house located about six blocks northeast of the hydroformer site. Although seven workers received injuries, none required hospitalization.[527]

The refining of oil always has the potential for disaster. Three things make the 1955 disaster stand out from the others: First, it was, by far, the most powerful explosion and the most spectacular fire in the refinery's history. The 1955 Standard Oil explosion was probably the most powerful to hit heavily industrialized Northwest Indiana. The only possible exception was a nitroglycerin explosion at the Aetna Powder Works in 1888 in what is now the Miller area of Gary. But even if the explosion of 3,000 pounds of nitroglycerin at Aetna was more powerful, there was no fire after that explosion to compare to the eight days of spectacular flames that blazed in Whiting in 1955.[528]

Second, although accidents had killed several workers at the Whiting Refinery over the years, only the 1955 explosion took the life of someone outside the refinery.

Third, while other fires and explosions led to evacuations from neighborhoods around the refinery, the 1955 explosion and fire was the only one to cause significant damage to a residential area. It wiped Stieglitz Park off the map.

"It was the worst in the history of the region," Whiting Mayor Michael Blastick and Police Chief James Mullaney said in the days that followed. It may also have been the most spectacular industrial explosion and fire in the history of Indiana and the Chicago area, as well.[529]

Even 60 years after the explosion, those who lived through it were still astounded that the death toll was not greater. "How do you blow up that much and have that little in the way of injuries, given the damage you saw across the street?" Tom Marciniak wondered. "Houses moved off their foundations, big chunks of pressure vessels laying over 129th Street. I mean, it was pretty spectacular, no matter how many ways you cut it." Thad Bogusz, who was just 100 feet from the hydroformer when it exploded, said, "It wasn't until the next day that I began to realize what a miraculous escape we made." Only four of the 13 men working on the hydroformer that morning lost any time on the job due to the explosion.[530]

Lawrence Broviak, who was at work inside the plant at the time, called it "...very fortunate. Thank God it happened at six o'clock in the morning. There was no traffic on the Boulevard at the time. That time of the year, everyone is going to the lake." Dennis Hittle agreed. "If this was going to happen, August on a Saturday at 6:12 a.m. was the best time. If it would have been on a school day, all of us probably would have been standing in the front of Uncle George's store, waiting for our bus." After the blast, newspaperman Fred Krecker talked to merchants along 119th Street, the city's main shopping district. "It was fortunate that the explosion occurred at the hour that it did," one merchant told him. "Had it happened later in the day when people would have been walking the sidewalks, serious injuries and fatalities would have resulted. People would have been hit by the flying glass and other debris."[531]

The newspapers of the time marveled at the relative good fortune of the city. "What might have happened if the winds had been high one can only guess," a *Chicago Tribune* editorial read. The newspaper said it was "good luck and good management" that prevented more injuries and death. The editorial was very complimentary of "the entire program of fighting the blaze, caring for refugees, and policing the area," all of which were "carried out with efficiency."[532]

The *Chicago Daily News* called the loss of life and destruction of property remarkably slight. "That no more were killed in the first blast appears to have been a matter of pure luck," a newspaper editorial said. "But more than luck must be credited for keeping the subsequent injuries to persons so low." The paper gave credit to a good community disaster plan. It complimented Standard Oil, the firefighters, the police, National Guard, and volunteers from the Red Cross and American Legion. They were among the many who "did their part and did it well," the *Daily News* said.[533]

Jesse Ducommun, who went on to become one of the oil industry's most respected experts on refinery safety, agreed. "It could have been a worse disaster, particularly in the number of lives lost and people hurt. Why wasn't it worse?" he asked. "I think simply because of modern safety engineering, trained personnel, and many factors of chance. Our traditional precautions and careful disaster planning won a victory over one of the worst industrial fires on record."[534]

If the measuring stick is the cost of damage, the Whiting Refinery fire was the second largest industrial accident in American history when it occurred. Losses within the refinery, including the loss of product, amounted to $19.7 million. Standard Oil's insurance companies paid all but one million of that. The company, however, had to foot the entire cost of damages outside the refinery. It's hard to know exactly how much those costs were, but some estimates put them at $30 million. Included in that figure was the cost to buy every piece of property in Stieglitz Park. It included compensation for property in other neighborhoods that received damage, and medical bills for some of the injured. It also included repairs to damaged infrastructure outside the plant, such as fire-damaged Indianapolis Boulevard. So the best estimate is that the Whiting Refinery explosion and fire caused almost $50 million in damage, in 1955 dollars. At the time, the only industrial accident in American history that resulted in greater damage was a

1953 fire that destroyed the General Motors Hydra-Matic transmission manufacturing plant in Livonia, Michigan, which resulted in $80 million in losses.[535]

Even before the flames died down, the hunt for a cause began. Since 1955 was in the heart of the Cold War era, the FBI came to Whiting to see if Communist sabotage was responsible. They were quickly satisfied that it was not, and they did not conduct further investigation.[536]

Plant manager Arthur Endres initially speculated that a material failure in the hydroformer might be the cause. Or maybe it was the introduction of water into the process, possibly through condensation. Representatives of the M.W. Kellogg Company, the prime contractor for building the unit, arrived to conduct an investigation of their own. Meanwhile, Standard Oil appointed a six-member committee to look into it. George Watts, Standard's director of engineering research, chaired the committee. They quickly ruled out water contamination as the cause, and they did not find evidence of structural failure.[537]

The committee began to think that a mixture of combustible material and oxygen somehow got into the hydroformer's reactor. "We're looking for the explanation of the presence of an explosive mixture within the unit," said A.H. Hayes, general superintendent of the refinery and a member of the committee. "We don't know yet how such a mixture may have got in."[538]

The committee examined fragments of the damaged hydroformer. They studied the control room charts. They interviewed the men working on the unit at the time of the explosion. The workers said there was no warning, no clue that a massive explosion was about to happen. "The explosion apparently occurred in the reactor and another vessel connected to it, probably simultaneously," Hayes said. The reactor was the large vessel at the bottom of the unit. Above it was the regenerator, "which merely dropped after the blast," Hayes said.[539]

In November 1956, Jesse Ducommun gave the most detailed public accounting of the committee's conclusions. He presented his report at a session on safety and fire protection at the annual meeting of the

American Petroleum Institute. The meeting was at the Conrad Hilton Hotel in Chicago.

Ducommun said that in the early days of his career in the oil refining industry, he was often reminded about the three sides of the fire triangle. If you allowed fuel, air (oxygen), and a source of ignition to combine, a fire was likely. In those days, he said, "We took many precautions to eliminate all of the air from equipment before the startup so that hydrocarbons and air would not come in contact. Once the unit was on-stream, only two sides of the triangle existed inside the processing equipment."[540]

That changed with the introduction of cat crackers in the early 1940s, and subsequently of hydroformers, to improve the octane readings of gasoline. Now, he said, "these three elements are needed to successfully carry out the desired chemical reactions." Engineers believed that thick steel walls, such as the two-inch walls of the hydroformer, were sufficiently strong to contain an internal explosion. They also believed that pressure-relieving devices would help prevent a complete failure of the vessel. On August 27, 1955, it didn't work that way.

The explosion occurred as workers were restarting the hydroformer after a maintenance shutdown. The process called for liquid naphtha to circulate through part of the system. The process also required the use of an inert gas to purge and heat the system. As the naphtha circulated, vapors from it mixed with the inert gas. As a result of that mixing, the inert gas became contaminated and highly combustible.

Valves were used as the relieving device, designed to keep such a dangerous mix away from the oxygen in an adjacent system. Before the startup, workers on the hydroformer completed an exterior inspection of those valves. The valves seemed to be in working order. They weren't. For unknown reasons, one or more of the valves had failed to close. As a result, oxygen leaked into the system and went undetected for several hours. During that time, it mixed with the contaminated and combustible inert gas. That volatile mixture circulated around tubes inside the unit. The skin-metal temperature of those tubes was high enough to ignite the mixture, resulting in a massive explosion. The two-inch thick steel walls did not contain the explosion, as anticipated. Instead, the explosion ripped the walls of the hydroformer into pieces.[541]

Could it happen again? Never say "never." But some changes instituted after 1955 led many to believe the likelihood was small. "Everything possible has been done to ensure that this, the largest refinery in the Middle West, will never be the scene of a disaster like the one which occurred 10 years ago," said Jesse Ducommun in 1965. The hydroformer explosion was, in part, caused by the accidental mixing of oxygen with combustible gasses. In the years that followed, engineers developed new technologies to lessen the chance of that happening. They developed new detection devices. Those devices increased the ability to spot potential problems more quickly. They also developed motor-operated double-block valves and inert gas sealing systems to assure the separation of fuel and oxygen.[542]

Another reason some say a similar explosion is unlikely is that Standard never built a similarly designed hydroformer. The company opted, instead, to build an ultraformer not far from the site where the hydroformer had stood. At the start of 1955, the hydroforming process appeared to be Standard's principal instrument for improving gasoline octane ratings. "Our company played an important role in the development of the original hydroforming process," the company proudly said in February 1955. "Standard scientists also helped develop the fluid hydroforming process to be used in Whiting." But in its end-of-the-year annual report, it never mentioned hydroforming. Instead, it touted ultraforming as "our new method of improving the octane quality of gasoline." By the end of 1955, it had 22 ultraformers built, or in the works, across all its refineries.[543]

By 1975, on the 20th anniversary of the explosion, Standard Oil Fire Chief Frank Horlbeck was retired from the refinery. He said he didn't think a similar fire could happen again at the plant. One reason for his optimism was a change the company made in the location of its oil storage tanks. "We knew the potential was there for a fire like that," Horlbeck said. "They had all those units stacked right next to each other, and when the first explosion started fires in six or eight places at a time, there was no way to stop it. But after 1955, when a new tank field was created to replace the storage tanks burned in the fire, it was located a mile away, far from any processing unit which had the potential to explode."[544]

The explosion and fire also sparked an awareness of fire prevention in American industries. In 1957, the United Press news agency reported, "...companies from the smallest lumber mill to the largest integrated oil firm are waging a steady war" in the battle against fires. Those efforts, United Press said, were due to what happened at the General Motors plant in Livonia and at Standard Oil in Whiting.[545]

Jesse Ducommun stressed that Standard Oil also needed to do whatever it took to lessen the chance of similar accidents. "It behooves us to keep in mind, at all times," Ducommun said, "the hazards which may be encountered in this type of equipment. This is the reason that we must be willing – and we are willing – to spend additional money to provide the safeguards."[546]

"These things happen pretty much continually where you're working with hazardous materials," Tom Marciniak said. "Something is going to let go somewhere, and you've got to prepare for those. You try to cover it by training, instrumentation, design, whatever you can do. Nevertheless, there's always a time where somewhere, something's going to happen."[547]

A 1988 explosion at the refinery was a reminder that efforts to prevent industrial accidents never end. Late that year, three men died in an explosion in the asphalt unit: 44-year-old Michael Zimmerman of Hammond, 37-year-old George Kusbel of Whiting, and 40-year-old Leo Gonzalez of East Chicago. It was the third significant accident in the refinery that year, and the first since 1955 to result in fatalities.[548]

Grace Kovach had lived near the refinery for over six decades by 2015, close enough to hear the refinery's fire whistles sound. She said she didn't hear them as often as she used to. "Maybe they learned something," she said. "Personally, I don't think they learned enough to shut down the units when they need it. The bottom line is still talking real loud."[549]

When something bad happens, people mourn, and then they need to move on. That lesson has been part of life for centuries. It's a lesson that Herbert Whiting and other survivors probably learned after the horrible Grand Crossing train wreck in 1853. It was certainly the lesson learned by the immigrants who made up much of the Whiting community in 1955. Those immigrants and their children lived through the hard times of the Depression and World War II. They had experience mourning their hardships and then moving on with life. The weekend after the 1955 explosion, Standard Oil's 36th annual Labor Day celebration was scheduled. It was not canceled. While fires still burned in the refinery, the employees of Standard Oil gathered in Whiting Park on the city's Lake Michigan shore. For two days, they had games and rides for the children. There were bingo games for the adults. The more active could face off in softball, boxing, and wrestling matches. There were boat races. They raffled off a new 1955 automobile. And, somewhat ironically, Dr. Llewellyn Heard performed his "Fire Magic" show, which featured "startling pranks with fire and explosions."[550]

Overall, Whiting felt good about itself after the fire. "Everybody in this town was fabulous," said City Nurse Ann Devoy. "Every organization, every church, started to organize, and they all did something. It was the most beautiful thing to see such cooperation in just the flash of a second." Jesse Ducommun joined in on the praise. "We shall always be grateful," he said, "as individuals and as a company, for this community spirit." An editorial in the *Gary Post-Tribune* also praised the response. "When catastrophe strikes," it said, "common sense and the Golden Rule take over to meet the situation."[551]

The firefighters received special praise. "Time and again in this fire we saw examples of courageous, effective action that was possible mainly because our men knew what they were doing," Frank Horlbeck later said. "I never saw one bit of hysteria."[552]

There were numerous stories of sacrifice – stories of how people gave tremendous amounts of time and effort to help those who needed assistance. There were stories about individuals who put their skills, abilities, and energies to good use, like Lillian Adams. Described as "spry and elderly," the 57-year-old was not equipped to man a fire hose, but she could cook, and she could organize. She put those skills to work by organizing the Community Center's kitchen and helping to get evacuees, firefighters, and other emergency workers the food and drink they needed to keep going. And she did it with only two hours of sleep over a 72-hour period.[553]

The 1955 explosion lived on in the memories of so many mainly because the blast was so powerful and the fire so fierce. *Chicago American* reporter George Murray called it, "the greatest fire any of us had ever seen." No one living in the vicinity of Whiting at the time could have missed what happened. In some ways, it was like a major storm - a shared experience that everyone could relate to and talk about.[554]

Brenda Wilson Felton never forgot it. "I was 13. I'm 72 now. And I can still, after all them years, remember when that happened." Her sister, Bonnie Wilson Faulkner, agreed. "It was like when Kennedy got shot, when the towers got hit. Things like that stick in your mind."[555]

When asked to name the most important event in her lifetime, Jo Ann Dudzik Jancosek replied, "World War II was probably the most important...but the single event that impressed me most was the [Standard Oil] fire."[556]

Pat Mazanek had no regrets about the explosion and fire trying to upstage her wedding day. "I'm not sorry we got married on that day because it's memorable," she said, happy to share her unique story of what it was like to get married while a major disaster took place about a mile away. "I tell everybody," she said, "'Oh, I got married the day that [Standard] blew up.'"

She and her husband Joe spent close to 59 years together. He passed away just three months before their 59th anniversary. On that anniversary date - August 27, 2014 - there was a relatively minor explosion at the Whiting Refinery, which many people in the city felt. "I mean, everybody called me that day when it happened," she said. "And they're laughing, 'Well, that's Joe letting you know he's still around.'"[557]

190

In the opinion of Mary Ann Stofcik Dominiak, "If you were alive in 1955, you remember the explosion...Lots of things we forget as we get older in life, but when you experience something like I did, it's hard to forget."

She was 16 when the explosion occurred. In the days that followed, she sat down and wrote a poem about it.[558]

"The Fire of '55"
By Mary Ann Stofcik Dominiak

First went the hydroformer tall and stern,
Then the fire began to burn.
Sirens were heard loud and clear,
Because to the houses the fire drew near.

Tanks exploded one by one,
Sounding like the shots from a gun.
As flames were rising higher in height,
People were running and fleeing with fright.

The fire was reaching the naphtha-filled tanks,
So bulldozers hurriedly shoveled sand banks.
The naphtha exploded with a loud roar,
Hundreds of feet through the air it did soar.

The houses nearby, so clean and neat,
Were touched by the fire and scorched from the heat.
The people inside had to take cover,
As a child who's lost, seeking its mother.

Taking their possessions, they began to flee,
Away from the fire, forgetting their key.
The houses were left alone and unguarded,
Because the dwellers had hastily departed.

The fire was spreading faster and faster,
Heading to bring newer disaster.
The tanks so near in every direction,
Would soon be without any protection.

The fire's still burning and turning grey,
Its embers diminished and went away.
In a few nights, it quieted down,
And Whiting again was a peaceful town.

REFERENCES

1   John Hmurovic & Frank Vargo, *George Timko: Memories of Standard Oil Fire of 1955*, transcript of an oral history conducted on September 22, 2014 by John Hmurovic & Frank Vargo (Whiting, Indiana: Whiting-Robertsdale Historical Society, 2014), 1.

2   Dave McLellan & Bill Warrick, *The Lake Shore & Michigan Southern Railway* (Polo, Illinois: Transportation Trails, 1989), 27; *Weekly Wisconsin*, February 25, 1852; "Boats and Railroads," *Kenosha Democrat*, February 21, 1852.

3   "Michigan Southern R.R. Open," *Sauk County Standard*, February 21, 1852; McLellan, 25.

4   Kenneth J. Schoon, *Calumet Beginnings* (Bloomington: Indiana University Press, 2003), 82; H.W. Brands, *American Colossus*, New York: Anchor Books, 2010), 290.

5   Mrs. Frank J. Sheehan, *The Northern Boundary of Indiana* (Indianapolis: Indiana Historical Society Publications, Vol. 8, No. 6, 1928), 312; Schoon, 15-16; Mark J. Camp & Graham T. Richardson, *Roadside Geology of Indiana* (Missoula, Montana: Mountain Press Publishing Company, 1999), 7-8.

6   "Whiting Changed from Sand Hills to Modern City," *The Whiting Times Historical Edition*, August 4, 1939, 4; "City Items," *Chicago Daily Journal*, January 13, 1852; "The Cold Weather," *Chicago Daily Journal*, January 20, 1852.

7   *Chicago Daily Journal*, February 21, 1852.

8   *Chicago Daily Journal*, ibid.; McLellan & Warrick, 27.

9   McClellan & Warrick, ibid.; "Through to Chicago," *Goshen Democrat*, February 25, 1852.

10   *New Albany Daily Ledger*, May 24, 1852; "Southern Michigan Road," *Burlington Weekly Telegraph*, February 28, 1852 [Reprinted from the *Chicago Journal*.]; "The Michigan Southern Railroad," *The New York Times*, May 25, 1852.

11   "Rapid Traveling," *Weekly Wisconsin*, June 30, 1852; "H.L. Whiting is Dead," *Chicago Evening Post*, June 25, 1897; *Whiting City Almanac* (Whiting: Whiting Savings and Loan Association, 1909), 11.

12   "Brimfield Births, Marriages & Deaths," Massachusetts Town & Vital Records 1620-1988, ancestry.com

13   *Chicago Evening Post*, ibid.

14 [The story of the collision at what became known as the Grand Crossing area of Chicago comes from numerous sources, including the following:] Edgar A. Haine, *Railroad Wrecks* (New York: Cornwall Books, 1993), 33; "The Chicago Collision," *New York Times*, May 3, 1853; "The Railroad Catastrophe," *Daily Chicago Journal*, April 27, 1853; "Terrible Accident!" *Chicago Democratic Press*, April 27, 1853; "Conclusion of Testimony before the Coroner," *Daily Chicago Journal*, April 28, 1853; "Verdict of the Jury," *Daily Chicago Journal*, April 28, 1853; "The Railroad Calamity," *Chicago Democratic Press*, April 28, 1853; "The Late Collision," *Chicago Democratic Press,* April 28, 1853; "The Late Railroad Collision," *Chicago Democratic Press*, April 29, 1853; "The Late Railroad Murder," *Daily Chicago Journal*, April 29, 1853.

15 *Whiting Democrat*, August 2, 1894.

16 "Souvenir Edition," *The Whiting Sun*, November 5, 1898.

17 "How the Chicago Suburbs Were Planted and Named," *Chicago Tribune*, March 4, 1900.

18 "Whiting Paradox Is Explained," *Lake County News*, March 13, 1907; "Momentous Masonic Banquet," *Whiting Call*, January 3, 1907.

19 "Early History of Whiting," *Golden Jubilee of Sacred Heart Church*, 1940; Rev. Edwin G. Kaiser, *1897-1947 – Fifty Years of Grace: History of St. John's Parish* (Whiting, Indiana, 1947), 19.

20 C. Exera Brown, compiler & publisher, *Michigan Southern and Northern Indiana Rail Road Business Gazetteer*, (Chicago: Printer's Co-Operative Association, 1868), 89; *Crown Point Register*, December 3, 1868.

21 "Pioneer Train Conductor Is Dead," Chicago Tribune, June 25, 1897; "The Railway Conductor," *The Conductor & Brakeman*, Vol.14 (Cedar Rapids, Iowa: The Order of Railway Conductors, 1897), 592.

22 "Whiting Changed from Sand Hills to Modern City," *The Whiting Times Historical Edition*, August 4, 1939, 4.

23 Powell A. Moore, *The Calumet Region: Indiana's Last Frontier* (Indianapolis: Indiana Historical Bureau, 1977), 179-180.

24 "Whiting Changed from Sand Hills to Modern City," *The Whiting Times Historical Edition*, August 4, 1939, 2.

25 Ibid.

26 Archibald McKinlay, *Oil and Water: A Pictorial History of Whiting, Indiana* (Virginia Beach, Virginia: The Donning Company Publishers, 2003), 55; "Whiting Changed from Sand Hills to Modern City," *The Whiting Times Historical Edition*, August 4, 1939; 1880 U.S. Federal Census, Whiting Station, Lake County, Indiana, June 17, 1880, pages 49-50, Supervisor's District 5, Enumeration District 66.

[27] Old-Timer Interviews, "Mutter Thamm Has Lived Here Fifty-Six Years," *The Whiting Times*, 1939.

[28] Roger Long, *Amazon.com* Review of *Twenty Years of Hus'ling*, by J.P. Johnston. Review written April 19, 2011.

[29] James Perry Johnston, *Twenty Years of Hus'ling* (Chicago: Hallet Publishing, 1887), 94 & 97.

[30] Old-Timer Interviews, "Henry Theobold Has Memories of Whiting in 1886," *The Whiting Times*, July 7, 1939.

[31] Paul H. Giddens, *Standard Oil Company (Indiana): Oil Pioneer of the Middle West* (New York: Appleton-Century-Crofts, Inc., 1955), 4.

[32] Information gathered from a variety of sources, including the displays on Kier and Drake at the Senator John Heinz History Center in Pittsburgh.

[33] Brands, 77-83.

[34] "Cheap Fuel for Chicago," *Chicago Tribune*, January 30, 1888.

[35] *Chicago Tribune*, August 15, 1888, 9.

[36] Giddens, 4; "The Standard Oil Company Makes a Purchase," *Chicago Tribune*, April 22, 1888; "Pushing the Big Pipe Line," *Chicago Tribune*, June 12, 1888; "Piping Petroleum to Chicago," *Chicago Tribune*, July 28, 1888.

[37] Giddens, 2, 4, 10; Thomas H. Cannon, H.H. Loring, Charles J. Robb, *History of the Lake & Calumet Region of Indiana* (Indianapolis: Historians' Association Publishers, 1927), 719.

[38] Giddens, 16; "Whiting Changed from Sand Hills to Modern City," *The Whiting Times Historical Edition*, August 4, 1939; Old-Timer Interviews, "Henry Theobold Has Memories of Whiting in 1886," *The Whiting Times*, July 7, 1939.

[39] Old-Timer Interviews, "Whiting Bride of 1889 Celebrates," *The Whiting Times*, May 12, 1939; "Mrs. Vogel Tells of the Good Times and the Hardships," *The Whiting Times*, 1939; *Lake County News*, August 10, 1905.

[40] Edward J. Nichols, *Danger! Keep Out* (Boston: Houghton Mifflin Company, 1943), 184.

[41] Ibid., 184-185.

[42] "Autoists Collide with Law," *Lake County News*, April 20, 1905; "Local Tips," *Whiting Sun*, August 18, 1906; "In Relation to Penal Offences," *Whiting Sun*, October 27, 1906.

[43] "A Brief History of the Origins of Whiting Refinery," duplicated from a Supervisory Orientation Manual published September 14, 1953, compliments of Materials Management, 1989, p. 23; William O. Lynch, "Editor's Page – A Transition Period: 1907-1911," *Indiana Magazine of History* (Bloomington:

Indiana University, June 1938), 222. [Lynch writes about talking with an "intelligent gentleman" on a train ride to Chicago in 1908 when it was still uncertain which fuel was best for the development of the automobile. The gentleman was convinced that steam, not gasoline, was the fuel of the future for cars, and it "would not be long until we would see no others."]

44   Works Project Administration, *The Calumet Region Historical Guide* (Gary, Indiana: Garman Printing Co., 1939), [Information throughout, but most can be found on pages 202-209, 215-223 & 228-235].

45   "Calumet Region Nears Its Destiny," *Lake County Times*, June 14, 1907.

46   U.S. Department of Commerce, Bureau of the Census, *14th Census of the United States, Vol. III, 1920*" (Washington: Government Printing Office, 1922), 297-299 & 304. [Whiting had 10,145 residents in 1920, and 1,017 of them, 10.0 percent, were born in Czechoslovakia. At 14.9 percent, Berwyn, Illinois had a higher percentage of Czechoslovak born residents in 1920, and even Cicero, Illinois at 11.4 percent had a higher percentage than Whiting. But the published 1920 census numbers do not indicate if Czechoslovakia born residents are Czech or Slovak. However, that information is available on individual census sheets. A look at those shows that Czechs, or Bohemians, made up most of Berwyn and Cicero's Czechoslovak population, while Slovaks far outnumbered Czechs in Whiting.]

47   Joseph Semancik, "Slovaks," *Peopling Indiana: The Ethnic Experience* (Indianapolis: Indiana Historical Society, 1996), 512, edited by Robert M. Taylor Jr. and Connie A. McBirney; John H.M. Laslett, *Colliers Across the Sea: A Comparative Study of Class Formation in Scotland and the American Midwest, 1830-1924* (Champaign, IL: University of Illinois Press, 2000), 81.

48   Old-Timer Interviews," Michael Kozacik, Bank President Remembers $9 Job," *The Whiting Times,* 1939.

49   Stieglitz Subdivision, Lake County (Indiana) Recorder's Office, Plat Book 2, Page 84.

50   "Can't Use John D. Rockefeller's Name," *Chicago Tribune*, August 5, 1895.

51   Advertisement, *Whiting Democrat*, August 29, 1895.

52   Sheet music of the *Rockefeller Park March*, composed by Hjalmer Frithief Neilsson (Hammond, Indiana: Tribune Printing Company, 1895).

53   "Protects His Name," *Whiting Democrat*, June 13, 1895.

54   Obituary for Gustav Stieglitz, *Chicago Tribune*, June 5, 1905.

55   "Davidson's Addition to East Chicago," Lake County (Indiana) Recorder's Office, Plat Book 2, Page 84.

56   "Homes in Area Bought by SO," *Whiting Refinery News*, September 9, 1955.

57   Giddens, 40-41.

58 "Son, Like His Father, Retiring from Standard," *Hammond Times*, July 17, 1956; Moore, 559-560.

59 Old-Timer Interviews, "Mutter Thamm Has Lived Here Fifty-Six Years," *The Whiting Times*, 1939.

60 "The Heart of the Octopus," *Chicago Tribune*, June 3, 1906.

61 "A Dirty Deal," *Whiting Sun*, June 9, 1906.

62 John Hmurovic & Frank Vargo, *Tom Marciniak: Memories of Standard Oil Fire of 1955*, transcript of an oral history conducted on September 11, 2014 by John Hmurovic & Frank Vargo (Whiting, Indiana: Whiting-Robertsdale Historical Society, 2014), 7.

63 John Hmurovic & Frank Vargo, *Dennis Zelenke: Memories of Standard Oil Fire of 1955*, transcript of an oral history conducted on September 4, 2014 by John Hmurovic & Frank Vargo (Whiting, Indiana: Whiting-Robertsdale Historical Society, 2014), 2.

64 Chuck Kosalko & Frank Vargo, *Lynn Larsen: Memories of Standard Oil Fire of 1955*, transcript of an oral history conducted on September 25, 2014 by Chuck Kosalko & Frank Vargo (Whiting, Indiana: Whiting-Robertsdale Historical Society, 2014), 7.

65 John Hmurovic & Frank Vargo, *Justine Bircher: Memories of Standard Oil Fire of 1955*, transcript of an oral history conducted on September 15, 2014 by John Hmurovic & Frank Vargo (Whiting, Indiana: Whiting-Robertsdale Historical Society, 2014), 2; Hmurovic & Vargo, *Tom Marciniak: Memories of Standard Oil Fire of 1955*, ibid.; Kosalko & Vargo, *Lynn Larsen: Memories of Standard Oil Fire of 1955*, ibid.

66 U.S. Department of Commerce, *1950 Census, Vol. II, Characteristics of the Population – Part 14 – Indiana*, Table 38 – General Characteristics of the Population for Urban Places (Washington: U.S. Government Printing Office, 1952), 14-80.

67 Francis A. Cizon & Joseph F. Scheuer, *Parishes in the Human Community: A Basic Study of the Five Roman Catholic Parishes of the Whiting-Robertsdale Social Area*, (LePlay Research, Inc., 1961).

68 James Hazzard, "A Girl from Connecticut Visited Whiting, Indiana," *New Year's Eve in Whiting, Indiana* (Milwaukee: Main Street Publishing Inc., 1985), 45.

69 "Public School Notes," *Whiting Sun*, January 16, 1904; U.S. Department of Commerce, *1950 Census, Vol. II, Characteristics of the Population – Years of School Completed – Persons 25 & Over* (Washington: US Government Printing Office, Washington 1952).

70 "Guardians Gather," *Lake County News*, February 8, 1906.

71   John Bodnar, *Leo Kus: Whiting, Indiana: Generational Memory, 1991-1993*, transcript of an oral history conducted on October 11, 1991 by John Bodnar (Bloomington: Indiana University Center for the Study of History and Memory, 1991), 91-143, 10; David Dabertin, *Elizabeth Herakovich: Whiting, Indiana: Generational Memory, 1991-1993*, transcript of an oral history conducted on May 30, 1991 by David Dabertin (Bloomington: Indiana University Center for the Study of History and Memory, 1991), 91-135, 16; John Hmurovic & Frank Vargo, *Evelyn Kortokrax, Memories of Standard Oil Fire of 1955*, transcript of an oral history conducted on October 1, 2014 by John Hmurovic & Frank Vargo (Whiting, Indiana: Whiting-Robertsdale Historical Society, 2014), 1.

72   John Bodnar, *Julia & Michael Pukac: Whiting, Indiana: Generational Memory, 1991-1993*, transcript of an oral history conducted on March 2, 1991 by John Bodnar (Bloomington: Indiana University Center for the Study of History and Memory, 1992), 91-153, 3; "Son, Like His Father, Retiring from Standard," *Hammond Times*, July 17, 1956.

73   Nichols, 113-114; Joseph Hmurovich was my grandfather, and I rode with him many times, worried that we were going to run out of gas.

74   "Refinery a Giant Among Giants," *Chicago Tribune*, August 28, 1955.

75   Andrew Jefchak, *Out of Stieglitz Park* (Grand Rapids, Michigan: Chapbook Press, 2011), 5.

76   Chuck Kosalko & Frank Vargo, *Larry Jennings: Memories of Standard Oil Fire of 1955*, transcript of an oral history conducted on August 22, 2014 by Chuck Kosalko & Frank Vargo (Whiting, Indiana: Whiting-Robertsdale Historical Society, 2014), 19; Jefchak, 7; Dennis Hittle, *Dennis Hittle: Memories of the Standard Oil Fire*, email correspondence with John Hmurovic in 2014, collected by Frank Vargo (Whiting, Indiana: Whiting-Robertsdale Historical Society, 2015).

77   Hittle, *Dennis Hittle: Memories of the Standard Oil Fire*, ibid.; Chuck Kosalko & Frank Vargo, *Raymond Gajewski: Memories of Standard Oil Fire of 1955*, transcript of an oral history conducted on July 23, 2014 by Chuck Kosalko & Frank Vargo (Whiting, Indiana: Whiting-Robertsdale Historical Society, 2014), 12; John Hmurovic & Frank Vargo, *Mary Ann Dominiak: Memories of Standard Oil Fire of 1955*, transcript of an oral history conducted on September 3, 2014 by John Hmurovic & Frank Vargo (Whiting, Indiana: Whiting-Robertsdale Historical Society, 2014), 6.

78   John Hmurovic & Frank Vargo, *Ann Gregorovich: Memories of Standard Oil Fire of 1955*, transcript of an oral history conducted on October 2, 2014 by John Hmurovic & Frank Vargo (Whiting, Indiana: Whiting-Robertsdale Historical Society, 8; Hittle, *Dennis Hittle: Memories of the Standard Oil Fire*, ibid.

79   Kosalko & Vargo, *Raymond Gajewski: Memories of Standard Oil Fire of 1955*, 4; John Hmurovic & Frank Vargo, *Leilani Suchanuk: Memories of Standard Oil Fire of 1955*, transcript of an oral history conducted on September 3, 2014 by John Hmurovic & Frank Vargo (Whiting, Indiana Whiting-Robertsdale Historical Society, 2014), 6.

80   "Classified Business Directory," *Polk's Hammond City Directory 1954* (Detroit: R.L. Polk & Company, 1955), 21-23, 19-20, 41-42; Hittle, ibid.; Kosalko & Vargo, *Lynn Larsen: Memories of Standard Oil Fire of 1955*, 8.

81   Hmurovic & Vargo, *Justine Bircher: Memories of Standard Oil Fire of 1955*, 3; Hittle, *Memories of the Standard Oil Fire*, ibid.

82   Hittle, *Dennis Hittle: Memories of the Standard Oil Fire*, ibid.

83   Ibid.

84   Hmurovic & Vargo, *Tom Marciniak: Memories of Standard Oil Fire of 1955*, 4; James Hazzard, "Gypsies in Whiting, Indiana," *New Year's Eve in Whiting, Indiana* (Milwaukee: Main Street Publishing Inc., 1985), 56.

85   Hittle, *Dennis Hittle: Memories of the Standard Oil Fire*, ibid.

86   Hmurovic & Vargo, *Justine Bircher: Memories of Standard Oil Fire of 1955*, 8.

87   David Dabertin, *Jim Sandrick: Whiting, Indiana: Generational Memory, 1991-1993*, transcript of an oral history conducted on January 23, 1991 by David Dabertin (Bloomington: Indiana University Center for the Study of History and Memory, 1991), 26.

88   John Hmurovic & Frank Vargo, *Betty Delinck: Memories of Standard Oil Fire of 1955*, transcript of an oral history conducted on October 1, 2014 by John Hmurovic & Frank Vargo (Whiting, Indiana: Whiting-Robertsdale Historical Society, 2014), 7; Hmurovic & Vargo, *Leilani Suchanuk: Memories of Standard Oil Fire of 1955*, 5-6.

89   Chuck Kosalko & Frank Vargo, *Jim Hoelzel: Memories of Standard Oil Fire of 1955*, transcript of an oral history conducted on September 12, 2014 by Chuck Kosalko & Frank Vargo (Whiting, Indiana: Whiting-Robertsdale Historical Society, 2014), 6; Hittle, *Dennis Hittle: Memories of the Standard Oil Fire*, ibid.; Jefchak, 7.

90   Hittle, *Dennis Hittle: Memories of the Standard Oil Fire*, ibid.; Chuck Kosalko & Frank Vargo, *Bill Haddad: Memories of Standard Oil Fire of 1955*, transcript of an oral history conducted on September 29, 2014 by Chuck Kosalko & Frank Vargo (Whiting, Indiana: Whiting-Robertsdale Historical Society, 2014), 9-10.

91   Hittle, *Dennis Hittle: Memories of the Standard Oil Fire*, ibid.

92   "Showers to Cool Region; 40 Days Over 90 Mark," *Hammond Times*, August 29, 1955; Vikki Ortiz Healy, "Cellphone Apps. Get Weather Fast, But Often Wrong," *Chicago Tribune*, June 11, 2015.

93   J.C. Ducommun, "6:12 at FHU-700," *American Petroleum Institute Proceedings*, Vol 36 [VI] 1956, 144.

94   "Expansion at Whiting...Up Goes the New," *Standard Torch*, February 1955, Vol. VIII, No. 2, 16; "Classified Business Directory," *Polk's Hammond City Directory 1954* (Detroit: R.L. Polk & Company, 1955), 3.

95   "Rapid Move to Put Refinery Back into Full Production," (Whiting) *Times-Graphic*, September 8, 1955; "Standard Oil to Build New Catalyst Unit," *Chicago Tribune*, September 9, 1953.

96   Giddens, p. 140-171; Phillip Britt, "Fuel for 21st Century," *The Times*, June 25, 1989.

97   Jefchak, 5; "Expansion at Whiting...Up Goes the New," *Standard Torch*, February 1955, 16.

98   "Expansion at Whiting...Up Goes the New," *Standard Torch*, February 1955, Vol. VIII, No. 2, p. 16; "$30 Million Whiting Fire Leaves 2 Dead, 26 Hurt," *Hammond Times*, August 28, 1955; "Fire Loss Tops 10 Million," *Chicago Tribune*, August 28, 1955.

99   "Standard's Balanced Gasolines Reach New High in Octane Ratings," *Standard Torch*, July 1955, Vol. VIII, No. 7, p. 22; "Refinery a Giant Among Giants," *Chicago Tribune*, August 28, 1955.

100   "Refinery a Giant Among Giants," *Chicago Tribune*, August 28, 1955.

101   "Standard's Balanced Gasolines Reach New High in Octane Ratings," *Standard Torch*, July 1955, Vol. VIII, No. 7, p. 22.

102   William Gaines, "Huge Whiting Oil Fire Was 10 Years Ago, But Memories Still Burn," *Chicago Tribune*, August 29, 1965; Bernie Bernacki, "Reason Behind the Big Blow-Up," *Compass II*, August 27, 1975.

103   Hmurovic & Vargo, *Mary Ann Dominiak: Memories of Standard Oil Fire of 1955*, 4.

104   Hmurovic & Vargo, *George Timko: Memories of Standard Oil Fire of 1955*, 1; Hmurovic & Vargo, *Dennis Zelenke: Memories of Standard Oil Fire of 1955*, 1.

105   Ducommun, 144.

106   Ducommun, ibid.

107   Frank Vargo, *Shirley Puello Christ: Memories of the Standard Oil Fire*, notes from a conversation in 2014 with Frank Vargo, collected by Frank Vargo (Whiting, Indiana: Whiting-Robertsdale Historical Society, 2015); John Hmurovic & Frank Vargo, *Pat Mazanek: Memories of Standard Oil Fire*

of 1955, transcript of an oral history conducted on September 4, 2014 by John Hmurovic & Frank Vargo (Whiting, Indiana: Whiting-Robertsdale Historical Society, 2014), 2; Chuck Kosalko & Frank Vargo, *Bonnie Wilson Faulkner & Brenda Wilson Felton: Memories of Standard Oil Fire of 1955*, transcript of an oral history conducted on September 18, 2014 by Chuck Kosalko & Frank Vargo (Whiting, Indiana: Whiting-Robertsdale Historical Society, 2014), 3.

[108] Dabertin, *Elizabeth Herakovich: Whiting, Indiana: Generational Memory, 1991-1993*, 91-135, 16; Robert J. Herakovich, *Robert J. Herakovich: Memories of the Standard Oil Fire*, collected by Frank Vargo (Whiting, Indiana: Whiting-Robertsdale Historical Society, 2015).

[109] Frank Vargo, *Sharon Fernando Reinke: Memories of the Standard Oil Fire*, notes from a conversation in 2014 with Frank Vargo, collected by Frank Vargo (Whiting, Indiana: Whiting-Robertsdale Historical Society, 2015).

[110] Frank Vargo, *Helen White Gray: Memories of the Standard Oil Fire*, notes from a conversation in 2014 with Frank Vargo, collected by Frank Vargo (Whiting, Indiana: Whiting-Robertsdale Historical Society, 2015).

[111] Frank Vargo, *Pam Cummings: Memories of the Standard Oil Fire*, notes from a conversation in 2014 with Frank Vargo, collected by Frank Vargo (Whiting, Indiana: Whiting-Robertsdale Historical Society, 2015).

[112] Kosalko & Vargo, *Jim Hoelzel: Memories of Standard Oil Fire of 1955*, 3; Frank Vargo, *Paul Stofcik: Memories of the Standard Oil Fire*, notes from a conversation in 2014 with Frank Vargo, collected by Frank Vargo (Whiting, Indiana: Whiting-Robertsdale Historical Society, 2015).

[113] John Hmurovic & Frank Vargo, *Grace Kovach: Memories of Standard Oil Fire of 1955*, transcript of an oral history conducted on September 17, 2014 by John Hmurovic & Frank Vargo (Whiting, Indiana: Whiting-Robertsdale Historical Society, 2014), 1.

[114] Frank Vargo, *Donald DeLong: Memories of the Standard Oil Fire*, notes from a conversation in 2014 with Frank Vargo, collected by Frank Vargo (Whiting, Indiana: Whiting-Robertsdale Historical Society, 2015).

[115] Kosalko & Vargo, *Larry Jennings: Memories of Standard Oil Fire of 1955*, 2; Larry McClelland, *Larry McClelland: Memories of the Standard Oil Fire*, collected by Frank Vargo (Whiting, Indiana: Whiting-Robertsdale Historical Society, 2015).

[116] Kosalko & Vargo, *Larry Jennings: Memories of Standard Oil Fire of 1955*, ibid.

[117] Hmurovic & Vargo, *Dennis Zelenke: Memories of Standard Oil Fire of 1955*, 2.

[118] Hmurovic & Vargo, *Dennis Zelenke: Memories of Standard Oil Fire of 1955*, 3.

[119] "'Like End of the World,'" *Hammond Times*, August 28, 1955.

[120] Kosalko & Vargo, *Bonnie Wilson Faulkner & Brenda Wilson Felton: Memories of Standard Oil Fire of 1955*, 3.

[121] Kosalko & Vargo, *Bill Haddad: Memories of Standard Oil Fire of 1955*, 1.

[122] David Dabertin, *Helen Dudzik: Whiting, Indiana: Generational Memory, 1991-1993*, transcript of an oral history conducted on February 10, 1991 by David Dabertin (Bloomington: Indiana University Center for the Study of History and Memory, 1991), 91-19, 20.

[123] "Eyewitness Stories; How Boy Died," *Chicago Sun-Times*, August 28, 1955.

[124] Frank Vargo, *Sharon Ross: Memories of the Standard Oil Fire*, notes from a conversation in 2014 with Frank Vargo, collected by Frank Vargo (Whiting, Indiana: Whiting-Robertsdale Historical Society, 2015).

[125] Frank Vargo, *Don Smith: Memories of the Standard Oil Fire*, notes from a conversation in 2014 with Frank Vargo, collected by Frank Vargo (Whiting, Indiana: Whiting-Robertsdale Historical Society, 2015).

[126] Frank Vargo, *Rosemarie Gomez: Memories of the Standard Oil Fire*, notes from a conversation in 2014 with Frank Vargo, collected by Frank Vargo (Whiting, Indiana: Whiting-Robertsdale Historical Society, 2015).

[127] "Aviation Gas New Threat," *Chicago American*, August 28, 1955; "More Whiting Blasts! *Chicago American*, August 27, 1955; "Fire Loss Tops 10 Million," *Chicago Tribune*, August 28, 1955; Fred Krecker, "Stillman 20 Ft. from Blast Tells Escape," *Hammond Times*, August 28, 1955.

[128] John Hmurovic & Frank Vargo, *Virginia Galvin: Memories of Standard Oil Fire of 1955*, transcript of an oral history conducted on September 23, 2014 by John Hmurovic & Frank Vargo (Whiting, Indiana: Whiting-Robertsdale Historical Society, 2014), 1.

[129] "Lakeshore Areas in Holland Feel Effects of Blast," *Holland Evening Sentinel*, August 27, 1955.

[130] Joe Gray, *Joe Gray: Memories of the Standard Oil Fire*, collected by Frank Vargo (Whiting, Indiana: Whiting-Robertsdale Historical Society, 2015).

[131] Frank Vargo, *Michael Goodson: Memories of the Standard Oil Fire*, notes from a conversation in 2014 with Frank Vargo, collected by Frank Vargo (Whiting, Indiana: Whiting-Robertsdale Historical Society, 2015).

[132] Hmurovic & Vargo, *Betty Delinck: Memories of Standard Oil Fire of 1955*, 1.

[133] "Anglers Tell First Oil Blast," *Chicago American*, August 28, 1955.

[134] Krecker, ibid.

[135] "Eyewitness Stories; How Boy Died," *Chicago Sun-Times*, August 28, 1955.

[136] Ducommun, ibid.

[137] Chuck Kosalko & Frank Vargo, *Marge Milligan: Memories of Standard Oil Fire of 1955*, transcript of an oral history conducted on September 29, 2014 by Chuck Kosalko & Frank Vargo (Whiting, Indiana: Whiting-Robertsdale Historical Society, 2014), 1; Ducommun, 147.

[138] Ducommun, ibid.

[139] Ducommun, ibid.

[140] Ducommun, ibid.

[141] "List of Dead and Wounded in Whiting Refinery Fire," *Chicago Tribune*, August 28, 1955; "Hunt Unknown Mixture in Blast Probe," *Whiting Refinery News*, September 9, 1955.

[142] "Oil Fire in Whiting Checked," *Chicago Tribune*, August 29, 1955; Ducommun, ibid.

[143] Ducommun, ibid.; "Damage Over $10,000,000," *Chicago American*, August 28, 1955.

[144] Krecker, ibid.

[145] Ducommun, ibid.

[146] Krecker, ibid.

[147] Ducommun, ibid.

[148] John Hmurovic & Frank Vargo, *Ronald Plewniak: Memories of Standard Oil Fire of 1955*, transcript of an oral history conducted on March 18, 2015 by John Hmurovic & Frank Vargo (Whiting, Indiana: Whiting-Robertsdale Historical Society, 2015), 5; Ronald Plewniak, *Memories of the Standard Oil Fire*, email correspondence with John Hmurovic on March 31, 2015, collected by Frank Vargo (Whiting, Indiana: Whiting-Robertsdale Historical Society, 2015).

[149] Sophia Joan Plewniak obituary, *The Times*, August 28, 2014; Hmurovic & Vargo, *Ronald Plewniak: Memories of Standard Oil Fire of 1955*, ibid.

[150] Hmurovic & Vargo, *Ronald Plewniak: Memories of Standard Oil Fire of 1955*, 4.

[151] "Eyewitness Stories; How Boy Died," *Chicago Sun-Times*, August 28, 1955.

[152] Hittle, *Dennis Hittle: Memories of the Standard Oil Fire*, ibid.

[153] "Flying Metal Flattens Grocery, Homes, Autos," *Hammond Times*, August 28, 1955.

[154] "More Whiting Blasts! *Chicago American*, August 27, 1955.

[155] Ibid.

156   Cindy Dressen, *Anne Jurbala: Memories of the Standard Oil Fire*, collected by Frank Vargo (Whiting, Indiana: Whiting-Robertsdale Historical Society, 2015).

157   Frank Vargo, *Darryle Smith: Memories of the Standard Oil Fire*, notes from a conversation in 2014 with Frank Vargo, collected by Frank Vargo (Whiting, Indiana: Whiting-Robertsdale Historical Society, 2015).

158   "Flying Metal Flattens Grocery, Homes, Autos," *Hammond Times*, August 28, 1955.

159   Frank Vargo, *Priscilla Springer McCarty-Reed: Memories of the Standard Oil Fire*, notes from a conversation in 2015 with Frank Vargo, collected by Frank Vargo (Whiting, Indiana: Whiting-Robertsdale Historical Society, 2015).

160   Ibid.

161   Ibid.

162   "6 Blasted from Bed," *Chicago American*, August 27, 1955; "Whiting Oil Blaze Out of Control," *Chicago Tribune*, August 28, 1955.

163   Hmurovic & Vargo, *Ronald Plewniak: Memories of Standard Oil Fire of 1955*, 1; "Fix-Up Job Ahead in Whiting," *The Daily Banner*, September 2, 1955.

164   Hmurovic & Vargo, *Ronald Plewniak: Memories of Standard Oil Fire of 1955*, ibid.; Leroy McHugh, "Dad Tells How Son Was Killed," *Chicago American*, August 27, 1955; Edward Ranzal, "City Imperiled as Blasts Fire Big Indiana Oil Refinery; 1,400 Flee, 2 Die," *New York Times,* August 28, 1955.

165   "Eyewitness Stories; How Boy Died," *Chicago Sun-Times*, August 28, 1955; McClelland, *Larry McClelland: Memories of the Standard Oil Fire*, ibid.

166   Nancy Lee Kane, "Flying 'Torpedo' Kills Boy, Injures Brother, *Hammond Times*, August 28, 1955.

167   Ibid.

168   Cheryl Macko Rosen, *Cheryl Macko Rosen: Memories of the Standard Oil Fire*, collected by Frank Vargo (Whiting, Indiana: Whiting-Robertsdale Historical Society, 2015).

169   Barry B. Burr, "Whiting's Great Fire – 20 Years Ago Today," *Compass II*, August 27, 1975.

170   "13,000 Fire Fighters," *Standard Torch*, October 1948; "How Whiting Refinery's Largest Fire Was Fought and Beaten," *Whiting Refinery News*, September 9, 1955.

171   Burr, ibid.; Rosen, *Cheryl Macko Rosen: Memories of the Standard Oil Fire*, ibid.

172   Ducommun, 147.

173   Ibid., 148; "Fire Loss Tops 10 Million," *Chicago Tribune*, August 28, 1955.

[174] Ranzal, ibid.; "How Whiting Refinery's Largest Fire Was Fought and Beaten," *Whiting Refinery News*, September 9, 1955.

[175] "Trained Crews on Alert, Keep Fire Danger Down," *Whiting Refinery News*, September 9, 1955.

[176] "Fire Finally Quenched at Whiting Oil Refinery," Gary Post-Tribune, August 31, 1955; "How Whiting Refinery's Largest Fire Was Fought and Beaten," *Whiting Refinery News,* September 9, 1955.

[177] Ibid.

[178] Ibid.

[179] "Walter E. Rhea," Obituary, *Hammond Times*, August 28, 1955; "Here's Brief Fire Resume," *Whiting Refinery News*, September 9, 1955; John Hmurovic, notes from a phone conversation with Richard Rhea, March 12, 2015 (Whiting, Indiana: Whiting-Robertsdale Historical Society, 2015).

[180] Ducommun, 153; Hmurovic, notes from a phone conversation with Richard Rhea, ibid.; Local Record of Death, City of Whiting Department of Health, Walter Elliott Rhea, filed August 29, 1955.

[181] "The Big Fire at Whiting," *Standard Torch*, October 1955, Vol. VIII, No. 10, p.2.

[182] "13,000 Fire Fighters," *Standard Torch*, October 1948; John Hmurovic & Frank Vargo, *Janet Tindall: Memories of Standard Oil Fire of 1955*, transcript of an oral history conducted on September 24, 2014 by John Hmurovic & Frank Vargo (Whiting, Indiana: Whiting-Robertsdale Historical Society, September 24, 2014), 1.

[183] "Know-How Is the Key to Effective Fire-Fighting," *Standard Torch*, October 1948; Ducommun, 152; "Trained Crews on Alert, Keep Fire Danger Down," *Whiting Refinery News*, September 9, 1955.

[184] John Bodnar, *Joyce & Jack Whiting: Whiting, Indiana: Generational Memory, 1991-1993*, transcript of an oral history conducted on March 5, 1992 by John Bodnar (Bloomington: Indiana University Center for the Study of History and Memory, 1992), 91-155, 35.

[185] Chuck Kosalko & Frank Vargo, *Steve Fusak: Memories of Standard Oil Fire of 1955*, transcript of an oral history conducted on February 12, 2015 by Chuck Kosalko & Frank Vargo (Whiting, Indiana: Whiting-Robertsdale Historical Society), 8.

[186] Frank Vargo, *Bob Usselman: Memories of the Standard Oil Fire*, notes from a conversation in 2014 with Frank Vargo, collected by Frank Vargo (Whiting, Indiana: Whiting-Robertsdale Historical Society, 2015).

[187] Chuck Kosalko & Frank Vargo, *Lawrence Broviak: Memories of Standard Oil Fire of 1955*, transcript of an oral history conducted on August 8, 2014

by Chuck Kosalko & Frank Vargo (Whiting, Indiana: Whiting-Robertsdale Historical Society, August 8, 2014), 2.

188 "The Big Fire at Whiting," *Standard Torch*, October 1955, Vol. VIII, No. 10, p.2.

189 "How Whiting Refinery's Largest Fire Was Fought and Beaten," *Whiting Refinery News*, September 9, 1955; Ducommun, 153.

190 Burr, ibid.

191 "Service Units Give Aid in Emergency," *Whiting Refinery News*, September 9, 1955.

192 "6 Gary Firemen, Reporter for P-T Burned at Oil Fire," *Gary Post-Tribune*, August 29, 1955.

193 "Damage Over $10,000,000," *Chicago American*, August 28, 1955; "Fight Flames After Blasts Peril Whiting," *Chicago Sun-Times*, August 28, 1955; "Chicago Offers Aid to Whiting," *Chicago Daily News*, August 27, 1955.

194 Burr, ibid.; Ducommun, 148.

195 "'Like A-Bomb' Says Flying Reporter," *Chicago American*, August 28, 1955.

196 "Whiting Refinery Blows Up," *Chicago American*, August 27, 1955.

197 "Fire Loss Tops 10 Million," *Chicago Tribune*, August 28, 1955.

198 "'Like A-Bomb' Says Flying Reporter," *Chicago American*, August 28, 1955.

199 Hmurovic & Vargo, *George Timko: Memories of Standard Oil Fire of 1955*, 2; "'Like A-Bomb' Says Flying Reporter," *Chicago American*, August 28, 1955.

200 Ray Sons, "Daily News Man at Inferno Scene," *Chicago Daily News*, August 27, 1955.

201 Frank Vargo, *Dennis Moore: Memories of the Standard Oil Fire*, notes from a conversation in 2014 with Frank Vargo, collected by Frank Vargo (Whiting, Indiana: Whiting-Robertsdale Historical Society, 2015).

202 John Hmurovic & Frank Vargo, *George Grenchik: Memories of Standard Oil Fire of 1955*, transcript of an oral history conducted on September 11, 2014 by John Hmurovic & Frank Vargo (Whiting, Indiana: Whiting-Robertsdale Historical Society), 1.

203 Hmurovic & Vargo, *Grace Kovach: Memories of Standard Oil Fire of 1955*, 2.

204 Frank Vargo, *Frank Vargo: Memories of the Standard Oil Fire*, collected by Frank Vargo (Whiting, Indiana: Whiting-Robertsdale Historical Society, 2015).

205 Ducommun, ibid.; "Showers to Cool Region; 40 Days Over 90 Mark," *Hammond Times*, August 29, 1955.

206   "Thousands Fleeing City; Fire May Rage for Days," *Chicago Daily News*, August 27, 1955; "Fire Loss Tops 10 Million," *Chicago Tribune*, August 28, 1955.

207   "Fight Flames After Blasts Peril Whiting," *Chicago Sun-Times*, August 28, 1955.

208   "Aviation Gas New Threat," *Chicago American*, August 28, 1955; "Fire Loss Tops 10 Million," *Chicago Tribune*, August 28, 1955.

209   Ducommun, ibid.; "Oil Plant Blast, Flames Threaten Whiting, Ind.," *Grand Rapids Press*, August 27, 1955; "$30 Million Whiting Fire Leaves 2 Dead, 26 Hurt," *Hammond Times*, August 28, 1955; Kosalko & Vargo, *Larry Jennings: Memories of Standard Oil Fire of 1955*, 4; Hmurovic & Vargo, *George Grenchik: Memories of Standard Oil Fire of 1955*, 2.

210   "Fire Loss Tops 10 Million," *Chicago Tribune*, August 28, 1955; "Aviation Gas New Threat," *Chicago American*, August 28, 1955; "Cars Forced to Detour," *Chicago American*, August 28, 1955.

211   Ducommun, 148; "How Whiting Refinery's Largest Fire Was Fought and Beaten," *Whiting Refinery News*, September 9, 1955.

212   "Fire Loss Tops 10 Million," *Chicago Tribune*, August 28, 1955.

213   Frank Vargo, *George Justak: Memories of the Standard Oil Fire*, notes from a conversation in 2014 with Frank Vargo, collected by Frank Vargo (Whiting, Indiana: Whiting-Robertsdale Historical Society, 2015); "$30 Million Whiting Fire Leaves 2 Dead, 26 Hurt," *Hammond Times*, August 28, 1955; Sons, ibid.

214   "Thousands Fleeing City; Fire May Rage for Days," *Chicago Daily News*, August 27, 1955; Sons, ibid.; Chuck Kosalko & Frank Vargo, *Earl Yoho: Memories of Standard Oil Fire of 1955*, transcript of an oral history conducted on September 18, 2014 by Chuck Kosalko & Frank Vargo (Whiting, Indiana: Whiting-Robertsdale Historical Society), 9.

215   Ducommun, 149.

216   Vargo, *Frank Vargo: Memories of the Standard Oil Fire*, ibid.

217   Hmurovic & Vargo, *Justine Bircher: Memories of Standard Oil Fire of 1955*, 1.

218   John Hmurovic & Frank Vargo, *JoAnne Samila: Memories of Standard Oil Fire of 1955*, transcript of an oral history conducted on September 23, 2014 by John Hmurovic & Frank Vargo (Whiting, Indiana: Whiting-Robertsdale Historical Society), 4.

219   "2,800 Back to Homes in Whiting," *Chicago American*, August 30, 1955.

220   Frank Vargo, *Patricia Macielewicz: Memories of the Standard Oil Fire*, notes from a conversation in 2014 with Frank Vargo, collected by Frank Vargo (Whiting, Indiana: Whiting-Robertsdale Historical Society, 2015).

221 "Whiting Center Puts Roof Over 125 Victims," *Chicago American*, August 29, 1955.

222 "Thousands Fleeing City; Fire May Rage for Days," *Chicago Daily News*, August 27, 1955.

223 "The Flight from Terror," *Gary Post-Tribune*, August 29, 1955.

224 Kosalko & Vargo, *Lynn Larsen: Memories of Standard Oil Fire of 1955*, 1; Vargo, *Shirley Puello Christ: Memories of the Standard Oil Fire*, ibid.

225 Hmurovic & Vargo, *Betty Delinck: Memories of Standard Oil Fire of 1955*, 2; "150 Whiting Families Still Out," *Gary Post-Tribune*, August 30, 1955.

226 Hmurovic & Vargo, *Justine Bircher: Memories of Standard Oil Fire of 1955*, 3.

227 Chuck Kosalko & Frank Vargo, *Frances Vanek: Memories of Standard Oil Fire of 1955*, transcript of an oral history conducted on August 4, 2014 by Chuck Kosalko & Frank Vargo (Whiting, Indiana: Whiting-Robertsdale Historical Society, 2014), 4.

228 Ibid.

229 Ibid., 5.

230 Kosalko & Vargo, *Bonnie Wilson Faulkner & Brenda Wilson Felton: Memories of Standard Oil Fire of 1955*, 3.

231 Hmurovic & Vargo, *Ann Gregorovich: Memories of Standard Oil Fire of 1955*, 3.

232 Kosalko & Vargo, *Frances Vanek: Memories of Standard Oil Fire of 1955*, 5.

233 Hmurovic & Vargo, *Betty Delinck: Memories of Standard Oil Fire of 1955*, 4.

234 "How One Family Fled Fire Terror," *Chicago Daily News*, August 27, 1955.

235 Kosalko & Vargo, *Bonnie Wilson Faulkner & Brenda Wilson Felton: Memories of Standard Oil Fire of 1955*, 6; John Hmurovic & Frank Vargo, *Nick Karin: Memories of Standard Oil Fire of 1955*, transcript of an oral history conducted on October 2, 2014 by John Hmurovic & Frank Vargo (Whiting, Indiana: Whiting-Robertsdale Historical Society, 2014), 12.

236 Frank Vargo, *Ann Kiraly: Memories of the Standard Oil Fire*, notes from a conversation in 2014 with Frank Vargo, collected by Frank Vargo (Whiting, Indiana: Whiting-Robertsdale Historical Society, 2015).

237 John Hmurovic, Chuck Kosalko & Frank Vargo, *Ann Devoy: Memories of Standard Oil Fire of 1955*, transcript of an oral history conducted on October 22, 2014 by John Hmurovic, Chuck Kosalko & Frank Vargo (Whiting, Indiana: Whiting-Robertsdale Historical Society, 2014), 26.

238 David Dabertin, *JoAnn Jancosek: Whiting, Indiana: Generational Memory, 1991-1993*, transcript of an oral history conducted on January 29, 1991 David

Dabertin (Bloomington: Indiana University Center for the Study of History and Memory, 1991), 91-16.

239 Vargo, *Frank Vargo: Memories of the Standard Oil Fire,* ibid.

240 Hmurovic, Kosalko & Vargo, *Ann Devoy: Memories of Standard Oil Fire of 1955,* 16.

241 "Whiting Oil Blaze Out of Control," *Chicago Tribune,* August 28, 1955; Frank Vargo, *Marge Strezo Zubay: Memories of the Standard Oil Fire,* notes from a conversation in 2014 with Frank Vargo, collected by Frank Vargo (Whiting, Indiana: Whiting-Robertsdale Historical Society, 2015).

242 Hmurovic, Kosalko & Vargo, *Ann Devoy: Memories of Standard Oil Fire of 1955,* 17.

243 "Mother Knocked from Bed Has 16th Child," *Hammond Times,* August 29, 1955; "Flying Metal Flattens Grocery, Homes, Autos," *Hammond Times,* August 28, 1955.

244 Krecker, ibid.; Photo Caption, [Whiting] *Times-Graphic,* September 8, 1955.

245 "Fire Loss Tops 10 Million," *Chicago Tribune,* August 28, 1955.

246 Hmurovic, Kosalko & Vargo, *Ann Devoy: Memories of Standard Oil Fire of 1955,* 20.

247 "Whiting Oil Blaze Out of Control," *Chicago Tribune,* August 28, 1955; "Relief Workers Speed Assistance to Victims," *Chicago American,* August 28, 1955.

248 McKinlay, 65.

249 "Refinery Fire Sidelites," *Times-Graphic,* September 8, 1955; Hmurovic, Kosalko & Vargo, *Ann Devoy, Memories of Standard Oil Fire of 1955,* 22.

250 "Service Units Give Aid in Emergency," *Whiting Refinery News,* September 9, 1955.

251 "Refinery Bears Few Scars of 1955 Disaster," *Chicago Tribune,* August 26, 1956; "Region Responds to Aid Whiting," *Hammond Times,* August 29, 1955; "Control Refinery Fire; Whiting A 'Ghost Town,'" *Chicago Daily News,* August 29, 1955; "Oil Fire in Whiting Checked," *Chicago Tribune,* August 29, 1955; "Area Cities Rush Aid To Stricken Community," *Hammond Times,* August 28, 1955; Edward Ranzal, "City Imperiled as Blasts Fire Big Indiana Oil Refinery; 1,400 Flee, 2 Die," *New York Times,* August 28, 1955; "Aviation Gas New Threat," *Chicago American,* August 28, 1955; "Fight Flames After Blasts Peril Whiting," *Chicago Sun-Times,* August 28, 1955; "Damage Over $10,000,000," *Chicago American,* August 28, 1955; "Whiting Center Puts Roof Over 125 Victims," *Chicago American,* August 30, 1955.

252 "Center Shelters 68 Victims," *Chicago American,* August 28, 1955.

253 Kosalko & Vargo, *Larry Jennings: Memories of Standard Oil Fire of 1955,* 4.

254   Hmurovic & Vargo, *JoAnne Samila: Memories of Standard Oil Fire of 1955*, 6.

255   "Refinery Fire Sidelites," [Whiting] *Times-Graphic,* September 8, 1955; Red Cross Issues Disaster Report, [Whiting] *Times-Graphic,* September 8, 1955.

256   "Center Shelters 68 Victims," *Chicago American,* August 28, 1955; Hmurovic, Kosalko & Vargo, *Ann Devoy: Memories of Standard Oil Fire of 1955,* 20.

257   Hmurovic, Kosalko & Vargo, *Ann Devoy: Memories of Standard Oil Fire of 1955,* 22.

258   "Cars Forced to Detour," *Chicago American,* August 28, 1955.

259   "Whiting Oil Blaze Out of Control," *Chicago Tribune,* August 28, 1955.

260   "Whiting Center Puts Roof Over 125 Victims," *Chicago American,* August 29, 1955.

261   David Dabertin, *Beatrice Stawitcke: Whiting, Indiana: Generational Memory, 1991-1993,* transcript of an oral history conducted on February 13, 1992 by David Dabertin (Bloomington: Indiana University Center for the Study of History and Memory, 1992), 91-158, 7; "Whiting Center Puts Roof Over 125 Victims," *Chicago American,* August 29, 1955.

262   Hmurovic, Kosalko & Vargo, *Ann Devoy: Memories of Standard Oil Fire of 1955,* 23.

263   Ducommun, 152; "Ranzal, ibid.; "Big Mushroom Cloud Visible 30 Miles Away," *Chicago Tribune,* August 28, 1955.

264   Hmurovic, Kosalko & Vargo, *Ann Devoy: Memories of Standard Oil Fire of 1955,* 23.

265   "Center Shelters 68 Victims," *Chicago American,* August 28, 1955; "Control Refinery Fire; Whiting A 'Ghost Town,'" *Chicago Daily News,* August 29, 1955.

266   Kosalko & Vargo, *Earl Yoho: Memories of Standard Oil Fire of 1955,* 2. 8, 14.

267   "$30 Million Whiting Fire Leaves 2 Dead, 26 Hurt," *Hammond Times,* August 28, 1955; "Thousands Fleeing City; Fire May Rage for Days," *Chicago Daily News,* August 27, 1955.

268   Kosalko & Vargo, *Earl Yoho: Memories of Standard Oil Fire of 1955.* [Interview with Earl Yoho talks about the roadblocks in general, as well as some of the locations of those roadblocks.]; Kosalko & Vargo, *Jim Hoelzel: Memories of Standard Oil Fire of 1955.* [Interview with Jim Hoelzel adds details about the Marktown roadblock.]; Hmurovic & Vargo, *George Grenchik: Memories of Standard Oil Fire of 1955.* [George Grenchik talks about the roadblock at Five Points.]; "More Whiting Blasts! *Chicago American,* August 27, 1955; "Fire Loss Tops 10 Million," *Chicago Tribune,* August 28, 1955.

269   "Big Mushroom Cloud Visible 30 Miles Away," *Chicago Tribune,* August 28, 1955; "Control Refinery Fire; Whiting A 'Ghost Town,'" *Chicago Daily News,*

August 29, 1955; "How One Family Fled Fire Terror," *Chicago Daily News*, August 27, 1955.

270   "How One Family Fled Fire Terror," *Chicago Daily News*, August 27, 1955.

271   "Standard Oil Starts Rebuilding," *The Calumet News*, August 31, 1955; "Control Refinery Fire; Whiting A 'Ghost Town,'" *Chicago Daily News*, August 29, 1955; Kosalko & Vargo, *Earl Yoho: Memories of Standard Oil Fire of 1955*, 5.

272   Kosalko & Vargo, *Steve Fusak: Memories of Standard Oil Fire of 1955*, 14.

273   "FBI Enters Probe of Whiting Fire," *Chicago Daily News*, August 29, 1955.

274   "Fire Loss Tops 10 Million," *Chicago Tribune*, August 28, 1955; "Thousands Fleeing City; Fire May Rage for Days," *Chicago Daily News*, August 27, 1955; Ducommun, 152.

275   Ranzal, ibid.

276   Clarence Hunter, "Legion at Whiting Scene Within Hour of Fatal Blast," *Gary Post-Tribune*, August 31, 1955; "Legion Gives Big Hand in Whiting," *Gary Post-Tribune*, August 29, 1955; "More Whiting Blasts! *Chicago American*, August 27, 1955; "Oil Fire in Whiting Checked," *Chicago Tribune*, August 29, 1955.

277   Gray, *Joe Gray: Memories of the Standard Oil Fire*, ibid.; "Mother Knocked from Bed Has 16th Child," *Hammond Times*, August 29, 1955.

278   Kosalko & Vargo, *Earl Yoho: Memories of Standard Oil Fire of 1955*, 6.

279   Kosalko & Vargo, *Earl Yoho: Memories of Standard Oil Fire of 1955*, 15; "Most of Evacuees Reoccupy Homes: Ban Return to Stiglitz Park," *Hammond Times*, August 29, 1955; "Many Return to Homes; Oil Fire Abating," *Chicago Tribune*, August 30, 1955; Donna Writt, *Memories of the Standard Oil Fire*, collected by Frank Vargo (Whiting, Indiana: Whiting-Robertsdale Historical Society, 2015).

280   "Thousands Fleeing City; Fire May Rage for Days," *Chicago Daily News*, August 27, 1955; Joseph Sjostrom, "A Look Back at Whiting Holocaust," *Chicago Tribune*, August 28, 1975.

281   Hmurovic & Vargo, *Grace Kovach: Memories of Standard Oil Fire of 1955*, 4; John Hmurovic & Frank Vargo, *Kay Rosinski: Memories of Standard Oil Fire of 1955*, transcript of an oral history conducted on October 2, 2014 by John Hmurovic & Frank Vargo (Whiting, Indiana: Whiting-Robertsdale Historical Society, 2014), 9.

282   David Dabertin, *Doris Wickhorst: Whiting, Indiana: Generational Memory, 1991-1993*, transcript of an oral history conducted on July 19, 1991 by David Dabertin (Bloomington: Indiana University Center for the Study of History and Memory, 1991), 91-136, 28; "Fire Loss Tops 10 Millions," *Chicago Tribune*,

August 28, 1955; "Damage Over $10,000,000," *Chicago American,* August 28, 1955; "Whiting Oil Blaze Out of Control," *Chicago Tribune,* August 28, 1955; John Hmurovic & Frank Vargo, *Jim Sandrick: Memories of Standard Oil Fire of 1955,* transcript of an oral history conducted on September 24, 2014 by John Hmurovic & Frank Vargo (Whiting, Indiana: Whiting-Robertsdale Historical Society, 2014), 1.

283   "Whiting Oil Blaze Out of Control," *Chicago Tribune,* August 28, 1955; "Damage Over $10,000,000," *Chicago American,* August 28, 1955; Kosalko & Vargo, *Larry Jennings: Memories of Standard Oil Fire of 1955,* 4.

284   Kosalko & Vargo, *Earl Yoho: Memories of Standard Oil Fire of 1955,* 16-17.

285   "Sabotage at Standard?" *Hammond Times,* September 24, 1941.

286   "Thousands Fleeing City; Fire May Rage for Days," *Chicago Daily News,* August 27, 1955.

287   Frank Vargo, *Bob Babbitt: Memories of the Standard Oil Fire,* notes from a conversation in 2014 with Frank Vargo, collected by Frank Vargo (Whiting, Indiana: Whiting-Robertsdale Historical Society, 2015); Vargo, *Donald DeLong: Memories of the Standard Oil Fire,* ibid.

288   Frank Vargo, *Geraldine Schultz: Memories of the Standard Oil Fire,* notes from a conversation in 2014 with Frank Vargo, collected by Frank Vargo (Whiting, Indiana: Whiting-Robertsdale Historical Society, 2015).

289   John Bodnar, *Betty Gehrke: Whiting, Indiana: Generational Memory, 1991-1993,* transcript of an oral history conducted on September 28, 1990 by John Bodnar (Bloomington: Indiana University Center for the Study of History and Memory, 1990), 91-4, 2; John Bodnar, *Clarence & Betty Gehrke: Whiting, Indiana: Generational Memory, 1991-1993,* transcript of an oral history conducted on October 11, 1991 by John Bodnar (Bloomington: Indiana University Center for the Study of History and Memory, 1991), 91-142, 23.

290   Hmurovic & Vargo, *Nick Karin: Memories of Standard Oil Fire of 1955,* 4.

291   Hittle, *Dennis Hittle: Memories of the Standard Oil Fire,* ibid.

292   Frank Vargo, *Elaine Gehring: Memories of the Standard Oil Fire,* notes from a conversation in 2014 with Frank Vargo, collected by Frank Vargo (Whiting, Indiana: Whiting-Robertsdale Historical Society, 2015); Hmurovic & Vargo, *JoAnne Samila: Memories of Standard Oil Fire of 1955,* 3.

293   Frank Vargo, *Dennis Fech: Memories of the Standard Oil Fire,* notes from a conversation in 2014 with Frank Vargo, collected by Frank Vargo (Whiting, Indiana: Whiting-Robertsdale Historical Society, 2015); Dabertin, *Helen Dudzik: Whiting, Indiana: Generational Memory, 1991-1993,* 20.

294   Frank Vargo, *Maurice Campbell: Memories of the Standard Oil Fire,* notes from a conversation in 2014 with Frank Vargo, collected by Frank Vargo (Whiting, Indiana: Whiting-Robertsdale Historical Society, 2015).

295   Kosalko & Vargo, *Jim Hoelzel: Memories of Standard Oil Fire of 1955*, 4.

296   "Big Mushroom Cloud Visible 30 Miles Away," *Chicago Tribune*, August 28, 1955; "Fight Flames After Blasts Peril Whiting," *Chicago Sun-Times*, August 28, 1955.

297   "The Big Fire at Whiting," *Standard Torch*, October 1955, Vol. VIII, No. 10, p.2.

298   "Fight Flames After Blasts Peril Whiting," *Chicago Sun-Times*, August 28, 1955; "Aviation Gas New Threat," *Chicago American*, August 28, 1955; "6 Gary Firemen, Reporter for P-T Burned at Oil Fire," *Gary Post-Tribune*, August 29, 1955.

299   "Fight Flames After Blasts Peril Whiting," *Chicago Sun-Times*, August 28, 1955; "6 Gary Firemen, Reporter for P-T Burned at Oil Fire," *Gary Post-Tribune*, August 29, 1955.

300   "6 Gary Firemen, Reporter for P-T Burned at Oil Fire," *Gary Post-Tribune*, August 29, 1955.

301   "Eyewitness Stories; How Boy Died," *Chicago Sun-Times*, August 28, 1955; "Mother Knocked from Bed Has 16th Child," *Hammond Times*, August 29, 1955.

302   Burr, ibid.; Rosen, *Cheryl Macko Rosen: Memories of the Standard Oil Fire*, ibid.

303   McClelland, *Larry McClelland: Memories of the Standard Oil Fire*, ibid.

304   "6 Gary Firemen, Reporter for P-T Burned at Oil Fire," *Gary Post-Tribune*, August 29, 1955.

305   "Dead, Injured in Explosions Listed," *Chicago Sun-Times*, August 28, 1955.

306   "Klein Recovering from Fire Burns," *Hammond Times*, August 31, 1955; "Damage Over $10,000,000," *Chicago American*, August 28, 1955.

307   Kosalko & Vargo, *Lawrence Broviak: Memories of Standard Oil Fire of 1955*, 2.

308   Hmurovic & Vargo, *Tom Marciniak: Memories of Standard Oil Fire of 1955*, 2.

309   Kosalko & Vargo, *Bill Haddad: Memories of Standard Oil Fire of 1955*, 2.

310   Frank Vargo, *Paula Tomera Timko: Memories of the Standard Oil Fire*, notes from a conversation in 2014 with Frank Vargo, collected by Frank Vargo (Whiting, Indiana: Whiting-Robertsdale Historical Society, 2015).

311   Hmurovic & Vargo, *Mary Ann Dominiak: Memories of Standard Oil Fire of 1955*, 1.

312   Hmurovic & Vargo, *George Timko: Memories of Standard Oil Fire of 1955*, 2.

[313] Hmurovic & Vargo, *George Timko: Memories of Standard Oil Fire of 1955*, 5.

[314] Frank Vargo, *Dave Sharp: Memories of the Standard Oil Fire*, notes from a conversation in 2014 with Frank Vargo, collected by Frank Vargo (Whiting, Indiana: Whiting-Robertsdale Historical Society, 2015).

[315] Hmurovic & Vargo, *Evelyn Kortokrax: Memories of Standard Oil Fire of 1955*, 1.

[316] Susan Brown, "Explosion Memories Don't Dim," *The Times*, August 27, 1988.

[317] Vargo, *Frank Vargo: Memories of the Standard Oil Fire*, ibid.

[318] "Whiting Observes 20th Anniversary of Safety Dep't and Plant Medical Service," *Stanolind Record*, July 1938, 1 & 2; "FBI Enters Probe of Whiting Fire," *Chicago Daily News*, August 29, 1955; Ducommun, 154; "Most of Evacuees Reoccupy Homes: Wind Shift Only Outbreak Threat," *Hammond Times*, August 29, 1955; "Whiting Workers' Record: Four Times Safer on Job," *Standard Torch*, December 1955, page MF, Vol. VIII, No. 12.

[319] Ducommun, 149; "The Cat and the Canary," *Standard Torch*, June 1951, 22.

[320] "Songless Birds Protect Workers," *Whiting Refinery News*, September 4, 1956; "The Cat and the Canary," *Standard Torch*, June 1951, 22.

[321] Kosalko & Vargo, *Steve Fusak: Memories of Standard Oil Fire of 1955*, 12.

[322] Hmurovic & Vargo, *Jim Sandrick: Memories of Standard Oil Fire of 1955*, 1.

[323] Jurbala, ibid.

[324] Frank Vargo, *Barb Poppen: Memories of the Standard Oil Fire*, notes from a conversation in 2014 with Frank Vargo, collected by Frank Vargo (Whiting, Indiana: Whiting-Robertsdale Historical Society, 2015); Dabertin, *Doris Wickhorst: Whiting, Indiana: Generational Memory, 1991-1993*, ibid.; Vargo, *Elaine Gehring: Memories of the Standard Oil Fire*, ibid.

[325] "Whiting Refinery Blows Up," *Chicago American*, August 27, 1955.

[326] Photo Caption, *Times-Graphic*, September 8, 1955.

[327] "Hello Girls Pitch-In in Pinch," *Hammond Times*, August 28, 1955.

[328] "Whiting Oil Blaze Out of Control," *Chicago Tribune*, August 28, 1955; "Hello Girls Pitch-In in Pinch," *Hammond Times*, August 28, 1955.

[329] Ducommun, 144 & 153; "Hello Girls Pitch-In in Pinch," *Hammond Times*, August 28, 1955.

[330] "Whiting Oil Blaze Out of Control," *Chicago Tribune*, August 28, 1955; "Hello Girls Pitch-In in Pinch," *Hammond Times*, August 28, 1955.

[331] "Big Mushroom Cloud Visible 30 Miles Away," *Chicago Tribune*, August 28, 1955; "Region Responds to Aid Whiting," *Hammond Times*, August 29, 1955; Kosalko & Vargo, *Jim Hoelzel: Memories of Standard Oil Fire of 1955*, 8.

[332] Lynn Boyd Hinds, *Broadcasting the Local News: The Early Years of Pittsburgh's KDKA-TV* (University Park, Pennsylvania: Penn State Press, 1995), 139; Hal Wolford, *When Cameras Were Round* (Evansville, Indiana: Evansville Bindery, 2001), 3.

[333] Robert Feder, robertfeder.com, October 19, 2013; Rosen, *Cheryl Macko Rosen: Memories of the Standard Oil Fire,* 2.

[334] Verda Klemm, *William Obermiller: Whiting, Indiana: Generational Memory, 1991-1993,* transcript of an oral history conducted on January 14 & 17, 1991 by Verda Klemm (Bloomington: Indiana University Center for the Study of History and Memory, 1991), 91-12, 7; Dan Nimmo and Chevelle Newsome, *Political Commentators in the United States in the 20th Century* (Westport, Connecticut: Greenwood Press, 1997), 31.

[335] "Fire Covered by Press, Radio, TV," *Whiting Refinery News,* September 9, 1955.

[336] Ibid.

[337] Frank Vargo, *Richard Joyce: Memories of the Standard Oil Fire,* notes from a conversation in 2014 with Frank Vargo, collected by Frank Vargo (Whiting, Indiana: Whiting-Robertsdale Historical Society, 2015).

[338] Kosalko & Vargo, *Earl Yoho: Memories of Standard Oil Fire of 1955,* 6; Vargo, *Frank Vargo: Memories of the Standard Oil Fire,* 3.

[339] "Fire Covered by Press, Radio, TV," *Whiting Refinery News,* September 9, 1955; Vargo, *Elaine Gehring: Memories of the Standard Oil Fire,* ibid.

[340] "Oil Co. Buys Homes South of 129th," *Hammond, Times,* September 4, 1955; "Sympathy, Gratitude, Courage – Warm Letters Speak Volumes," *Whiting Refinery News,* September 30, 1955; "Paints Fire," *Holland Evening Sentinel,* September 28, 1955.

[341] Frank Vargo, *Fred Behrens: Memories of the Standard Oil Fire,* notes from a conversation in 2014 with Frank Vargo, collected by Frank Vargo (Whiting, Indiana: Whiting-Robertsdale Historical Society, 2015).

[342] Kosalko & Vargo, *Raymond Gajewski: Memories of Standard Oil Fire of 1955,* 1.

[343] Hmurovic & Vargo, *Justine Bircher: Memories of Standard Oil Fire of 1955,* 2.

[344] John Bodnar, *Joseph Sotak: Whiting, Indiana: Generational Memory, 1991-1993,* transcript of an oral history conducted on November 6, 1991 by John Bodnar (Bloomington: Indiana University Center for the Study of History and Memory, 1991), 91-144, 24-25.

[345] Frank Vargo, *Dale Seliger: Memories of the Standard Oil Fire,* notes from a conversation in 2014 with Frank Vargo, collected by Frank Vargo (Whiting,

Indiana: Whiting-Robertsdale Historical Society, 2015); Hmurovic & Vargo, *Betty Delinck: Memories of Standard Oil Fire of 1955*, 2.

346 Frank Vargo, *Rose Lubeck: Memories of the Standard Oil Fire*, notes from a conversation in 2014 with Frank Vargo, collected by Frank Vargo (Whiting, Indiana: Whiting-Robertsdale Historical Society, 2015).

347 David Dabertin, *Rosemary Kraly: Whiting, Indiana: Generational Memory, 1991-1993*, transcript of an oral history conducted on January 22, 1992 by David Dabertin (Bloomington: Indiana University Center for the Study of History and Memory, 1992), 91-156, 26-27.

348 Herakovich, *Robert J. Herakovich: Memories of the Standard Oil Fire*, ibid.; Dabertin, *Elizabeth Herakovich: Whiting, Indiana: Generational Memory, 1991-1993*, ibid.

349 John Bodnar, *Ann Marie Kaminsky: Whiting, Indiana: Generational Memory, 1991-1993*, transcript of an oral history conducted on May 14, 1991 by John Bodnar (Bloomington: Indiana University Center for the Study of History and Memory, 1991), 91-26, 34; "Sympathy, Gratitude, Courage – Warm Letters Speak Volumes," *Whiting Refinery News*, September 30, 1955.

350 Frank Vargo, *Doris Cinotto: Memories of the Standard Oil Fire*, notes from a conversation in 2014 with Frank Vargo, collected by Frank Vargo (Whiting, Indiana: Whiting-Robertsdale Historical Society, 2015).

351 Kosalko & Vargo, *Bill Haddad: Memories of Standard Oil Fire of 1955*, 1.

352 Kosalko & Vargo, *Lynn Larsen: Memories of Standard Oil Fire of 1955*, 1.

353 Hmurovic & Vargo, *Janet Tindall: Memories of Standard Oil Fire of 1955*, 1-2.

354 John Wolford, *Barry Klemm: Whiting, Indiana: Generational Memory, 1991-1993*, transcript of an oral history conducted on December 18, 1992 by John Wolford (Bloomington: Indiana University Center for the Study of History and Memory, 1992), 3.

355 Hmurovic & Vargo, *Pat Mazanek: Memories of Standard Oil Fire of 1955*, 1-3.

356 Frank Vargo, *Bob Hanchar: Memories of the Standard Oil Fire*, notes from a conversation in 2014 with Frank Vargo, collected by Frank Vargo (Whiting, Indiana: Whiting-Robertsdale Historical Society, 2015); Dabertin, *Elizabeth Herakovich: Whiting, Indiana: Generational Memory, 1991-1993*, 91-135, 16.

357 Dabertin, *JoAnn Jancosek: Whiting, Indiana: Generational Memory, 1991-1993*, 2; Hmurovic & Vargo, *Mary Ann Dominiak: Memories of Standard Oil Fire of 1955*, 1.

358 "Blast Speeds Baby Arrival," *Chicago Sun-Times*, August 29, 1955; "Mother Knocked from Bed Has 16th Child," *Hammond Times*, August 29, 1955; "Blast Hurries Stork," *Gary Post-Tribune*, August 29, 1955.

359 Frank Vargo, *Ina Kizziah: Memories of the Standard Oil Fire*, notes from a conversation in 2014 with Frank Vargo, collected by Frank Vargo (Whiting, Indiana: Whiting-Robertsdale Historical Society, 2015); Vargo, *Dale Seliger: Memories of the Standard Oil Fire*, ibid.; "Control Refinery Fire; Whiting A 'Ghost Town,'" *Chicago Daily News*, August 29, 1955; "Mother Knocked from Bed Has 16th Child," *Hammond Times*, August 29, 1955.

360 Diane Donovan & Nancy Banks, "'Big Fire' Memories Rekindled," *The Times*, August 21, 1983; Don & Joyce Coleman, *Don & Joyce Coleman: Memories of the Standard Oil Fire*, collected by Frank Vargo (Whiting-Robertsdale Historical Society, 2015).

361 Hmurovic & Vargo, *Pat Mazanek: Memories of Standard Oil Fire of 1955*, 1-3; "Legion Gives Big Hand in Whiting," *Gary Post-Tribune*, August 29, 1955.

362 Dabertin, *Beatrice Stawitcke: Whiting, Indiana: Generational Memory, 1991-1993*, 6.

363 John Hmurovic & Frank Vargo, *Teresa Zebracki: Memories of Standard Oil Fire of 1955*, transcript of an oral history conducted on September 24, 2014 by John Hmurovic & Frank Vargo (Whiting-Robertsdale Historical Society, 2014), 1-2.

364 Hmurovic & Vargo, *George Grenchik: Memories of Standard Oil Fire of 1955*, 1; Kosalko & Vargo, *Bill Haddad: Memories of Standard Oil Fire of 1955*, 2; "'Like A-Bomb' Says Flying Reporter," *Chicago American*, August 28, 1955; Hmurovic & Vargo, *Dennis Zelenke: Memories of Standard Oil Fire of 1955*, 2.

365 "How Whiting Refinery's Largest Fire Was Fought and Beaten," *Whiting Refinery News*, September 9, 1955.

366 "$30 Million Whiting Fire Leaves 2 Dead, 26 Hurt," *Hammond Times*, August 28, 1955.

367 Hmurovic & Vargo, *George Timko: Memories of Standard Oil Fire of 1955*, 1.

368 Hmurovic & Vargo, *Betty Delinck: Memories of Standard Oil Fire of 1955*, 2.

369 "Huge Refinery Fire at Whiting Checked," *Chicago Sun-Times*, August 29, 1955; "Most of Evacuees Reoccupy Homes: Wind Shift Only Outbreak Threat," *Hammond Times*, August 29, 1955; Kosalko & Vargo, *Earl Yoho: Memories of Standard Oil Fire of 1955*, 9. [Both the *Chicago Sun-Times* and the *Hammond Times* mention the tactic of firing bullets into the storage tanks. Additionally, National Guardsman Earl Yoho states that while he was on duty at the refinery during the fire, he heard comments about using their rifles, or even the National Guard's machine gun, to shoot bullets into the storage tanks, though he never knew if anyone actually did it.]

370 "Fight Flames After Blasts Peril Whiting," *Chicago Sun-Times*, August 28, 1955; "$30 Million Whiting Fire Leaves 2 Dead, 26 Hurt," *Hammond Times*, August 28, 1955.

371 Ranzal, ibid.

372 "Cars Forced to Detour," *Chicago American*, August 28, 1955; "The Wreckage," *Chicago Sun-Times*, August 28, 1955; Verne Seehausen, *Verne Seehausen: Memories of the Standard Oil Fire*, collected by Frank Vargo (Whiting-Robertsdale Historical Society, 2015); Mike Ramey told his story to John Hmurovic in 2004.

373 Hmurovic & Vargo, *Leilani Suchanuk: Memories of Standard Oil Fire of 1955*, 4; "Aviation Gas New Threat," *Chicago American*, August 28, 1955.

374 Dabertin, *Helen Dudzik: Whiting, Indiana: Generational Memory, 1991-1993*, 20.

375 Hmurovic & Vargo, *Pat Mazanek: Memories of Standard Oil Fire of 1955*, 2.

376 Ducommun, 149.

377 Hmurovic & Vargo, *JoAnne Samila: Memories of Standard Oil Fire of 1955*, 4-5, 8-10; Obituary, *Hammond Times*, November 3, 1955. [More information about Charlie Fizer's life was obtained on ancestry.com, particularly from 1940 Census records and the Soundex Index to Naturalization Petitions for the United States District and Circuit Courts, Northern District of Illinois, Reels F-241 through F-356.]

378 "Fight Flames After Blasts Peril Whiting," *Chicago Sun-Times*, August 28, 1955.

379 "Evacuated Families Back Home," *Gary Post-Tribune*, August 29, 1955; "Oil Fire in Whiting Checked," *Chicago Tribune*, August 29, 1955.

380 "Most of Evacuees Reoccupy Homes: Ban Return to Stiglitz Park," *Hammond Times*, August 29, 1955.

381 "2,800 Back to Homes in Whiting," *Chicago American*, August 30, 1955; "Evacuated Whiting Families Begin Return to Blast-Stricken Area," *Chicago Sun-Times*, August 30, 1955; "Fate of Area Now Depends on Winds," *Chicago American*, August 29, 1955.

382 Ibid.

383 "2,800 Back to Homes in Whiting," *Chicago American*, August 30, 1955.

384 Vargo, *Frank Vargo: Memories of the Standard Oil Fire*, ibid.

385 Hmurovic & Vargo, *George Timko: Memories of Standard Oil Fire of 1955*, 3.

386 "Families Returning After Indiana Blast," *New York Times*, August 30, 1955; "60 Whiting Homes Opened to Residents," *Chicago Daily News*, August 30, 1955; "Huge Refinery Fire at Whiting Checked," *Chicago Sun-Times*, August

29, 1955; "Control Refinery Fire; Whiting A 'Ghost Town,'" *Chicago Daily News*, August 29, 1955.

[387] "Control Refinery Fire; Whiting A 'Ghost Town,'" *Chicago Daily News*, August 29, 1955; "Most of Evacuees Reoccupy Homes: Ban Return to Stiglitz Park," *Hammond Times*, August 29, 1955.

[388] "Fire Finally Quenched at Whiting Oil Refinery," *Gary Post-Tribune*, August 31, 1955; "75 More Families Return to Homes in Oil Fire Area," *Chicago Tribune*, August 31, 1955.

[389] George Lindberg, "A Look at Dying Oil Fires Revives Memories of War," *Gary Post-Tribune*, August 31, 1955.

[390] Vargo, *Priscilla Springer McCarty-Reed: Memories of the Standard Oil Fire*, ibid.

[391] Lindberg, ibid.

[392] Hmurovic & Vargo, *JoAnne Samila: Memories of Standard Oil Fire of 1955*, 5; Hittle, *Dennis Hittle: Memories of the Standard Oil Fire*, ibid.; "Control Refinery Fire; Whiting A 'Ghost Town,'" *Chicago Daily News*, August 29, 1955.

[393] Emmett Dedmon, *Challenge and Response: A Modern History of Standard Oil Company (Indiana)* (Chicago: The Mobium Press, 1984), 52-55.

[394] Ranzal, ibid.; "Standard Head Pledges Quick Aid to Victims," *Chicago Tribune*, August 28, 1955; Ducommun, 153.

[395] Ducommun, ibid.

[396] "More Than 1,000 Fire Claims Paid Off," *Whiting Refinery News*, September 9, 1955.

[397] "150 Whiting Families Still Out," *Gary Post-Tribune*, August 30, 1955; "Evacuated Families Back Home," *Gary Post-Tribune*, August 29, 1955.

[398] Hmurovic & Vargo, *Justine Bircher: Memories of Standard Oil Fire of 1955*, 4 & 6.

[399] Kosalko & Vargo, *Marge Milligan: Memories of Standard Oil Fire of 1955*, 1.

[400] "Standard Oil Tells of Purchase Plan," *Hammond Times*, September 1, 1955; "More Than 1,000 Fire Claims Paid Off," *Whiting Refinery News*, September 9, 1955.

[401] "Final Blaze Out at Whiting Refinery," *Gary Post-Tribune*, September 6, 1955.

[402] "Standard Oil Tells of Purchase Plan," *Hammond Times*, September 1, 1955.

[403] "More Than 1,000 Fire Claims Paid Off," *Whiting Refinery News*, September 9, 1955; "The Big Fire at Whiting," *Standard Torch*, October 1955, Vol. VIII, No. 10, 2.

404 Frank Vargo, *Martha Thompson: Memories of the Standard Oil Fire*, notes from a conversation in 2014 with Frank Vargo, collected by Frank Vargo (Whiting, Indiana: Whiting-Robertsdale Historical Society, 2015); Red Cross Issues Disaster Report, *Times-Graphic*, September 8, 1955; "Remove Troops from Whiting; 2 Tanks Burn On," *Chicago Tribune*, September 1, 1955; "Many Return to Homes; Oil Fire Abating," *Chicago Tribune*, August 30, 1955; "Fire Covered by Press, Radio, TV," *Whiting Refinery News*, September 9, 1955.

405 "Most of Evacuees Reoccupy Homes: Wind Shift Only Outbreak Threat," *Hammond Times*, August 29, 1955; "53 Hours on Job at Big Blaze," *Hammond Times*, August 30, 1955; Ducommun, 149; Sjostrom, ibid.

406 Rosen, *Cheryl Macko Rosen: Memories of the Standard Oil Fire*, 2-3.

407 Nancy Nemeth Moore, *Nancy Nemeth Moore: Memories of the Standard Oil Fire*, collected by Frank Vargo (Whiting, Indiana: Whiting-Robertsdale Historical Society, 2015).

408 "Fate of Area Now Depends on Winds," *Chicago American*, August 29, 1955; "Most of Evacuees Reoccupy Homes: Wind Shift Only Outbreak Threat," *Hammond Times*, August 29, 1955.

409 "150 Whiting Families Still Out," *Gary Post-Tribune*, August 30, 1955; "3-Inch Rainfall; Farmers Happy," *Hammond Times*, August 30, 1955; "60 Whiting Homes Opened to Residents," *Chicago Daily News*, August 30, 1955.

410 "2,800 Back to Homes in Whiting," *Chicago American*, August 30, 1955; "150 Whiting Families Still Out," *Gary Post-Tribune*, August 30, 1955; "Evacuated Whiting Families Begin Return to Blast-Stricken Area," *Chicago Sun-Times*, August 30, 1955; "Families Returning After Indiana Blast," *New York Times*, August 30, 1955.

411 "75 More Families Return to Homes in Oil Fire Area," *Chicago Tribune*, August 31, 1955; "Fire Finally Quenched at Whiting Oil Refinery," *Gary Post-Tribune*, August 31, 1955; George Lindberg, "A Look at Dying Oil Fires Revives Memories of War," *Gary Post-Tribune*, August 31, 1955.

412 "One Tank Burns On," *Hammond Times*, September 1, 1955; "Oil Co. Offers to Buy 155 Fire Area Homes," *Gary Post-Tribune*, September 2, 1955; "Standard Oil Bids for Homes in Blast Area," *Chicago Tribune*, September 3, 1955.

413 "150 Whiting Families Still Out," *Gary Post-Tribune*, August 30, 1955; "Control Refinery Fire; Whiting A 'Ghost Town,'" *Chicago Daily News*, August 29, 1955.

414 "1 Tank Still Burning at Standard Oil," *Gary Post-Tribune*, September 3, 1955; "Oil Co. Buys Homes South of 129th," *Hammond, Times*, September 4, 1955.

415 "Fire Finally Quenched at Whiting Oil Refinery," *Gary Post-Tribune*, August 31, 1955.

416 "150 Whiting Families Still Out," *Gary Post-Tribune*, August 30, 1955.

417 "Fire in Whiting Oil Refinery Finally Out," *Chicago Tribune*, September 5, 1955; "Final Blaze Out at Whiting Refinery," *Gary Post-Tribune*, September 6, 1955.

418 "Final Blaze Out at Whiting Refinery," *Gary Post-Tribune*, September 6, 1955.

419 "Standard Oil Tells of Purchase Plan," *Hammond Times*, September 1, 1955; "Whiting Oil Blaze Out of Control," *Chicago Tribune*, August 28, 1955.

420 Vargo, *Marge Strezo Zubay: Memories of the Standard Oil Fire*, ibid.

421 "Standard Oil Tells of Purchase Plan," *Hammond Times*, September 1, 1955.

422 "Oil Co. Offers to Buy 155 Fire Area Homes," *Gary Post-Tribune*, September 2, 1955; "Standard Oil Bids for Homes in Blast Area," *Chicago Tribune*, September 3, 1955; "Oil Co. Buys Homes South of 129th," *Hammond, Times,* September 4, 1955.

423 Ducommun, 153; "Here's Brief Fire Resume," *Whiting Refinery News*, September 9, 1955.

424 "Thousands Fleeing City; Fire May Rage for Days," *Chicago Daily News*, August 27, 1955, [Counted 33 injuries.]; "Damage Over $10,000,000," *Chicago American*, August 28, 1955, [Says, "At least 56 were injured severely enough to require hospital treatment."]; "Fire Loss Tops 10 Millions," *Chicago Tribune*, August 28, 1955, [Says that "Most of the injured were treated in St. Catherine's St. Catherine's Hospital, East Chicago.]; "Fire in Refinery Under Control After 24-Hour Fight With Blasts," *New York Times*, August 29, 1955, [Says 40 were injured.]

425 Edward Ranzal, "City Imperiled as Blasts Fire Big Indiana Oil Refinery; 1,400 Flee, 2 Die," *New York Times*, August 28, 1955; "Whiting Blaze Costly to Firemen of Black Oak," *Gary Post-Tribune*, September 1, 1955.

426 "Fight Flames After Blasts Peril Whiting," *Chicago Sun-Times*, August 28, 1955; "Fate of Area Now Depends on Winds," *Chicago American*, August 29, 1955; Bernie Bernacki, "Reason Behind the Big Blow-Up," *Compass II*, August 27, 1975; "Control Refinery Fire; Whiting A 'Ghost Town,'" *Chicago Daily News*, August 29, 1955.

427 "6 Gary Firemen, Reporter for P-T Burned at Oil Fire," *Gary Post-Tribune*, August 29, 1955.

428 "Eyewitness Stories; How Boy Died," *Chicago Sun-Times*, August 28, 1955; "6 Gary Firemen, Reporter for P-T Burned at Oil Fire," *Gary Post-Tribune*, August 29, 1955.

429 "Dead, Injured in Explosions Listed," *Chicago Sun-Times*, August 28, 1955.

430 "Evacuated Families Back Home," *Gary Post-Tribune*, August 29, 1955; "FBI Enters Probe of Whiting Fire," *Chicago Daily News*, August 29, 1955; "List of

Dead and Wounded in Whiting Refinery Fire," *Chicago Tribune*, August 28, 1955.

[431] Vargo, *Priscilla Springer McCarty-Reed: Memories of the Standard Oil Fire*, ibid.

[432] Hmurovic & Vargo, *George Timko: Memories of Standard Oil Fire of 1955*, 3.

[433] "Mom Clutches Teddy Bear of Son Killed in Oil Blast," *Chicago Daily News*, August 29, 1955.

[434] "Tiny Blast Victim Buried in Whiting," *Chicago Daily News*, August 30, 1955; "75 More Families Return to Homes in Oil Fire Area," *Chicago Tribune*, August 31, 1955.

[435] "It's your World," *Long Beach (CA) Press Telegram*, November 23, 1955; "Ducks Grounded by Oil Slick Getting Back in Condition for Flight," *Logansport (IN) Pharos Tribune*, November 22, 1955.

[436] Anne Douglas, "Lake Oil Slick Engulfs Birds," *Chicago Tribune*, November 22, 1955; "Ducks Grounded by Oil Slick Getting Back in Condition for Flight," *Logansport (IN) Pharos Tribune*, November 22, 1955.

[437] Douglas, ibid.

[438] "Winds Send Oil Slick to Front Door of City," *Chicago Tribune*, November 23, 1955; Douglas, ibid.

[439] "The Oil Slick Is Still Unexplained," Chicago Tribune, December 28, 1955; "Winds Send Oil Slick to Front Door of City," *Chicago Tribune*, November 23, 1955.

[440] "Winds Send Oil Slick to Front Door of City," Chicago Tribune, November 23, 1955; "Oil Identified; Seek Source of Lake 'Slick,'" *Chicago Tribune*, December 29, 1955.

[441] "Hint Whiting Fire Source of Lake Oil Slick," *Chicago Tribune*, January 19, 1956; "The Oil Slick Is Still Unexplained," *Chicago Tribune*, December 28, 1955.

[442] "Standard Oil Starts Rebuilding," *The Calumet News*, August 31, 1955.

[443] Ann Powers, "Federal Water Pollution Control Act (1948)," *Major Acts of Congress* (The Gale Group, 2004), http://www.encyclopedia.com/doc/1G2-3407400129.html.

[444] Hmurovic & Vargo, *JoAnne Samila: Memories of Standard Oil Fire of 1955*, 5.

[445] "'Like A-Bomb' Says Flying Reporter," *Chicago American*, August 28, 1955; "Lay Gas Odor on South Side to Wind Shift," *Chicago Tribune*, September 5, 1955.

[446] Vargo, *Frank Vargo: Memories of the Standard Oil Fire*, ibid.; Hmurovic & Vargo, *George Timko: Memories of Standard Oil Fire of 1955*, 4.

447 "Cars Forced to Detour," *Chicago American*, August 28, 1955.

448 "Relief Workers Speed Assistance to Victims," *Chicago American*, August 28, 1955; Hmurovic & Vargo, *Betty Delinck: Memories of Standard Oil Fire of 1955*, 4.

449 Kosalko & Vargo, *Lynn Larsen: Memories of Standard Oil Fire of 1955*, 1.

450 Frank Vargo, *John Tokoly: Memories of the Standard Oil Fire*, notes from a conversation in 2014 with Frank Vargo, collected by Frank Vargo (Whiting, Indiana: Whiting-Robertsdale Historical Society, 2015).

451 "Disaster," *Chicago Daily News*, August 29, 1955.

452 Hmurovic & Vargo, *George Timko: Memories of Standard Oil Fire of 1955*, 8.

453 Hmurovic & Vargo, *JoAnne Samila: Memories of Standard Oil Fire of 1955*, 6; Hmurovic & Vargo, *Janet Tindall: Memories of Standard Oil Fire of 1955*, 2.

454 Kosalko & Vargo, *Larry Jennings: Memories of Standard Oil Fire of 1955*, 16.

455 John Bodnar, *John Marcisz: Whiting, Indiana: Generational Memory, 1991-1993*, transcript of an oral history conducted on March 3, 1992 by John Bodnar (Bloomington: Indiana University Center for the Study of History and Memory, 1992), 91-152, 15-16.

456 John Bodnar, *Dorothy & Edward Tokarz: Whiting, Indiana: Generational Memory, 1991-1993*, transcript of an oral history conducted on March 2, 1992 by John Bodnar (Bloomington: Indiana University Center for the Study of History and Memory, 1992), 91-150, 30.

457 Nichols, 12.

458 Dabertin, *Jim Sandrick: Whiting, Indiana: Generational Memory, 1991-1993*, 91-18, 23; Bodnar, *Betty Gehrke: Whiting, Indiana: Generational Memory, 1991-1993*, 23.

459 "Whiting," *Lake County News*, August 23, 1906.

460 Bodnar, *Clarence & Betty Gehrke: Whiting, Indiana: Generational Memory, 1991-1993*, 48.

461 David Dabertin, *George Brown: Whiting, Indiana: Generational Memory, 1991-1993*, transcript of an oral history conducted on November 28, 1990 by David Dabertin (Bloomington: Indiana University Center for the Study of History and Memory, 1990), 91-10, 29.

462 Hmurovic & Vargo, *Dennis Zelenke: Memories of Standard Oil Fire of 1955*, 7-8

463 Hmurovic & Vargo, *Tom Marciniak: Memories of Standard Oil Fire of 1955*, 3.

464 Hmurovic & Vargo, *Mary Ann Dominiak: Memories of Standard Oil Fire of 1955*, 7.

465 Bodnar, *Betty Gehrke: Whiting, Indiana: Generational Memory, 1991-1993*, 2.

466 Hmurovic & Vargo, *Pat Mazanek: Memories of Standard Oil Fire of 1955*, 11; Kosalko & Vargo, *Bonnie Wilson Faulkner & Brenda Wilson Felton: Memories of Standard Oil Fire of 1955*, 2-3.

467 "Oil Co. Buys Homes South of 129th," *Hammond, Times*, September 4, 1955; "Four Replace Blood Given Ronnie Plewniak," *Whiting Refinery News*, September 30, 1955; "Sympathy, Gratitude, Courage – Warm Letters Speak Volumes," *Whiting Refinery News*, September 30, 1955.

468 Hmurovic & Vargo, *Ronald Plewniak: Memories of Standard Oil Fire of 1955*, 4.

469 Ibid., 2.

470 Frank Vargo, *Ron Gaspar: Memories of Standard Oil Fire of 1955*, transcript of an oral history conducted on September 5, 2014 by Frank Vargo (Whiting, Indiana: Whiting-Robertsdale Historical Society, 2014), 1.

471 Hmurovic & Vargo, *Ronald Plewniak: Memories of Standard Oil Fire of 1955*, 2; Hmurovic & Vargo, *Justine Bircher: Memories of Standard Oil Fire of 1955*, 2, 9-10.

472 Hmurovic & Vargo, *Ronald Plewniak: Memories of Standard Oil Fire of 1955*, 3 & 6.

473 "Boy Injured in Whiting Blast Gets $150,000," *Chicago Tribune*, May 10, 1957; "Awarded $150,000," *Chicago Tribune*, June 23, 1957; John O. Holland, "Liability Lawyer Works for Air-Passenger Rights," *Christian Science Monitor*, October 3, 1986; "Oil Firm Named in Damage Suit," *Anderson (Indiana) Herald Bulletin*, May 10, 1956.

474 Hmurovic & Vargo, *Ronald Plewniak: Memories of Standard Oil Fire of 1955*, 8; Olivia Clarke, "Survivor: 'It's Pretty Traumatic,'" *The Times of Northwest Indiana*, August 27, 2005.

475 Hmurovic & Vargo, *Ronald Plewniak: Memories of Standard Oil Fire of 1955*, 10.

476 Ibid., 6 & 13.

477 Obituary, *The Times of Northwest Indiana*, August 27, 2014; Hmurovic & Vargo, *Ronald Plewniak: Memories of Standard Oil Fire of 1955*, 5.

478 "Homes in Area Bought by SO," *Whiting Refinery News*, September 9, 1955.

479 Hittle, *Dennis Hittle: Memories of the Standard Oil Fire*, ibid.

480 Rosen, *Cheryl Macko Rosen: Memories of the Standard Oil Fire*, 3.

481 Kosalko & Vargo, *Raymond Gajewski: Memories of Standard Oil Fire of 1955*, 1-2.

[482] Frank Vargo, *Eleanor Kincheloe: Memories of the Standard Oil Fire*, notes from a conversation in 2014 with Frank Vargo, collected by Frank Vargo (Whiting, Indiana: Whiting-Robertsdale Historical Society, 2015).

[483] Burr, ibid.

[484] "Refinery Bears Few Scars of 1955 Disaster," *Chicago Tribune*, August 26, 1956; Kosalko & Vargo, *Earl Yoho: Memories of Standard Oil Fire of 1955*, 25. [Chuck Kosalko quoted his wife, Gayle Faulkner Kosalko while interviewing Earl Yoho]; Phil Hermanek, "Relinquish Stieglitz," *The Calumet Day*, May 30, 1973; Hmurovic & Vargo, *Betty Delinck: Memories of Standard Oil Fire of 1955*, 8.

[485] Jefchak, 57.

[486] Hermanek, ibid.

[487] United States Census Bureau, Census of Population and Housing, 1930 through 2010; Burr, ibid.

[488] Chad Berry, *James & Sara Etter: Whiting, Indiana: Generational Memory, 1991-1993*, transcript of an oral history conducted on June 25, 1992 by Chad Berry (Bloomington: Indiana University Center for the Study of History and Memory, 1992), 91-171, 33; Thomas M. Whiteside Jr., *Program for the Redevelopment of Central Business District in Whiting, Indiana* (Department of Architecture, University of Illinois, 1972), 4.

[489] Purdue Calumet Development Foundation, *An Urban Improvement Program for Whiting, Indiana* (Hammond: October 1958), 9.

[490] Bodnar, *Leo Kus: Whiting, Indiana: Generational Memory, 1991-1993*, 21.

[491] Hmurovic & Vargo, *Justine Bircher: Memories of Standard Oil Fire of 1955*, 9.

[492] Bodnar, *John Marcisz: Whiting, Indiana: Generational Memory, 1991-1993*, 26.

[493] Dabertin, *Jim Sandrick: Whiting, Indiana: Generational Memory, 1991-1993*, 91-18, 22-23.

[494] Ken Otterbourg, "Hormel's New Recipe for Success," *Fortune*, June 15, 2016, 209.

[495] "The Big Fire at Whiting," Standard Torch, October 1955, 2; "Evacuated Families Back Home," *Gary Post-Tribune*, August 29, 1955; "Oil Fire in Whiting Checked," *Chicago Tribune*, August 29, 1955; "Fate of Area Now Depends on Winds," *Chicago American*, August 29, 1955; "Many Return to Homes; Oil Fire Abating," *Chicago Tribune*, August 30, 1955; "150 Whiting Families Still Out," *Gary Post-Tribune*, August 30, 1955.

[496] "Fire Finally Quenched at Whiting Oil Refinery," *Gary Post-Tribune*, August 31, 1955; "1 Tank Still Burning at Standard Oil," *Gary Post-Tribune*, September 3, 1955; David Dabertin, *Robert Herakovich: Whiting, Indiana: Generational*

Memory, 1991-1993, transcript of an oral history conducted on May 30, 1991 by David Dabertin (Bloomington: Indiana University Center for the Study of History and Memory, 1991), 91-48, 32.

497   Gray, *Joe Gray: Memories of the Standard Oil Fire*, ibid.; Hmurovic & Vargo, *George Grenchik: Memories of Standard Oil Fire of 1955*, 2; Kosalko & Vargo, *Earl Yoho: Memories of Standard Oil Fire of 1955*, 9.

498   Lindberg, ibid.

499   Lindberg, ibid.

500   "Clear Debris, Rush Repairs on Key Units," *Whiting Refinery News*, September 9, 1955; "Final Blaze Out at Whiting Refinery," *Gary Post-Tribune*, September 6, 1955.

501   "30 Million Whiting Fire Leaves 2 Dead, 26 Hurt," *Hammond Times*, August 28, 1955; "Gas Ample in Chicago," *Chicago American*, August 28, 1955; "Fire in Refinery Under Control After 24-Hour Fight with Blasts," *New York Times*, August 29, 1955.

502   "A Statement by the President of Standard Oil Company Concerning the Whiting Fire," *Gary Post-Tribune*, September 6, 1955.

503   "Integration, Hard Work Kept Customer Supply Lines Open," *Whiting Refinery News*, September 30, 1955.

504   "Port Washington Area Is Reporting A Fuel Shortage," *Sheboygan Press*, January 6, 1956.

505   "Widespread Effects of Fire," *Sheboygan (Michigan) Press*, October 15, 1955; "Oil Industry Feels Whiting Fire Impact," *Greeley (Colorado) Daily Tribune*, October 19, 1955.

506   Ducommun, 154; "Integration, Hard Work Kept Customer Supply Lines Open," *Whiting Refinery News*, September 30, 1955; "Oil Industry Feels Whiting Fire Impact," *Greeley (Colorado) Daily Tribune*, October 19, 1955.

507   "Standard Oil (Indiana)," *New York Times*, November 2, 1955; Annual Report for 1955, Standard Oil of Indiana, 2.

508   Annual Report for 1956, Standard Oil of Indiana, 12; Annual Report for 1955, Standard Oil of Indiana, 14; "Insurance Cut Then --- Boom!" *Chicago Daily News*, August 27, 1955.

509   Annual Report for 1955, Standard Oil of Indiana, 7.

510   Bodnar, *Leo Kus: Whiting, Indiana: Generational Memory, 1991-1993*, 6; Kosalko & Vargo, *Lawrence Broviak: Memories of Standard Oil Fire of 1955*, 2; Hmurovic & Vargo, *Tom Marciniak: Memories of Standard Oil Fire of 1955*, 3.

511   Hmurovic & Vargo, *George Timko: Memories of Standard Oil Fire of 1955*, 6.

[512]   Bodnar, *Clarence & Betty Gehrke: Whiting, Indiana: Generational Memory, 1991-1993*, 21.

[513]   Hmurovic & Vargo, *Grace Kovach: Memories of Standard Oil Fire of 1955*, 2.

[514]   Bodnar, *Joseph Sotak: Whiting, Indiana: Generational Memory, 1991-1993*, 23.

[515]   "Chairman Prior Stresses Importance of Profits," *Whiting Refinery News*, July 21, 1959.

[516]   Bodnar, *Joseph Sotak: Whiting, Indiana: Generational Memory, 1991-1993*, ibid.

[517]   Bodnar, *Dorothy & Edward Tokarz: Whiting, Indiana: Generational Memory, 1991-1993*, 17-18.

[518]   Dabertin, *George Brown: Whiting, Indiana: Generational Memory, 1991-1993*, 6.

[519]   Steve Zabroski, "Whiting Thinks Marina for Lakefront," *The Times*, April 13, 2006.

[520]   "BP Gives $1 Million to Lake Michigan Restoration Projects," British Petroleum News Release, bp.com, Press Releases, June 30, 2015.

[521]   Joseph S. Pete, "BP Seeks Another Big Whiting Investment," *The Times*, August 7, 2016.

[522]   Sarah Reese, "40 Arrested During Climate Change Protest," *The Times*, May 15, 2016.

[523]   Jerry Davich, "Foul Odor Prompts Whiff of Noxious Rationalization," *Post-Tribune*, June 1, 2016.

[524]   "Fatal Blast of Oil Tank an Accident," *Gary Evening Post*, July 8, 1921.

[525]   "Sabotage at Standard?" *Hammond Times*, September 24, 1941; "Standard Oil Fire," *Hammond Times*, September 25, 1941.

[526]   "5,000 Watch Buildings Go Up in Flames," *Hammond Times*, June 13, 1946; "Fire and Explosions Rip Whiting Plant of Standard Oil; 1 Hurt," *Chicago Tribune*, June 13, 1946.

[527]   "New Blast in Oil Refinery!" *Chicago Tribune*, September 11, 1955.

[528]   "Terrible Explosion," *Chesterton Tribune*, April 12, 1888.

[529]   "$30 Million Whiting Fire Leaves 2 Dead, 26 Hurt," *Hammond Times*, August 28, 1955; Gaines, ibid.

[530]   Hmurovic & Vargo, *Tom Marciniak: Memories of Standard Oil Fire of 1955*, 2; Gaines, ibid.; Ducommun, 147.

[531]   Kosalko & Vargo, *Lawrence Broviak: Memories of Standard Oil Fire of 1955*, 4; Hittle, *Dennis Hittle: Memories of the Standard Oil Fire*, 4; Krecker, ibid.

[532]   "The Whiting Fire," *Chicago Tribune*, August 30, 1955.

533   "Disaster," *Chicago Daily News*, August 29, 1955.

534   Ducommun, 153.

535   Burr, ibid.; Diane Donovan & Nancy Banks, "'Big Fire' Memories Rekindled," *The Times*, August 21, 1983; "Determination of Loss in Whiting Fire Delayed," *Chicago Tribune*, September 5, 1955; Jonathan Cox, "Hydra-Matic Fire," prezi. com, May 6, 2014.

536   "FBI Enters Probe of Whiting Fire," *Chicago Daily News*, August 29, 1955.

537   "Many Return to Homes; Oil Fire Abating," *Chicago Tribune*, August 30, 1955; "Hunt Unknown Mixture in Blast Probe," *Whiting Refinery News*, September 9, 1955.

538   "Hunt Unknown Mixture in Blast Probe," *Whiting Refinery News*, September 9, 1955.

539   Ibid.

540   Ducommun, 153.

541   Ducommun, 147 & 158.

542   Sjostrom, ibid.; Gaines, ibid.

543   "Expansion at Whiting…Up Goes the New," *Standard Torch*, February 1955, Vol. VIII, No. 2, p. 16; Annual Report for 1955, Standard Oil of Indiana, 22; Annual Report for 1955, Standard Oil of Indiana, 25; "Standard Oil to Build Second Ultraformer Unit," *Hammond Times*, June 29, 1956; "3rd Ultraformer Set at Whiting," *Hammond Times*, December 28, 1956.

544   Sjostrom, ibid.

545   "Industry Aids in Fire Fighting," *Pasadena Star News*, January 12, 1957.

546   Ducommun, 154.

547   Hmurovic & Vargo, *Tom Marciniak: Memories of Standard Oil Fire of 1955*, 7.

548   Richard Bryant, "Amoco Inspection Planned," *The Times*, November 4, 1988.

549   Hmurovic & Vargo, *Grace Kovach: Memories of Standard Oil Fire of 1955*, 4-5.

550   "Standard's Whiting Plant to Hold Two-Day Picnic," *Gary Post-Tribune*, August 31, 1955; "SO Public Service Film, 'Fire Magic,' Shows Fire Chemistry, *Standard Torch*, December 1955, page MG, Vol. VIII, No. 12.

551   Hmurovic, Kosalko & Vargo, *Ann Devoy: Memories of Standard Oil Fire of 1955*, 18; Ducommun, 144; "Meeting an Emergency," *Gary Post-Tribune*, September 1, 1955.

552   "Trained Crews on Alert, Keep Fire Danger Down," *Whiting Refinery News*, September 9, 1955; "The Big Fire at Whiting," *Standard Torch*, October 1955, 2.

[553] "Whiting Center Puts Roof Over 125 Victims," *Chicago American*, August 29, 1955.

[554] "'Like A-Bomb' Says Flying Reporter," *Chicago American*, August 28, 1955.

[555] Kosalko & Vargo, *Bonnie Wilson Faulkner & Brenda Wilson Felton: Memories of Standard Oil Fire of 1955*, 5.

[556] Dabertin, *JoAnn Jancosek: Whiting, Indiana: Generational Memory, 1991-1993*, 1.

[557] Hmurovic & Vargo, *Pat Mazanek: Memories of Standard Oil Fire of 1955*, 3.

[558] Hmurovic & Vargo, *Mary Ann Dominiak: Memories of Standard Oil Fire of 1955*, 5-6.

INDEX

Printed in the United States
By Bookmasters